Music for the Dance

Recent Titles in
Contributions to
the Study of Music and Dance

Music and Musket: Bands and Bandsmen
of the American Civil War
Kenneth E. Olson

Edmund Thornton Jenkins: The Life and Times
of an American Black Composer, 1894–1926
Jeffrey P. Green

Born to Play: The Life and Career of
Hazel Harrison
Jean E. Cazort and Constance Tibbs Hobson

Titta Ruffo: An Anthology
Andrew Farkas, editor

Nellie Melba: A Contemporary Review
William R. Moran, compiler

Armseelchen: The Life and Music of Eric Zeisl
Malcolm S. Cole and Barbara Barclay

Busoni and the Piano: The Works, the Writings,
and the Recordings
Larry Sitsky

Music as Propaganda: Art to Persuade, Art to Control
Arnold Perris

A Most Wondrous Babble: American Art Composers, Their Music,
and the American Scene, 1950–1985
Nicholas E. Tawa

Voices of Combat: A Century of Liberty and War Songs, 1765–1865
Kent A. Bowman

Edison, Musicians, and the Phonograph: A Century in Retrospect
John Harvith and Susan Edwards Harvith, editors

The Dawning of American Keyboard Music
J. Bunker Clark

Mozart in Person: His Character and Health
Peter J. Davies

Music for the Dance

REFLECTIONS ON A COLLABORATIVE ART

Katherine Teck

Contributions to the Study of Music and Dance, Number 15

GREENWOOD PRESS

New York · Westport, Connecticut · London

For Rachel and Daniel

Library of Congress Cataloging-in-Publication Data

Teck, Katherine.
Music for the dance : reflections on a collaborative art / Katherine Teck.
p. cm. — (Contributions to the study of music and dance, ISSN 0193–9041 ; no. 15)
Bibliography: p.
Includes index.
ISBN 0–313–26376–0 (lib. bdg. : alk. paper)
1. Ballet dance music—History and criticism. 2. Dance music—History and criticism. 3. Ballet. 4. Modern dance.
I. Title. II. Series.
ML3460.T4 1989
782.9′5—dc19 88–38551

British Library Cataloguing in Publication Data is available.

Library of Congress Catalog Card Number: 88-38551
ISBN: 0-313-26376-0
ISSN: 0193-9041

First published in 1989

Greenwood Press, Inc.
88 Post Road West, Westport, Connecticut 06881

Printed in the United States of America

The paper used in this book complies with the Permanent Paper Standard issued by the National Information Standards Organization (Z39.48-1984).

10 9 8 7 6 5 4 3 2

Copyright Acknowledgments

A quotation from the unpublished report written by Ian Horvath in 1987 about Meet the Composer's Composer/Choreographer Project appears by permission of Meet the Composer.

The three line drawings by Roy Doty appear by permission of Roy Doty.

Contents

Preface vii

CREATION 1

1. Choreographers Talk about Music 3
2. Call in the Composers! 27
3. The Partnership of Movement and Sound 51
4. Composer-Conductor-Instrumentalists 67

PERFORMANCE 83

5. Free-Lancers in the Pits 85
6. The Orchestra for American Ballet Theatre 103
7. *La Bayadère:* From Rehearsals to Curtain Calls 113
8. Maestro, Please. . . . 123

SILENT ARTISTS SPEAK 147

9. Dancers' Tales 149
10. What Is Musicality in a Dancer? 167

TOWARD THE FUTURE 185

11. Building Theaters, Patronage, and Artistry 187
12. Obtaining New Music for Choreography 193
13. A Festival of Ballets to American Music 199

Appendix 209

Notes 213

Bibliographic Essay 221

Index 225

Preface

Music is the most constant partner for the dancer in America today. Yet it is often the aspect of dance performances that is least written about, least understood, most expensive, and most challenging to work with effectively.

How have some of our leading choreographers collaborated with composers, arrangers, conductors, and instrumentalists? What kind of music makes a good dancy companion? What is needed, for example, to help a dancer to jump for joy or portray an anguished character, to set the mood for a virtuosic display, to accomplish an extended adagio lift, or merely to keep up with the rest of a chorus line?

Even professional dancers are not always sure about what they want from music—or how to get it—although they glowingly assert that they could not perform without this aural companion. And some of these artists are among the most astute listeners that music has ever had. On the other side of the footlights, both theater-goers and performing musicians have an increasing appreciation for the dancers' art, as well as a great curiosity to know more about how successful dance collaborations come into being.

Who decides what music will be played—and how it will be played? What is it like to be a musician performing in theater pits? How do dance companies manage to pay for interesting new music? How is electronic sound technology being put to imaginative artistic use for theatrical dance? And what is "musicality" in a dancer?

When I first started working as a musician for ballet and modern dance, I was disappointed to find relatively little information in print concerning these and other questions. And so it seemed that a good way to learn more about the interaction between music and dance would be to go directly to some outstanding choreographers, dancers, conductors, and orchestral instrumentalists, and to ask them about their experiences. This effort has resulted in the present volume.

* * *

While visiting the choreographer Agnes de Mille, I recalled a striking quotation from her volume, *The Book of the Dance* (New York: Golden Press, 1963):

> A fine dance never mimics the musical plan exactly; it sometimes joins; it sometimes departs. Music and dance should supply two separate designs with form and life of their own which, when experienced together, create an impression neither could possibly achieve alone. (p. 208)

How such collaboration is best achieved is the subject of this exploration, which focuses on the creation and performance of music for ballet and modern concert dance in twentieth-century America.

It is hoped that the reader will gain not only specific information about how some of our leading artists have worked together, but also a general sense of the pleasures, challenges, difficulties, amusing mishaps, and craft involved in combining music and movement. This is not a how-to guide, though it is hoped that readers will be stimulated to use some of the ideas presented here.

Material for this book was gathered by the author in personal interviews with individual artists, and in direct observation, unless otherwise indicated in the text or notes.

This book has been made possible only by the generosity and interest of all the artists mentioned in the text—and of some who are not named here. They have all shared their time, their knowledge, their opinions, their memories, and their artistry. In addition, they have frequently extended personal invitations to the author to visit in their homes or studios, or to attend private showings and rehearsals not normally open to the public.

A special note of appreciation must be added for the encouragement extended by Donald York, Oliver Daniel, Agnes de Mille, Richard Philp, and Richard Jackson. Marilyn Brownstein of Greenwood Press provided valuable guidance in the writing, and Ruth Adkins, also of Greenwood Press, did a superb job of copyediting. Elizabeth Lee read the manuscript—as did Alan Teck, whose suggestions were helpful throughout the preparation of this volume.

I hope that this book may give pleasure not only to those who contributed to it, but also to other dance professionals, teachers, students, musicians of all kinds, and especially to some of that devoted multitude of theater-goers who love the dance.

CREATION

1

Choreographers Talk about Music

Some of the finest music that exists for American dance today had its beginnings somewhere in the minds and feelings of choreographers. It is their creativity, their artistic desires—and sometimes their budgets—that determine not only the general musical atmosphere, but also the overall structural forms, instrumentation, and even the very melodies that dance audiences will hear.

AGNES DE MILLE REMINISCES ABOUT BALLET AND BROADWAY

"There are two ways of working in dances and ballets," said Agnes de Mille in a spirited interview with the author.[1] "The choreographer has two choices," she explained. "Either he can take a piece of music that's already composed (famous or otherwise) and pattern his own designs exactly according to the musical dictation, or he can design his own ballet and then ask a composer to follow his general outlines."

When she herself worked directly with composers, Miss de Mille found that they generally asked her to break a dance down into sections and minutes. "Take *Rodeo,* which I did with Aaron Copland," she gave as an example. "He wanted to know, for the cowboy entrance, how much dancing there would be, in terms of minutes, until the girls arrived and walked across the scene . . . and so forth."

The choreographer seemed rather amused to recall that she herself had made a suggestion to Copland. "I gave him one tune. There is the little party scene with the running set in it, a 3/4. It's an old cowboy tune that Virgil Thomson used to sing, and I got it from him. I don't think he knew I was going to give it to Aaron! Aaron grabbed it. Virgil has also used it—but a little differently."

Touching upon how problems can arise when there are last-minute changes in the choreography, Miss de Mille pointed out: "Aaron has a very strict and marvelous sense of the musical form he's deriving from. He never ruptures it for any dance needs or any dramatic needs or anything.

"I remember on the train going West with the Ballet Russe de Monte Carlo, Freddy Franklin said, 'You know, the cowboy doesn't get the girl; he just becomes an *also ran*. I don't like it. I'll dance the opening, but I have to get out.' "

"So," continued Miss de Mille, "I thought, 'Why *shouldn't* he get the girl?' I knew *that* would be a nice twist, and it suddenly seemed absolutely a fine idea. So I said, 'Well, you're going to have the girl! I'm going to fix it.'

"But then she had to make up her mind—I think she had four bars of music for it—that she didn't love one boy that she *thought* she had right along, but was crazy about the other. I said, 'This is insane. No girl can do that in four bars!' And Aaron said, 'You cannot have another bar, because it's a strict form.' "

"Well, I was caught with the dramatic dilemma of having the heroine change her mind from one man to the other just like that," said Miss de Mille, snapping her fingers. "Of course," she continued, "that's ridiculous. So I fooled him. On a measure seven, I had a very long tacet, and we sat on that, and sat and sat, and then the whole orchestra exploded when they came back in. Aaron bought that. That was all right, for I had broken the music at a proper moment."

"Now, those are the kinds of problems that are faced all the time in dramatic ballet," she pointed out.

If choreographers sometimes make musical suggestions, it also happens that composers contribute to a collaboration above and beyond their musical creation. For instance, Miss de Mille mentioned that composer Morton Gould was responsible for a great deal in her ballet *Fall River,* based on the true story of the Lizzie Borden murder trial.[2]

"In real life," Miss de Mille observed, "Lizzie was acquitted and lived out a long and very unsatisfactory life all by herself in Fall River [Massachusetts]. Well, that's not dramatic, and everything in the ballet pointed to guilt and repayment of guilt. That was the story—the story of someone who was a good woman, an ordinary woman, who suddenly commits a heinous crime."

The choreographer took a deep breath and continued: "Well! The father died of eleven blows of an axe straight through the skull, and the stepmother had twenty-two blows of the axe. It was simply a mashing. Now if you do *that,* you're out of your skull! So I was doing a ballet about how an ordinary person could reach the state where they were capable of doing that. If you let the girl go scott free, where's your dramatic statement? She *had* to die.

"We were in the Russian Tea Room, and I said to Morton, 'You know, everything's building to the judgment, and there isn't any; it's a miscarriage of justice.' He said, 'Hang her!' I said, 'Well, I don't think I can do that; it isn't history.' He said, 'Do it!' So I called lawyers and found out that you cannot libel a dead person." In the end, the composer's advice was followed for the ballet: Lizzie was hanged.

"I have to choose composers that can work with me," the choreographer said, "because we work very closely. We're married in a way."

One collaborator that gave Miss de Mille particular satisfaction in working together on Broadway shows was Trude Rittmann. "Oh!" exclaimed the choreographer, perking up visibly, "She'd knock her teeth out . . . dismember herself. She—now *she* goes into the rehearsal hall with you. Of course, the way shows were done, it's like pancakes being done on the griddle while you eat. I'd tell her what I wanted, then I'd start moving around the floor. She'd doodle at the piano. I wouldn't pay much attention to her, and she wouldn't pay much attention to me—or at least I think she wouldn't. And then she'd say, 'Agnes, repeat that if you can.' So then I'd try."

The composer would then enlist some of the more musical dancers to observe closely and count accurately. "I would have girls watching me," explained the choreographer, "because when I start composing that way on my own body, I turn off certain recording areas in my mind. All the critical and recording areas are just numb, and I just go. I don't even know what I've done. I say, 'Tell me what I did.' "

"It takes highly skilled and highly trained girls to say 'You did this and this,' " observed Miss de Mille. "I would say 'That's fine,' or 'That's no good.' Then Trude would say, 'Now wait. I'm not going to take it in this tempo. You keep going in your tempo; don't vary a thing; don't change a count. I'm going to play an entirely different rhythm. See if you like it.'

"And she'd do it. This makes a dichotomy. Then she'd say, 'You like that? Well, I'll go home and work on it awhile.' Then she'd come the next day and say 'I threw it all away.' And I'd say, 'But Trude, you *couldn't*. Go through the wastebaskets and get it.' "

"Oh, the goings-on!" declared Miss de Mille, adding with a sigh, "But she had the loveliest stuff you can imagine."

When the big Broadway musicals were being put together, it was usual for a special arranger to be brought in for the dance music. Even though Kurt Weill, for example, wanted to do the dance music for his own shows, time did not allow it, and Miss de Mille would tell him, "I *have* to have Trude." But then, according to the choreographer, Weill would take Rittmann's work and weave it into his own final musical version. "He was terribly finicky," commented Miss de Mille. "He would orchestrate sitting in the back of the theater with everything spread out. He was an absolute musician. Dick Rodgers was a good musician, but he never orchestrated or arranged for dance—not four bars!"

Some of the other outstanding orchestrators that Miss de Mille worked with in the theater were Robert Russell Bennett, Hershy Kay, and Don Walker.

"You know," she explained, "you never can tell what an orchestrator has done on a thing. One man takes the job and gets the pay. Then he sublets a great deal of the work because it has to be done in a week—the entire score.

"The main figure comes into the rehearsal hall, makes notes, writes them all down, and disappears. And he has maybe four or five men working for him like slaves, in hotel bedrooms. You never see them; you never meet them. And piles of work, music, come into the theater. There are always some anonymous silent people huddled around the orchestrator, and maybe these are the men that work . . . but we never know."

When asked what it was that Trude Rittmann gave her for her dances that was most needed, Miss de Mille reflected: "Well, she gave me a *composition*. I needed good rhythm. I'm terrific with rhythm. And I needed melody—not just the song melody. Generally you already had the song; you'd sung it juiceless; you'd just milked every bit of everything out of it. Then when the tenor or the soprano retired and the dancers took over the stage, you couldn't have the same tune over again—obviously. Well, Trude said the dance had to be rooted in the tune some way. She was the only one who worked into the fiber of the tune and played around with the rhythms of the tune—inverting, changing patterns, changing accents. But it was all from the same material, basically. Then she would come back to a restatement of the main theme at the end, as a rule. Her dances were simply fascinating."

"But this sense of what kind of sound to put with movement . . . when to change keys, when to change the rhythm . . . this is all art, and I cannot give you a recipe for this," said the choreographer. "All I can tell you is that most of the composers who work with dancers haven't the faintest idea about it!"

"Big-name composers usually don't want to be bothered," she observed, "because they don't want to be restrained by another art form. Balanchine was able to work with Stravinsky, but Balanchine just took the music and placed patterns on the stage that visually complemented the score, without changing a note or anything. And his ballets don't have a story, as a rule."

When it was suggested that some audience members are surprised to find that the music for a ballet doesn't have to follow the movements precisely at all times, the choreographer answered: "And vice versa. This is *art!*"

Some of Agnes de Mille's most rewarding collaborations were for her concert dances. In the early days of her career, for her own solo dances she would take music and "cut it up and do whatever I wanted with it . . . paste it together."

"I was a pretty good pianist," she related, "so I could cut my own music, arrange my own music, and play through things to see what I wanted. But that's really hard, because it takes attention to read the music and play it, and then attention was off the fantasy of the movement. Now, I can make tapes, play them back, and really just go to town and do anything I want."

"When I'm thinking of movement generally," she continued, "I always used to put music on the gramophone, because it was like taking a drink: I get high on music. It opened up all sorts of areas in me: emotional and imaginative, and so on. And I would start moving then. If in two hours of this I got just a little tiny phrase of movement, that would be considered fruitful by me. But anyway, I would *not* use the music I was going to dance to, because it gets worn out. I would use Mozart or Boccherini or lots of Scarlatti, and some of the pre-Elizabethans. With this, I would work out *ideas* for the choreography.

"Then Trude had to come and put it into form, into patterns. Then she would return and announce 'I haven't changed a count; I haven't changed any of the accents, and you have time to do everything you wanted to do. But this *is* different.' And generally, it was perfectly lovely."

When asked, in conclusion, if she felt that any music could be danced to, or if some music is more danceable than other pieces, Miss de Mille replied: "For me, yes. I think Webern is regrettable for dancing; I wouldn't touch him. All this very abstract music: just sound, like trouble in the radiator. Maybe it has form; maybe if I studied it I'd see it. I would just simply have to dance in *spite* of it. There's nothing there for me. I can't say it can't be done, but *I* couldn't!"

DORIS HUMPHREY'S VIEWS ON MUSIC

The pioneer modern dance choreographer Doris Humphrey also suggested that not all music is suitable for concert dances. For example, in her book *The Art of Making Dances,* she ruled out:

> the intellectual composition, made to illustrate a theory; the kind musicians call "eye music," interesting to follow on a score, but usually dry and technical to the ear; the bravura piece, made to show off the virtuosity of a performer and the resources of a single instrument; the impressionistic composition, such as a tone poem, in which timbre and tonal color are the *raison d'être;* the "big" piece, such as the more opulent symphonies, overwhelming in complexity and volume and so complete that it is both futile and impertinent to attempt to add anything; the well-known programmatic piece, unless the composer's thought is going to be followed exactly; the too-complex composition in general, which is so demanding of attention that it cannot make a good partner; and of course, the cliché-ridden and the commonplace.[3]

Commenting on changing tastes and varying traditions in music, Humphrey observed:

> In general, there is no part of the dance which differs so much from time to time and from place to place as the choices and uses of the music which accompanies it. Isadora Duncan danced alone to whole symphonies. Now this would be unthinkable. In some quarters, romantic music is considered the only suitable style for dance; in others, it is thought to be passé. Many dance directors think a strict adherence to musical phrasing and beat is correct practice and that anything else is unmusical. In short, there are vast differences in approach.[4]

PAUL TAYLOR'S MUSICAL TASTES

In search of further opinions concerning what makes suitable music for the dance, the author asked Paul Taylor to describe his process of choosing music for his choreography.[5]

"Sometimes," said Mr. Taylor, "I have sort of an idea for a dance, and I'm looking for something that I think might go with it, or against it . . . something to complement or help it. Other times, I'm just looking around to hear something I can stand, because you have to hear it over and over; it takes a lot of work. If the music is not going to hold up well on several hearings, I don't want to get stuck with it."

However, he does not agree with the opinion of others that only some music is danceable. "I think *anything* can be good for dance," he asserted. "There's no such thing as sound or silence that can't be used for dance! It depends on *how* it's used, how suitable it is, how it's made to sound to the audience (by its relationship to the dance). Whether it's acceptable or not, and whether it's successful, depends on this. There are no rules; there are no laws. The individual choreographer makes his laws; he's selecting what *he* feels would be right."

"He's wrong lots of times," Mr. Taylor conceded, "but nevertheless, he's not to be told that he 'can't use that because it's not dance music.' Anything is fair game. The sky is the limit. The possibilities that are open to us are infinite, and we choose which ones are suitable—to *us*."

Although he has mounted a number of stunning dance works set to older classical music, Mr. Taylor says that given his choice, he would rather always have new music. However, his choices are often dictated by finances. "I like old music. I've learned a lot from it—and most of it is new to *me*," he added with a laugh.

"But to commission a new score is more exciting if not for any reason except that you don't know what you're going to end up with," Mr. Taylor suggested. "Also, if you're in tune with the right composer and you have an idea for a dance, it's very, very convenient to have the music commissioned rather than trying to cram your ideas into a prewritten piece that you can't change. You can cut and take a section off here and there. But my attitude about that is: try not to tamper with what the composer has done. Again, it depends on what kind of piece it is and what kind of music it is. Certainly, I've done patchworks using many combinations and many composers, but it's not ideal."

One deliberate overlaying of disparate pieces of music was originally Paul Taylor's idea. For his *Cloven Kingdom,* he wanted to combine some percussion pieces of the late Henry Cowell with other music by Arcangelo Corelli and Malloy Miller. Together with the late composer-conductor John Herbert McDowell, the choreographer juxtaposed these vastly different works to heighten the almost startling onstage amalgam of social formalities and animal-like behavior. Mr. Taylor explained that the music for *Cloven Kingdom* was worked out initially by splicing tapes. Later, the final version was written down so that it could be played live—as it continues to be done, requiring several conductors.

Among the contemporary composers with whom Paul Taylor has joined forces is Carlos Surinach. "He was wonderful to work with," said the choreographer. Recalling *Agathe's Tale,* he explained, "I don't usually work with a script, but for this, we had a preplanned plot. I discussed it with him, and I knew what I *thought* I wanted."

Depending on the piece and the composer, Paul Taylor has used different methods of collaborating. For instance, in speaking of Donald York (who for some years has also been the company's conductor), Mr. Taylor mentioned: "He's gotten to know my work so well and has a wonderful sense of what I'm about, that we usually don't discuss it in any detail. I'll tell him about how long the piece will be, and maybe about some sections. But mostly, with some people, my attitude is that it's best to kind of just step back and let them do what they want. Then when they've got something that I can hear, I begin my work. I very rarely ask for musical changes—although there have been several times when I've started with one piece of music and completely thrown it out and ended up with something entirely different. "But with a composer like Don, there are very few changes. I think there was one—he wanted to make the end of *Diggity* a little longer, and added a few measures, which helped considerably."

This choreographer does not require certain specific counts for phrase lengths. "I did it once, with Don," he said, "and it was not fair to him. I don't think you should throttle composers that way."

When it was observed that some choreographers do specify certain counts, Mr. Taylor remarked: "I know they do, and they may have good reasons for them, but they're not mine. I wouldn't want to give them. If you have a dance already made, then the composer is just going to go in and fit the music to what's already there. That's one way to do it, I suppose, but that's terribly restrictive for the composer."

Yet choreographers often do just the reverse of that procedure: they choose extant music and then must set their choreography to fill the time—or else make cuts and arrangements to fit better with their dances as they develop.

Even when no basic musical changes are made, a choreographer must still make additional choices between widely varying versions of the same work. For instance, in his setting of Stravinsky's *Le Sacre du Printemps,* Paul Taylor settled immediately upon the rarely heard two-piano version.

"It has things that you don't have in the orchestral version," he explained. "It's my feeling that the rhythms sound clearer. And the idea of it for that dance was that it was more suitable to have something that sounded like a 'rehearsal' situation rather than a performance. That was important to the plot of the dance. But mainly, I chose it just because I liked it. I listened to the piano version for quite some time. In fact, we put it on instead of the other just for my own pleasure. Not that I wouldn't like to choreograph the orchestra version someday, but with certain scores like that, the volume and the richness of the orchestration can swamp you if you don't handle it right in the dance. They usually try to get around that in dance by big sets and large casts of dancers, which I don't think is a solution. But there *are* other solutions."

Commenting on the metrical changes in *Sacre,* Mr. Taylor said: "It's not complex. It's one of the easiest things to dance to I've ever done. It's easy as pie! The rhythms remain constant; they don't retard or speed up. And so, they're easy to count—for a dancer. At least nowadays. When it was first done, because it was so different, the dancers were thrown for a loop. But you see, the basic tempo is not fluctuating, and once you get the basic beat, then it's easy. There's no problem for the dancer."

"As far as convenience to choreograph to," he continued, "*Sacre* is written in very short sections, and that sort of helps with the problem of having things go on too long. If there is a long section of music and it doesn't change much, you really have to fill it up with movement ideas, or dramatic ideas, or some kind of something to keep the audience's interest. It just has to be real good. *Everything* is supposed to be real good, but it's a little easier when—as in *Sacre*—those sections last just the right time, and by coincidence, an amount of time that you can say something and then go on to something else in your dance; you don't have to keep padding it."

When asked how audience members can heighten their experiences of dance performanced to music, Mr. Taylor replied: "Well, I think that the more you can see a piece, the more you can see in it and hear in it. Sometimes pieces aren't made for seeing only once. So if someone wants to have a wider experience with a piece, then go back and discover it again."

"I think the technical things about both music and dance are not so important for audiences to be aware of," Mr. Taylor cautioned. "Some people are interested in that and want to make a study of it. I think that's fine. But your mind can get in the way of seeing and hearing. So often, I think the best an audience can do is to go to the theater and simply open their pores to what may be intended from the stage and the pit, and not come with a lot of preconceived notions that they try to force into what they are hearing and seeing."

From his own touring, Mr. Taylor recalled: "One of the best audiences I ever had was of Colombian Indians—about thirty thousand of them. They approached the work, though they had never seen anything remotely like it. I remember the program. We didn't get all the way through it because it rained. But their reaction I remember better than that of any audience we've ever had. They were like wonderful children who are seeing something for the first time, and they were delighted and amused . . . and so open and direct with their responses."

"So I think," Mr. Taylor continued, "that if we so-called civilized people could go into the theater and open ourselves and receive something new without a lot of book-learning—not that that isn't helpful; it *is* good in some cases. But I think the main thing for people to do is just relax and look at it.''

''With dance,'' he pointed out, ''it's a language that everybody is familiar with. Gesture is something that we 'read' in each other every day. We can't put the meanings in words quite often, but we're all familiar with the communication through our bodies—when we talk to each other, and the gestures we see across the street. We know what these things mean.''

''It's the same in watching dance,'' he concluded. ''People don't trust their own knowledge. It may be knowledge that's way in the back of their head or in their bloodstreams or nerve endings or in their spines. It's that kind of knowledge. They don't trust it . . . and it's to *be* trusted.''

HANYA HOLM'S EXPERIENCES WITH MUSIC

Hanya Holm: The very name conjures up the near-legendary aura of her skillfully crafted, serious concert works for barefoot modern dancers in Vermont and Colorado. Yet in contrast, one might also remember images of the stylish, witty, and lavishly costumed *Kiss Me Kate* and *My Fair Lady,* for which she also did the choreography.

In the music for her dances, there is an equally wide stylistic range, from a procession of simple percussion played by the dancers themselves, to the fullest theatrical instrumentation of tunes by Lerner and Loewe, to the crusty modernist orchestral counterpoint of Wallingford Riegger.

Sitting in the sunshine by her window one morning, Hanya Holm serenely recalled some of her varied experiences.[6] Back in 1938, her musical choices were capable of evoking almost wrathful ire. For instance, critic Jerome D. Bohm attended the New York premiere of Miss Holm's *Trend* and wrote that for her music she had used ''*Ionization* and *Octandre* of Varèse, performed in a recorded version which does nothing to ameliorate the exacerbating noises conceived by the composer, and which by no stretch of the imagination can be included in the category of music.''[7]

Writing some years later, the more sympathetic critic Walter Sorrell pointed out that ''what also distinguished Hanya's dancing was her intimate relationship to music, which strongly motivated her.''[8] It was this aspect of her artistry that the author discussed with Hanya Holm.

''You know, before I became a dancer, I was a very good musician,'' said Miss Holm. She liked to play Beethoven and all the classics on the piano, but in her youth, she didn't perform much contemporary music. However, she did get rigorous basic training in the Dalcroze music school. ''I would thoroughly recommend it for every child,'' she said.[9]

Miss Holm went on to explain that in the Dalcroze method, movement is used to help teach children the basics of music. ''The movement, unlike dance training, was *natural*—whatever you could do with it,'' she pointed out. ''With the music, mostly we analyzed the rhythms and the dynamic.'' Asked if this was good preparation for being a dancer, Miss Holm exclaimed, ''It couldn't be better!''

''I never had trouble with musicians,'' she went on to say. ''I always understood and could say precisely what a musician understands. I mean, not vaguely, but one could speak about the dynamic, about different rhythms: sharp rhythm, dynamic rhythm, uneven rhythm.''

Yet getting all the grammar of musical terms right was not enough. Collaboration also demanded some instincts and perceptions which cannot always be taught. For instance, Miss Holm remembered her extensive work with composer-arranger Trude Rittmann. ''Oh! She was very good. She understood. But you know, when you talk about music,'' advised the choreographer, ''you don't nail it down; you say it in 'percent.' There's always a mixture between facts of timing and emotional impact, and dynamic. And that you have to understand. It was easy with Trude; she understood so easily, she could feel it herself.''

''You see,'' she continued, ''it is very important in all the arts, to describe. You want this—what the value is emotionally. But the emotion is different for me, different for you. Everybody feels differently. To make a musician understand 'I want just this,' you have to get the right words, and you have to understand them; and then you have to say 'Yes, that is precisely what I want.' Precise it should be. What do we want? How should it be? It is so vague, and we have so many different opinions. The one feels that way and that way and that way; what for one is joy is probably not joy for another one.''

So the fact that she knew musical terms helped Miss Holm to say what she wanted more exactly. ''But,'' she qualified, ''you *still* have to use descriptions which are not always direct; they are sometimes indirect. And you have to know the people a little bit: how they work, how they translate a work themselves. If you say it's a happy piece, well it can be gay; it can be just a little bit more emotional, or less. There are degrees, and they are so fine, and so important. You have to *feel* how, and you have to try it out. You can't open a drawer and find on page number six there is a description. That doesn't work.''

In collaborating for musicals on Broadway, Miss Holm of course had to make use of the song tunes from the show, just as did Agnes de Mille. ''I cannot use Bach all of a sudden; they would say that's funny,'' she said playfully. ''It has to be in the idiom of the musical.''

During her career, Hanya Holm's ideas about how movement should relate to music varied, depending upon what project she was working on. In her early concert days, she had pianist Harvey Pollins improvise for the dancers during class. Out of his improvisations would come music which was used for the lecture-demonstrations that Miss Holm took on tour, particularly to college campuses. Another person she worked well with was composer-pianist John Colman, who also came from a Dalcroze background. There were times, however, when the choreographer dispensed with piano and just had percussion.

"When I didn't need so much melody," she explained. "I made sets of rhythms. For sound, hit a bell, and it rings."

"The Dalcroze music was not made for dancing," emphasized the artist. "There was improvisation on the piano, not with percussion. So I had to learn to improvise. You have to do it to become thoroughly acquainted with the structure of music: chords, how they are related; how to lead a melody; how to make a countermelody . . . all of this has to be thoroughly known."

At one point, Miss Holm taught Dalcroze classes herself, and that involved some musical improvisation on her part. In making music for movement, she advised, "you don't illustrate it, but you give the core, the basic structure of rhythm, timing, pattern, melody, harmony, voicing, phrasing—all that you have to learn and master."

"I still have a collection of a lot of instruments," Miss Holm continued. "I have drums, flute, Blockflute [recorder]. I played the recorder for [Mary] Wigman while she danced. I had to use the same tunes for her, always a certain repetition, because she depended on it. No improvisation there. It was interesting, though. I travelled with her for several years. That was the beginning. No orchestra or anything. We made it all ourselves."

By the time Hanya Holm was in America on her own and collaborating with the composer Wallingford Riegger, her musical needs had become more complicated. She would describe to Riegger what she wanted, and then "he went and searched around until he found the right thing," the choreographer recalled. She would work out parts of her dances alone, "and *with* him," she emphasized. "Sometimes I had to take his development. This was necessary to do, because after all, the music has its own laws, and we have to respect that. It was a very close relationship. He would sit at the piano and search it out and say 'Is this right? I don't know how you will develop it.' And he would play a little bit, and I would say, 'That's the right way.' So we understood; we talked it over."

Miss Holm never requested specific instrumentation from the composer. "I could only say at the end if it was workable or not, that it feels the right mood and temperament," she explained. "You see, sometimes one sees that a dance should go on, and then the music goes on quite differently. Then you say so! 'I'm not ready; I'm in the middle of a movement; the movement has to go on to the end.' You have to bring the dance to a climax, and the composer has to do something too for a climax in the music." Hanya Holm sometimes changed her choreography to go with the music, "but very rarely," she noted. "The music usually can make adjustments."

Wallingford Riegger was at Bennington College in those early days of modern dance. "He was here in New York, too," Miss Holm recalled. "I had my studio on the corner of 11th Street, and he would come there, and sit at the piano, and he could stay up sometimes half of the night, working."

Other composers, it seems, were not so dedicated to the dance. For example, the choreographer found it quite different to work with Roy Harris, whom she called "a musician's musician. I explained what I wanted. He had to watch the movement; he had to understand that a little bit. Sure, you have to accept it. If you don't accept the dancers, you'd best stay out," she advised. "But Harris didn't pay any attention to the fact that there is another art like dance involved in it."

When asked what music made her feel most like dancing, Hanya Holm immediately named percussion. She recalled in particular the playing of Franziska Boas, the daughter of the famous anthropologist. "She understood breath control. It wasn't mechanical," noted the choreographer.

Referring again to her early use of music by Edgard Varèse, she commented: "I liked Varèse because he too was a dynamic man. I took his *Octandre* and *Ionization* and he liked it, because he *saw* what he had *felt*. His later music, I couldn't quite agree with. It was mechanical, and that wasn't as good. I didn't like it—and I told him so, too!" laughed the artist.

Dwelling on Varèse's use of dissonance, she observed: "Some people couldn't understand the dissonance, because in this, several tones of different nature come together; it wasn't always harmony like Bach, Beethoven, and Mozart. Varèse used dissonances—lots of them, but they were so en passant, you see, that they 'belonged' to it. Otherwise, if you stop and make a big thing of the dissonances, it becomes overblown, and jars the listener. All musicians, even the classicists, used dissonance. The moment you dwell on it and make something out of it, it becomes strange. But Varèse used the dissonances for effect."

"We couldn't count Varèse the usual way," confided the choreographer. "We'd say 'One—two—three—carrumba!' "

Yet when needed, Hanya Holm knew how to talk precisely to musicians. She mentioned working on a ballet in Israel with a conductor who was "very good, but afraid. I said, 'Come on; have courage!' and worked with him very closely. And he took it, too, because he knew what I was talking about. I used his language. I think it's important. When you approach the musicians and talk fantasy, they resent it. You have to talk their language."

THE INFLUENCE OF SOUND ITSELF: MARY WIGMAN

Hanya Holm's creative work was all done in the United States. Nevertheless, she and other early modern dancers here drew enormous inspiration from the German dancer Mary Wigman. Today, even the writings of Wigman can indicate the kind of emotional response to basic sound that impels many choreographers.

In this excerpt from Walter Sorrell's translation, Mary Wigman pointed out the practical importance of counting beats in the process of collaboration:

Counting is spelled with capital letters by us dancers. We need it especially in our choreographic work during the process of creation and the rehearsing of group works in the modern dance or ballet . . . to account for the structure of the two cooperating artistic languages, dance and music, to attune them to each other in their temporal course and bring them together in harmonious understanding. We need it to define the beats, to clarify the transitions from one theme to the next, to be precise in giving the necessary accents, the moments of arrested movement and breathing. There is always counting. The musicians count and the dancers count. And sometimes they miss one another in counting, because the musicians count along the musical line whereas the dancers arrive at their counting through the rhythm of movement.[10]

The more mystical influence of basic sounds—in this case, of a gong—was recorded by Wigman in this way:

From everywhere, from all directions, a bewitching whispering and humming came toward me. . . . I felt as if I were witnessing an hour of birth. Now, from the whispering and murmuring, from shimmer and glimmer, the sound-turned-tone emerged in all its purity. . . . Full, warm, and dark, it was the voice of the depth, playfully alive in all its shadings. With breath-taking urgency it grew to its full strength, bronze that sounded and sang, in whose embrace the beating of one's own blood seemed to determine the rhythm of its vibrating revolutions. . . . Then, with imperial calm, suddenly it seemed to be still; and as if under the force of a majestic command, the natural order of things was restored. . . . *Monotony,* a solo dance from the group work *Celebration,* came about because of this "tone experience" given to me as a present by the Chinese gong. Only long after the genesis of the dance did I become aware of how deeply it was rooted in that experience.[11]

THE LEGACY OF GEORGE BALANCHINE

The choreography of George Balanchine continues to be a major influence upon the entire world of theatrical dance, not just at the New York City Ballet.[12] Highly regarded by both orchestral instrumentalists and conductors as one of the most musical choreographers of our time, Balanchine was the son of a composer. Furthermore, the choreographer himself was thoroughly trained in piano, theory, and composition.

Balanchine did not leave Russia until he was a young man, and some of his most formative work as a choreographer was developed in the artistic ferment of the Diaghilev troupe in Europe. It is not surprising, therefore, that Balanchine's musical tastes were grounded in the European classics, and that he was so deeply drawn to the works of Igor Stravinsky.[13]

Once transplanted to America, George Balanchine may have started wearing cowboy shirts, working in Hollywood, and choreographing for Broadway. But for his dances developed for the New York City Ballet, he drew mainly from the huge repertoire of European orchestral concert music of the past, and from the music of his friend Stravinsky. However, he did venture to choreograph some more serious concert works by American composers—for instance, some of Charles Ives' music in the ballet *Ivesiana.*

Balanchine used both older classics and new music in ways that large audiences have found uniquely tasteful and satisfying. A tremendous part of his artistry lay in his understanding and feeling for the structure and styles of classical music. So influential was his approach to merging music and dance that younger generations now sometimes find it difficult to believe that Balanchine's art was such a departure from previous theater. Balanchine was able to strip ballet of its previous dependence on grand costumes, scenery, pantomime, and elaborate plots. He presented dancers in simple tunics, with no backdrop whatsoever—and still created expressive, neoclassic dances that to many audience members seem to epitomize the tasteful merging of music and movement.

George Balanchine died in 1983. He left relatively little in the way of public writings, but the following excerpt from an essay he wrote in the late 1940s seems to reveal the heart of his approach to combining movement and music. It also touches upon his affinity for Stravinsky's music:

> Speaking for myself, I can only say Stravinsky's music altogether satisfies me. . . . When I listen to a score by him I am moved . . . to try to make visible not only the rhythm, melody and harmony, but even the timbres of the instruments. For if I could write music, it seems to me this is how I would want it to sound. . . . *Apollon* I look back on as the turning point of my life. In its discipline and restraint, in its sustained oneness of time and feeling, the score was a revelation. It seemed to tell me that I could dare not to use everything, that I, too, could eliminate. . . . I examined my own work in the light of this lesson; I began to see how I could clarify, by limiting, by reducing what seemed to be multiple possibilities to the one that is inevitable. . . . It was in studying *Apollon* that I came to understand how gestures, like tones in music and shades in painting, have certain family relations. As groups they impose their own laws. The more conscious an artist is, the more he comes to understand these laws, and to respond to them. Since this work, I have developed my choreography inside the framework such relations suggest.[14]

Decades later, when speaking at a press conference to announce the ambitious Stravinsky Festival given by the New York City Ballet in June 1972, George Balanchine commented further on his use of this composer's music:

> Stravinsky is who is responsible for anything we are using in music. . . . He made *musique dansante*. There have been only three who could do it: Delibes, Tchaikovsky, and Stravinsky. They made music for the body to dance to. They invented the floor for the dancer to walk on.[15]

Balanchine's approach to choreographing to music seems to have been very exact, and apparently he was quite conscious of the specifics of the music with which he worked. In speaking with Solomon Volkov, for example, he downplayed any mystical feelings that an artist might have, explaining:

> When I do a ballet I don't think about happiness or sadness; I think about the composer and his music. I can't cry over The Prodigal Son or Orpheus because they've gotten

themselves into a mess. I have enough problems with the music; it's very hard to come up with movements that don't contradict the music, that suit it. And then you think, how do I do it so that in this spot the man's arms go up and call the woman. And so that it will be interesting, elegant, or funny, and so on. That's our whole art! And it's difficult; you have to think a lot about it.

So you sit and think, how do you make the movement go with the musical line and not with the accents within a bar? If in the music there is a strong accent, the dance doesn't have to have one. You look, the music is in three-quarter time, but in the notes it could be six-eight. And in turn, six-eight isn't simply six even parts; the accent can fall on the even note or on the odd one. You have to keep all this in your mind. And so, when I'm doing a *pas de deux* to music by Tchaikovsky, I don't think about the *pas de deux* but about the music, about Tchaikovsky.[16]

Though the predominant part of his repertoire was drawn from classical music and Stravinsky, Balanchine did also from time to time collaborate with other living composers. One of these was Hershy Kay, who after arranging some British tunes for *Union Jack* wrote: "Mr. Balanchine is a fine musician and thinks his choreography in a musical manner. Form is primary with him, and one can never go wrong in taking his suggestions. This does not mean that he will not listen to other suggestions—there is always give and take."[17]

ERICK HAWKINS: COMMISSIONING AMERICAN MUSIC

Of all the American choreographers working in the twentieth century, Erick Hawkins has been one of the most dedicated in eliciting beautifully crafted new scores for his own company. And though this isn't widely known, it was also he who was in large measure responsible for arranging the commissioning of some important pieces when he was associated with the Graham Company, both as a principal dancer and as Martha Graham's husband.

For his own dances, he has enlisted such outstanding symphonic composers as Henry Cowell, Alan Hovhaness, David Diamond, Ross Lee Finney, Lou Harrison, Lucia Dlugoszewski, Wallingford Riegger, Virgil Thomson, and others. Yet interestingly enough, to prepare his dancers for moving to modern scores, the choreographer long ago decided to lead his company classes each day in "silence," so that they would not come to depend on exterior sound in order to feel and maintain a basic pulse or complicated metric and rhythmic patterns.

After one such class in his studio, Mr. Hawkins met with the author to discuss the music in his theatrical works.[18] *Ahab* had just been premiered as part of the 350th anniversary celebrations at Harvard University, and this work still very much preoccupied the choreographer.

Since 1948 he had been thinking about combining dance, music, and spoken lines based on Melville's novel *Moby Dick.* But it was not until nearly four decades later that Mr. Hawkins was satisfied with a scenario and a general idea of costumes, movement, and staging focusing on the obsessed whaling captain—whom the choreographer himself portrayed. At that point, Mr. Hawkins telephoned Ross Lee Finney, and within just a few months, the composer was able to provide an original score for *Ahab*.

''He did a wonderful job of integrating the text and the music,'' commented the choreographer. ''I had given him a scenario that told practically down to the second how long anything should be. He was extremely skillful and very humble—that's not the word exactly, but there *is* a humility of a kind. He took it for granted that I could get what I wanted on the stage, and he did it that way, so I had absolutely no trouble in the lengths of time he gave me. I think it's a terrific score! He followed my scenario so carefully, and with such subtlety!''

Mr. Hawkins had not given any demonstration of movement whatsoever to the composer. ''I couldn't give him any,'' he explained. ''I would describe what the section was *apt* to be, but until I did it with the music, I wouldn't know.''

''Practically everybody who tries to tell a real story on the stage in dancing has trouble in finding the right movement metaphors for their ideas,'' remarked Mr. Hawkins. ''If it's a narrative, the ideas are not literally on that stage; it's talking about something that's *not* on the stage. And so to try to find the equivalent poetically and imagine something that will work with that, is the problem.''

Consequently, the final movement patterns themselves could not be set until Mr. Hawkins had the score to *Ahab* in hand. ''Then I had our players come and make a tape of it,'' he recounted.

''I don't compose ordinarily just by hearing the music and having it kick me in the pants and make me do the movement,'' the choreographer said. ''All these recent years when the score has been written for our orchestra, I know the music very well from the first run-through that the musicians would do for a tape. I can't read a score the way a skilled musician would, but I can tell what the character of the melody is, be conscious pretty much of the rhythm, and so forth. I can get a pretty good notion of the *area* of sound that it's going to have.''

''So,'' he continued, ''I start out in a section of the music that I know I want to embody, and I work it out from an image. Then it's a long process of testing, to have the rhythms work. I work from the idea, but even in a piece where it's just a 'pure' dance and not narrative in any way, I try to let the movement come out. I am stimulated by the fact that I know what *area* the music is in, so *that* determines the general character of the movement.

''Then I just keep inventing all kinds of things, and we have a way of notating it down. Afterwards, it's a process of selecting out of that material—selecting what movement would go with that music. For example, if I am inventing the movement for one section, then I would put the metronome on and be conscious of what the tempo was, or the meter. If the meter was in three, then in general, I wouldn't want to do something that was too complicated in five. No matter how many variations or modifications I made, you would have to have some common denominator.''

Erick Hawkins is justifiably proud of his invention of movement in relation to music. Speaking of his early apprenticeship as a dancer, he recalled: ''I sat at Balanchine's feet for four years. He was a great artist, and I loved it. Everybody talks about how you could 'look at the movement and hear the music.' But I had one enormous advantage over him!'' declared Mr. Hawkins somewhat gleefully. ''He was locked into a vocabulary that was rather set, and when *I* hear a new passage in the music, I swing along with its essence, and I don't have to stick in an arabesque because that's all I can think of to do, when the music is *not* saying 'arabesque.' ''

As a young man, Mr. Hawkins related, he sought out the artists whom he considered the top people of that time, namely Balanchine and Graham. ''I was sitting in there watching them compose,'' he reminisced, ''and I was in the first dance that Balanchine ever composed in America! I had been studying dance not more than a year and a quarter. And I was in some of Martha's best pieces.''

''So I watched these two very fine artists proceed, and I learned from them,'' continued the choreographer. ''But I just feel that I've had certain achievements because I took a harder way than either one of them did. I was in a *purer* position.'' Clarifying the point, he explained: ''I once said to Lincoln Kirstein, after a performance at the City Center, 'Lincoln, you've got these big audiences, but I've never made a compromise.' ''

''Balanchine made all kinds of compromises,'' observed Mr. Hawkins. ''Like *Stars and Stripes* and *Union Jack,* where he brought a live donkey on the stage. He did all kinds of things that were slightly towards the pot-boiler. They were not a fresh statement, if you did Donizetti variations or Harlequin or something like that. He was reworking *old* subject matter, *old* material, *old* vocabulary . . . and *old* music!'' declared Mr. Hawkins vehemently.

A similar viewpoint was held by the composer Ned Rorem, who wrote:

> Only two American composers have come up with memorable ballet scores in thirty years—that is, since the happy postwar collaborations of Martha Graham with Copland, Schuman, Barber, and Dello Joio. They are Lucia Dlugoszewski, whose concoctions for Erick Hawkins' choreography are a hypnotic joy to both ear and eye . . . and Leonard Bernstein. Balanchine's caused nothing in American music.[19]

Mr. Hawkins himself suggested: ''You see, Balanchine was still thinking about dear old St. Petersburg, even if he lived here. His psychology was St. Petersburg, so he didn't give a hoot about—well, in the first place, he couldn't! He grew up with another ambiance.''

''I suppose artists can be transported to another country,'' he reflected. ''But look: I was born out where the plains meet the Rockies! All my formative years were here; I absorbed something that came out of the way *this* society thinks and feels, and the way *its* bodies move, and *its* psychology—the psychology of how an American girl might dance: instead of being a Czar's mistress, she might be something else. The astringent limitation of wearing a toe shoe does not fit with our American psychology. Isadora Duncan knew that in 1900, but others *still* don't know it!''

There are many observers who do cherish what Erick Hawkins has accomplished, as witnessed, for example, by this review in *The New York Times,* by Anna Kisselgoff:

> Mr. Hawkins, the choreographer, is so wonderful at getting to the essence of things! ''Plains Daybreak'' and ''Hurrah'' . . . are masterpieces of artistic integrity, of specifically American material made universal. ''Plains Daybreak'' gives us creation of the world poetically filtered through a vision inspired by American Indian ceremonials. The imagery in ''Hurrah'' conspires with the music of Virgil Thomson to create an unsentimental but nostalgic view of an American fairground romance at the turn of the century.
>
> In ''Plains Daybreak'' here is the human who finds his proper place in the evolutionary scale among his animal friends at the dawn of creation. Everything is beautiful about this work.[20]

Another perspective was offered by Jamake Highwater, in *Dance Magazine:*

> Hawkins has steadfastly created an exacting and imaginative theatrical ritual out of American experience. Hawkins combines our heritage as animals within various American ethnic traditions. It is this unique blend of native resources that places him among the most important artists of the twentieth century.
>
> In this era when dance has come of age, Erick Hawkins' works have a particularly important significance. For they talk to us in a language that is at once ultramodern and ancient. . . . Yet Hawkins is a chronicler of the American experience. Despite the fact that there are strong Oriental influences on his work, he remains a quintessentially *American* choreographer.[21]

As Erick Hawkins himself put it, ''Right off the bat, I knew that if you were going to have a new dance, you had to have a new music.''

Among his outstanding collaborations are more than a dozen pieces created with the composer Lucia Dlugoszewski. ''For those many years,'' explained the choreographer, ''I did the movement first, and then she wrote the music. There is no other composer that I would do that with.[22] Most of them are not humble enough, and they are not aesthetically interested enough to really see the relationship of the music to the dance. So I have to take that responsibility.

''Too many musicians and composers are too limited, too egocentric, and so they are not seeing that it would be marvelous to collaborate—that if they liked the choreographer and believed in the idea, it would be worth collaborating in a very subtle and intense way. They just kind of want to do a score and have a little *réclame* from having worked with the dance. But deeply loving it, theatrically—we just don't have a tradition of that."

Railing a bit at the avant-garde, intellectual type of composers, the choreographer suggested: "In recent years, our composers have, in general, gotten so dumb, so antitheatrical, so antiphysicality, that they don't know *how* to write scores for dance. So then the alternative has been by all the dumb people in dance, to go and use rock music. Well, that's no solution; that's a retrograde, psychologically destructive area of music, and the rock music goes with drug culture. There's no question; they're part of the same thing."

"So the refined art of music, the way it has been, is getting to be almost nonexistent," observed Mr. Hawkins. "There are very few composers that have real life in them. That's why Ross Lee Finney is so good," he offered in contrast. "He's very poetic, very sensitive. And his music is fresh. It doesn't have anything that's copying somebody else or copying some intellectual program or some slogan. It's done out of real invention, imagination, and feeling."

Speaking generally, Mr. Hawkins went on to say: "Most people don't see that the music and dance are two parts that have come together to make one thing. And there are too many of our audiences who are too obtuse—including critics. They act as if they didn't hear the music. Here I have these fine composers write, and they don't even mention the music! They don't even know whether it's Bach or Podunk!" said the choreographer in exasperation, adding: "They're too illiterate. They don't see the capability of making an intense theatrical art."

Yet for all his own intensity, there is also a streak of gentle charm in Erick Hawkins' work—as exhibited in his *Trickster Coyote,* for instance, with its score by Henry Cowell. "This piece was for my first solo concert in New York, in 1941," recalled the choreographer with feeling. "Henry played the flutes and did some squawks on the Chinese oboe. He travelled with me and played the parts also on the Hungarian pipe and English recorder. Then he gave me some instruments like a gourd rattle and a bone scraper that Chavez [the composer] had brought from Mexico." Mr. Hawkins waved towards a box in his studio: "There are the masks, and the costumes."

Trickster Coyote continues to be performed, and Henry Cowell's little melodies for it continue to please. "Melody has charm, and it relates very much to being at one with the world," emphasized the choreographer. He also agreed that another aspect of Cowell's music that was so good for dances was the fact that it had marked rhythmic swing and a physicality in it.

In contrast, Mr. Hawkins noted, "what Balanchine did was go back to the old classics to get his swing. He'd go back to Tchaikovsky. The works that he did *were* marvelous. But I just know: it's like the bird that doesn't build its own nest but goes and uses somebody else's nest. Build your own nest!"

"And so," concluded the choreographer, "the adventure is in finding the composers that are valid. Now that gets pretty difficult, and like this business of using tape recordings, people say, 'Well, we don't have the money for new or live music.' " To such comments, Erick Hawkins replies: "*Find* the money! Or else have one player do something beautiful!"

ALWIN NIKOLAIS: ALL-IN-ONE CREATOR

Money was the reason cited by choreographer-composer Alwin Nikolais for his venturing to make electronic music for his own dances. But artistically, he has produced interesting and effective sound scores that would not have been possible without electronic equipment. His work seems to epitomize what authors Lynne Anne Blom and L. Tarin Chaplin imagined when they wrote:

> Ideally, the sound score for a dance is the sound of the movement—what the dancer-choreographer hears as she creates her dance. What would happen, then, if the choreographer were doubly blessed, having the ability to compose as well as choreograph? Such a "choreoposer" could produce a score perfectly suited to the needs of each particular dance.[23]

Though most of the theater-going world tends to think of Alwin Nikolais primarily as a visual artist, he in fact came to dance originally through his activities as a professional musician.

Cheerfully reminiscing in his studios one day, Mr. Nikolais spoke about his first experiences in merging movement and music: playing for silent films in Westport, Connecticut.[24] "For that," he explained, "I played the organ. Most people flash into their minds immediately the tin pan piano for films. But no, that was very sophisticated music. If you played in a small theater, as I did—I wasn't yet 17—you advertised for a job saying that you played the Wurlitzer or whatever, and that you had a library of three or four *thousand* pieces of music, which meant that you would compile a score for a film, and the film companies would give you a cue sheet. They would say 'love scene, lasting sixty seconds,' or whatever, and so you could stack up your music."

"Well, I couldn't do that five times a week," explained Mr. Nikolais. "It would be a laborious thing. So I began to improvise. With the cue sheet, they would give a sample of the *kind* of music needed—just one line of music—and I would use that as a jump-off point for my improvisation. I was incredibly good at improvisation, which I was able to transfer to the piano later for dance."

"I played for silent movies for three years. This meant playing from four to seven or eight hours a day, almost nonstop—just getting up from the organ bench and running off for a milkshake and coming back quickly," laughed Mr. Nikolais.

But then talkies came in, and the young organist was out of work. So he hit upon the idea that he might find employment with the local dance teacher, who did "ballet, kind of Isadora Duncan style," according to the artist. "It was one of those small hodgepodge things," he added. "She did tap . . . everything from batons to hulas, you know. There again, I improvised a great deal, now on the piano.''

''But I first started to dance because I had gone with that dance teacher to see Mary Wigman perform,'' said Mr. Nikolais. ''This was 1933, and she used exotic instruments played offstage: percussion things, mostly big gongs and cymbals and wood blocks. I was completely captivated by the kind of accompaniment she used. From there, I went to Truda Kaschmann, who was from the Wigman school, and I wanted to find out about percussion accompaniment from her. She said, 'Well, you'll have to learn how to dance to do this.' So I accepted this rather gleefully and changed my profession!''

''The following year,'' Mr. Nikolais related, ''we both went to Bennington, where Franziska Boas taught percussion, and she had this roomful of absolutely glorious instruments. She was the world's worst teacher and also the world's best, because all she did was put you there and say 'Go play.' So you did, and she would say, 'No, no' or 'Yes, yes,' but never why; you had to find out yourself. She would just tell us a task of making a series of sounds that would correlate into something that one could call music.''

''So from there,'' continued the choreographer-composer, ''I went back to Hartford—this was 1937–38—and I'd go into automobile junkyards and collect brakedrums, U-bolts, and gas tanks. I filled my studio with this junk and then proceeded to use it as the basis for sound.''

Around this time, Alwin Nikolais also started to do some of his own choreographing, incorporating his knowledge of percussion techniques and passing on these skills to his dancers. After his service in the Army, Mr. Nikolais returned to the dance world and worked with Hanya Holm for about a year. Then he ''landed at the Henry Street Playhouse,'' where he stayed for twenty-two years, becoming director in addition to teaching, choreographing, and staging theatrical works for both children and adults.

''I played the piano for a long time for my own classes,'' he related. ''I would get up and demonstrate and then sit down and play. At the Henry Street Playhouse, the classes were up on the stage, and since the piano was in the pit, I would have to leap up on the stage. So this was kind of an athletic job which kept my legs in fine fettle for a while.''

Mr. Nikolais also continued his experiments with sound. ''At that time,'' he said, ''I brought in a series of dance and music artists, including Henry Cowell, who did his inside-the-piano spiel, and I began to play inside the piano during my accompaniment as well. I became fairly skilled in that. So after the War, I did much of my own sound stuff.''

''You see,'' he explained, ''the whole thing was that at Henry Street Playhouse, we had no money. Dancers would be onstage, and sometimes I would just improvise on the piano or play percussion. They obviously had never heard what I was playing before—because it *was* improvised. And this would be done, actually, in performance; *nothing* was written.''

Searching through file cards that listed all his repertoire, Alwin Nikolais indicated that his early formal works featured music by a string of other composers—names not necessarily well-known now. ''I couldn't afford a 'great' composer,'' explained the artist, ''whereas very often the student composers were inadequate. They would do very strange things. I remember one in particular. I gave him the whole rhythmic structure of the dance itself, and he went away and then came back with a piece of music, and the dancers went through their piece exactly right. At the end, he was still playing. I said, 'Eugene, the piece is over.' He said, 'Yes, but the music isn't!'

''My first professional choreography was commissioned by Chick Austin, who was a big name in art in Hartford. He was very much involved with the avant-garde particularly, and he commissioned me and Truda Kaschmann to do a ballet, and Ernst Krenek to do the score. It worked out very well, because of course Ernst was a marvelous musician.''

That particular project could come under the category of collaboration by air mail. ''Krenek was lecturing all over the country,'' recalled the choreographer, ''and I would send him my notes by special delivery. I wrote out, specifically, whole rhythmic structures. Of course, being a musician myself, I could do that very well. He would then, a few days later, send back a musical piano score, which later took the shape of a piece for chamber orchestra.''

''He was an exponent of the Schoenberg technique of twelve tones, which I hated at first, but after I worked with it for a while, I began to see and hear it . . . and love it,'' said Mr. Nikolais. ''I thought it was good. So the final piece of music was stunning, especially with the orchestra.''

It wasn't until his *Forest of Three* that the choreographer-composer used a wire tape recorder for the first time. ''It was an economic necessity!'' he laughed ruefully. ''Yes! I couldn't often afford to engage a composer. I used student composers, but that to me was often disastrous, because I *was* a good musician, and I *could* understand what music could do to dancing. Of course, most of them had no experience with it whatsoever.''

''So as soon as the tape recorder came out, I began to put sounds on tape, using voices—anything. I liked the idea of *musique concrète* [the use of natural sounds manipulated on tape]. I still think it's probably the most challenging and the most rewarding of any sound process,'' observed the artist. ''Nothing is prearranged beforehand; you have to have the guts to choose a sound out of the air—wherever—and of course, nothing is precooked or prefrozen for you: no scale, no harmonic structure. You have to work as an honest-to-God musician; you have to choose from moment to moment what you want to listen to. You stamp on the floor, shuffle your feet, punch somebody in the stomach, hit a piece of wood or an old gas tank, whatever, mixing already-recorded sounds on there.''

''In the process,'' related Mr. Nikolais, ''I discovered. I grew like Topsy. If the tape broke, I'd put it in accidentally backwards and then decide I liked that better. Then I also discovered the changing of speeds that altered the sounds. And so I began to be a tape composer, manipulating the tape, squeezing it, changing the speed, pinching it, and doing all sorts of things to make a succes-

sion of sounds—and then making endless splices and putting it all together again,'' he said. ''This was a monk's job, but I loved it.''

The next step was to use electronically reproduced sound, which Alwin Nikolais did in his path-breaking work *Imago,* first presented in May 1963 at the McMillan Theatre at Columbia University. Experimenting in the university's sound labs with engineer James Seawright, the choreographer-composer found this a new kind of collaboration. ''I would talk to him, and he would have me listen to some sounds, and then I would indicate where I wanted to go from there. He would punch on the piano roll, and it would come back. It was a laborious task,'' noted Mr. Nikolais.

''Shortly after that,'' he recalled, ''Jimmy informed me that there was a big electronic show and suggested I go with him. We came upon the Moog, and I immediately ordered one. So I have the very first synthesizer that Bob [Moog] sold.''

With this equipment, the artist no longer had to bother with punch cards, and he had no need for an intermediary engineer. ''Immediately I could manipulate it,'' he emphasized. ''I still know nothing about electronics or how they operate. If any one minor thing went wrong, I would be in a complete dither; I wouldn't know what to do. But I followed Bob's handwritten instructions about what to push where and what to plug in and so on, and I just played with it, and through trial and error got what I wanted, and immediately fed it through the tape recorder. I went along with that for years.''

That first Moog is somewhat of an antique now, and Alwin Nikolais has updated his electronic equipment, recently making use of his sophisticated Synclavier and an Emulator.

Since acquiring all his electronic systems, this choreographer-composer has evolved an interesting way of working up his theatrical productions. He usually does the whole choreography first, in silence, or to counts. Thinking of his Columbia-Princeton lab days, he remarked that even then he had begun to work in arhythmical material.

''We used a stop watch,'' he explained. ''We could measure sound exactly on tape. The way I frequently did the score if it had no meter was to have the dancers do the dance, and I would indicate moments of cue. There might not be a cue for as long as forty seconds or one minute, and then I would say 'Cue 44: jump,' and 'Cue 45: turn,' and so on. All this was recorded on tape with microphone. Now I had a time measurement on the tape, so I would be able to make a sound and would match it up with the length of time before the cue, then splice on the next one, and so forth, and I would have a perfectly timed, regulated score.''

As for introducing his dancers to the actual sounds they will have for a performance of a new work, the choreographer commented: ''In the first place, I don't consider the Mickey Mouse quality of the music; I like the music and the movement to run simultaneously as two separate strata of reception for the hearing and the eye.''

There are, as he explained, certain landmarks with the cues—places where certain things have to happen in the movement in conjunction with the sound score. But in between, the counts may be different for the two media—or there may be no regular counts at all. ''Recently, I've been going back a lot to a metrical and rhythmic structure. But still a lot of work is done without meter and without pulse.''

Turning again to the compositional aspects of his multimedia creations, Alwin Nikolais said: ''Very often I will know two weeks in advance the kind of choreography I'll be doing, so I'll start searching for sound all day. I will have a 'sound bank' available so that when the choreography is done, I can choose from that.''

''I think the one convenience about the electronic instruments,'' he emphasized, ''is that you can do it all yourself, and you don't have to depend upon the skill of other people.''

2

Call in the Composers!

LOUIS HORST: SPEARHEADING A NEW MOVEMENT

Most choreographers do not have the time, training, or inclination to compose music for their own dances. When Martha Graham, for instance, was first exploring a new path in modern dance, she had at the piano her musical mentor, Louis Horst, who coaxed, taught, composed, and performed for her. His influence was such that some have even considered him the father of modern choreography. The historian Ernestine Stodelle has written that "more accurately, from a historical standpoint, he could be called modern dance's first pioneer," and she went on to observe:

> Like every great leader, Louis Horst cut through the wilderness of ignorance with a machete of convictions. With his pioneer-partners Martha Graham, Doris Humphrey and Charles Weidman, he ripped away the undergrowth of an effete, European-dominated ballet. The four artists made up the modern dance *avant-garde* of the twenties and thirties. With youthful fervor they dedicated themselves to the ideals underlying contemporary art: to express the inner conflicts, the dynamic rhythms and the stark realities of twentieth century life.[1]

Born in Kansas City in 1884, Horst died in New York in 1964. He first became involved with dance as a collaborator with Ruth St. Denis. Subsequently, in addition to his impact as music director for Graham, he influenced many other choreographers and dancers through his courses and books on preclassic and modern forms in music for the dance.[2]

Ernestine Stodelle has summarized his contributions to the field:

It was Louis Horst, the composer, who led the way for a new relationship between music and the dance. Certainly, such productive collaborations as the Agnes de Mille-Aaron Copland ballet *Rodeo* and the Jerome Robbins-Leonard Bernstein Broadway musical *West Side Story* could never have become realities without Horst's pioneer innovations. Though Doris Humphrey and the German modern dancer, Mary Wigman, used musical accompaniment in various unorthodox ways, it was Louis Horst's score for Martha Graham's solo, *Fragments: Tragedy and Comedy,* performed in 1928, which according to him, was the first original musical score to be written for a dance after the dance had been composed. A new precedent was set, and from that time on, many first-rate musicians rallied to the exciting demands of composing scores in broken rhythms, changing dynamics and unresolved dissonances to match the tensions of the new dancing. Wallingford Riegger, Henry Cowell, Hunter Johnson, Freda Miller, Norman Dello-Joio, Norman Lloyd, William Schuman, Vivian Fine, Halim El-Dabh, Robert Starer, even Paul Hindemith, were among those who lent their musical talents to the modern dance.[3]

Writing twenty years later, the distinguished critic Walter Sorrell still depicted a forceful musical presence in Louis Horst:

Louis never thought of himself as a great composer, yet he was proud of having written *Frontier* for Martha, and *Primitive Mysteries,* and *El Penitente*—not as music that stands by itself, but as music that was for the dance it accompanied. Some dancers who commissioned scores from him felt sure that whatever he would compose for them would be in the right key for their ideas. . . . He did not mind the term Gebrauchsmusik [functional music] for what he did. The composer, he felt, gains a vitality and rhythmic strength from association with dance. Music serves, or should, not only to limit, to accentuate, to confine, to deepen the choreography, but specifically to discipline the very plastic instrument of the dancer. The body is not the simplest of instruments. Music is only . . . a frame for a dance.[4]

Summing up Horst's contribution, Sorrell paid a rather astonishing tribute:

Dance history can boast of three outstanding nondancers who have vastly contributed to the development of the art. What Diaghilev and Kirstein were to ballet, Horst was to modern dance. He had little or none of their organizing abilities, but was much more of a creative artist himself: as accompanist-composer, writer, and above all, as teacher.[5]

OTTO LUENING: ON BENNINGTON, ELECTRONICS, AND MULTIMEDIA

Another composer who not only collaborated with Doris Humphrey, but who was also very much in on the ground floor of the whole early modern dance movement in this country is Otto Luening.

His work for Humphrey was *Theatre Piece No. 2,* which the composer discussed one day in his apartment overlooking the Hudson River.[6] He recalled: "Doris Humphrey had a kind of scenario that had a certain dramatic shape to it, that she had thought about and that I could respond to. I could say, 'What do you need—kind of loud music here, or not so much?' At first, it was not too precise; rather a general idea."

The drama, as the composer understood it, was to depict a progression from chaos to prehistoric earth people, then developing in various ways—some of them serious, some of them satirical—finally into a free dance. It included, along the way, some take-offs of popular dance clichés in the thirties.

"It was something that I rather liked doing myself," Mr. Luening remarked. "Before that, I had written a little set of chamber pieces called *Four Cartoons*. Two of these were takeoffs on dance music: first I wrote an ancient dance, with the accompanying clichés of the time; and then I did the same with the modern, except I 'messed it up' on purpose so it was very dissonant."

In the Humphrey piece, there was also one section with a 1930s aesthetic. While the dance was going on, a singer performed music for which Otto Luening had made up some phony German—as he described it, "a long, soul-searching piece, with twelve-tone accompaniment."

The vocalizing in the first movement had no words: "Just the human voices coming out of the chaos," explained the composer. "First you heard nothing, then a stamping, then gradually you heard this voice coming. There was nothing else but stamping and percussion in the 'orchestra'—which consisted of electronic sounds, suggesting the mystery of chaos. Then we had a kind of primitive dance, and so on, moving gradually into the more advanced things, and we got into these satires. I even wrote texts and some dialogue for them."

"It was a broad sense of dance," emphasized Mr. Luening; "It was a theatrical *event* that included dance . . . and of course, Humphrey was the one that used the electronic music that I could do. I used an electronic score, and I also used brass—but I didn't need anything more."

Explaining how the unchanging electronic score was merged with the movement, the composer mentioned that Humphrey whittled her scenario down and timed it very carefully. "She actually made a time chart, a measure chart: 'we have three measures of 4/4 time here at about this tempo, and now we need two measures of 6/8.' She had enough musical knowledge to put that all down. She was a very precise artist."

When asked if Humphrey ever gave him impulses or movement to accompany musically, the composer said: "Well, yes; she would give *sort* of an idea. I'd see a rehearsal, then I'd be on my own. It was quite a job then to put that score together electronically. I told her, 'Now listen, you don't have Louis Horst here as a dance accompanist. Every time that you make one change like that, of one measure, it takes *hours* to get this work back on track; so make up your mind!' "

After Humphrey had devised her score, said the composer, "then I'd play things; I'd test things for her. I'd try out something electronically and say, 'This is about the way it seems we ought to do this.' On the whole, she went along with my musical ideas."

Distinguishing this use of specifically tailored electronic music from the kind of experience provided when dancers merely put a needle on a phonograph record, Ruth and Norman Lloyd noted in their article "Un-Can the Music":

> Doris Humphrey's new *Theater Piece No. 2* . . . is a most successful experiment in dance and sound. The work has a score for tape-recorder and chamber orchestra written by Otto Luening. The tape-recorder with its unearthly electronic sounds, bathed the dance in a surrealistic form of music. It contributed something that could not be done by any other means. It was inventive—not ersatz.[7]

"I had had a lot of experience with dancers," Mr. Luening explained. "I was chairman of the Bennington music department when that dance school started, and I always had some contact with dance. I also performed flute in some things for Martha Graham's premieres and conducted operas with ballets. All the things we did at Bennington did involve cooperation between music and dancing and drama; that was part of the whole Bennington idea," noted the composer-educator.

Ernestine Stodelle gave a graphic description of the Bennington scene: "Striding the campus like a superfluity of royalty, resident practitioners of the various arts conferred with the dancers. Among them was Otto Luening, future pioneer in tape and electronic music."[8] Upon hearing this description, Mr. Luening laughed and remarked: "We *had* to cooperate with all this stuff. If we didn't, nothing would happen. We were out there on this hill in Vermont, you know, and there wasn't much to do, so what were the faculty—even in other departments—to do, particularly in the winter? So entertainment became very essential. The arts became part of the intellectual entertainment, because it *was* a very sophisticated arts school. And the dancers got in on the ground floor because they wanted to make the dance equal to the other arts. So the dance was now an art, no longer in the gymnasium, but out and equal with the other arts. That was the notion."

"Then of course," he added, "the question was: with music and drama, how much of both of them do you use for the dance? There was an enormous cooperation between dancers and composers, and also with the drama people."

Concerning his association at Bennington with Louis Horst, Mr. Luening was asked if he thought it fair to call Horst the father of modern choreography. Mr. Luening observed: "Well, he was. He really helped Martha Graham with music. He'd play things over for her, and taught all her students about the old forms."

"Louis was a conventionally trained musician," he continued. "He had a lot of practical experience, including being a pit musician, and vaudeville playing. Well, when he met me, I was a pal, so I could talk his language, about the musicians and the composers or whatever. But my relationship with Louis and Martha goes way back before Bennington. When I was in Rochester in '25 on the faculty of the Eastman School of Music, Martha was a dance instructor in the opera department of the same school. After rehearsals, we would have some food at the Fern Restaurant and talk a lot about how we ought to do things. I was working on a piece called *Sister Beatrice,* which also used movement. So we'd talk about combining all these media, very early in the game.''

Other vignettes of his dance associations occurred to Mr. Luening: ''Around 1929, when I was free-lancing around New York, Louis hired me to play John Powell's *Dirge* for the Dance Repertory Theater. It was for two pianos, eight hands. There were two players at each piano, and I was one of them. And then, he hired me to do a set of arrangements of Basque folksongs that Kurt Schindler had collected, and that Martha was using in one of her dances. I arranged a lot of them for small chamber combinations—one of Louis' little combos, you know. I used to sit there late hours with him and her and write out the parts, while she was sewing the costumes for the performance. We had to do everything by hand.''

Mr. Luening also performed with Horst for the premiere of Martha Graham's *El Penitente.* ''Horst made an arrangement for piano, flute, and clarinet, and I played it with Bob McBride,'' he noted.

''Horst, in referring to himself, always said he was not a composer; he was an 'accompanying composer,' '' Mr. Luening recalled. ''In other words, he filled the bill for the music that was needed, and let the dancer—let Martha—be creative in her total concept of what went on.''

''I don't think Martha cared much about the details of music,'' Mr. Luening ventured to say, ''but she knew *instinctively.* It was a very subjective experience for her, whether a musical score felt right or not. She'd talk to Louis, and he would make the adjustments musically. So it was back and forth between her and Louis. That was very successful for many years.''

''Louis Horst was sort of a grandfather of this whole movement—and a solid musician,'' remarked Mr. Luening. ''He was like me—or Wally Riegger; he had a solid basic foundation, from which one took off. But you didn't take off just because you were being 'inspirational'; that was much too risky, because you had to deal with theaters, and with audiences.''

''The next step was that they began getting other composers like Bill Schuman. And it got bigger and bigger: orchestras, more theater, then people doing recitations. So gradually out of this dance movement, they moved into a new *kind* of theatrical event. So you see that multimedia was not invented last week!'' observed Mr. Luening with a flourish.

Elaborating on the subject of multimedia, the composer related: ''I actually wrote a piece of music in Chicago called *The Soundless Song* for chamber ensemble, voice, movement, and colored lights. That piece came alive because of my preoccupation with theosophy. I saw all of these possible things, unification not only in words or only in sound; you had to have *everything* and work it out with symbols. Mixed media: that was it, because no one media could really tell the whole story. It was a sort of metaphysical philosophical idea behind my works. That happened a lot too with certain of the dancers. It was in the air at that time.''

When asked what he explored philosophically in those early discussions with Martha Graham and Louis Horst, he replied: ''At the time we were all feeling around, about getting a different kind of unity for the different media—one different from Wagner or Strauss. We didn't want to go on in the big European tradition; we wanted to make our own thing here, to express things in simpler terms without always having a colossal orchestra or enormous stage sets. But of course, that's all expanded now. In later years, you have Martha at the Metropolitan Opera and running things on a pretty big scale.''

When asked if the reason for his doing those early small arrangements was financial, or if it was because the kind of sound desired then was a sparse one, the composer responded: ''Well, both. In those Basque folksongs, the music is very simple and very powerful, and you didn't have to have a symphony; that was not necessary. There were some economic reasons to do it with a small combination, but also some artistic ones. Art isn't *all* enormous and big and expansive; you don't have to make it that way. The universe is not only infinitely large, but also infinitely small. Infinity is not only expansive. So we had those notions, and we also felt we didn't want to be cut out just because you didn't have a big opera house at your command. Without a symphony orchestra, you ought *still* to be able to make your artistic statement.''

Turning to the seemingly infinite possibilities now beckoning with electronics, Mr. Luening suggested: ''But you see, if they use the sounds like Christmas tree decorations, you don't have to be a musician to hang them all right. You can work with sound effects.'' He felt, in contrast, that trained composers have much to offer in the way of deciding how to put sounds together to make balanced structures.

Asked to comment about more haphazard methods, in which chance and dance and music are the ingredients to be blended for public performances, the composer said, ''Well, that's a new business that's happened. You have a lot of that with computers. You can do random choices and so on. I can't say just what I feel about it, but I think it's somewhat of an illusion to think that anything like that—that art—can be completely free, because it always has to stop at some point. And so you have a framework of some sort: a beginning and an ending.''

''I've always accepted that,'' he went on to say, ''because I don't think you can orchestrate the cosmos. Some of the people go around and make tape recordings of everything, like taking a picture of nature: if you do enough of it, you'll get it all in. But we don't have any canvas big enough for this kind of thing. That's only my opinion—only one man; I never cared to play God, so I'd rather let other people do it. I must say that I've seen some things that John Cage has done that are very attractive, for example . . . *some* things. But he generally stops at some point too. He doesn't want to go on forever, and I don't want to sit there for a month and listen to him!'' laughed the composer.

Looking back over the whole canvas of performing arts in this century, Otto Luening remarked that, ''in the United States, the arts had always been rather the plaything of the elitist patrons for music, for chamber music, for paintings; they weren't really integrated into the national life, excepting the popular arts like musical comedy and pop music. But that was business, and 'Business is the business of America'; that was understood.''

''But the whole function of art, and what it meant, and what you had to do . . . and that you could *learn* some things from it, *that* had not been established in the twenties or thirties,'' Mr. Luening explained. ''So when we got to Bennington, it was accepting the arts as a part of the academic scene with the same privileges, the same respect, that was given to mathematics or language, or anything. And this was new.''

''Dance was not 'established' in those days,'' he noted. ''Now it's all over the place—an established activity in the United States, and a pretty honored one.''

''What happened in this business, including with the dance,'' Mr. Luening mused, ''is that it's gone so fast and we have such a mass of stuff, that it's very hard for people to have any type of judgement about it.''

''Do we need quality? Or is it enough just to produce over and over again?'' he asked. ''Is it all right if we just *do* things—or do you have to hear them too and see them and absorb them? And can you get sick from too much music listening?'' asked this composer, who among his many honorary offices served on the environmental committee for noise control in New York City.

''Everybody has all this available sound,'' Mr. Luening concluded. ''But how can you *use* it? I mean, what's there for *you?* Everybody has to find that out, and see.''

HENRY COWELL'S VANTAGE POINT

Just as the physical sources of musical sound have been enlarged, so too the stylistic possibilities available for American theatrical performances have expanded enormously. As we approach the end of the century, the music for dance is increasingly apt to be drawn from cultures spanning the globe, as well as from the ethnic heritage and the personal imagination of individual American composers.

This enlargement of both available musical repertoire and collective audience taste owes much to the explorations and persistence of a few early twentieth-century American composers, notably the late Henry Cowell. What he suggested over a quarter of a century ago is perhaps even more pertinent to composers currently at work:

It is true that I have devoted more time to the study of non-European musical systems than other Western composers, but that is because I took it for granted that a 20th-century composer would need to know and to choose from among many kinds of musical inheritance in the world, not just the French and the German alone. It seemed natural for an American to stretch his mind beyond the limitations of European traditions and to welcome the infinite variety and vitality of the human imagination as it has expressed itself in the music of the world.

I soon found, of course, that every continent has developed literally dozens of musical styles, all of which had beauty and meaning for their practitioners. This great sea of musical imagination seemed to me my natural inheritance, within which I must find my own music. The multiplicity of musical experience to which I subjected myself seemed to me to be a fact of modern life—useless to turn one's back on it.

Today every composer is faced with the problem I embraced for myself in my youth: How may one learn to live in the whole world of music—to live, and to create? No single technique, no single tradition is any longer enough.[9]

In the dance world, each piece can present intriguing puzzles to composers—puzzles that have many possible solutions. And each composer may work in entirely different ways depending upon the choreographer with whom he is collaborating.

WILLIAM SCHUMAN: COMPOSING FOR GRAHAM AND TUDOR

"I first met Martha in 1940," recalled composer William Schuman as he spoke to a gathering of students and friends at the Graham School.[10] "It was in Boston, at the Boston Symphony Orchestra, which was under [Serge] Koussevitsky at that time. They introduced my *Third Symphony*. I went backstage to receive guests with the conductor, and Katherine Cornell—the actress, who was a great friend of Martha's—introduced herself to me and said that Martha Graham would like to meet me."

"Then those *eyes* looked at me, and Martha Graham said, 'Mr. Schuman, your music moves me.' I wanted to yell 'Mama!' I knew I would never be the same again. . . . and I have never *been* the same again!" laughed the composer.

The first work on which the two artists collaborated was *Night Journey*. Mr. Schuman recalled the method of their joint creation: "When we agreed that we would try and work together, she sent me a letter—a long and involved letter describing the ideas she had for a ballet with a folk singer, and it really didn't appeal to me very much. I was wondering how I could say that. Then there was a postscript: 'I am considering a work on the Oedipus theme from Jocasta's point of view.' So I wrote that I liked the idea in the postscript! But from the composer's point of view, I needed to know a little more."

"I think of the composer as an assisting artist," explained Mr. Schuman. "Don't let me sound modest, because an enormous part of the drama that comes from the stage has to come from the pit; I am not downgrading the role of the composer. But I asked: 'What is the aural ambiance that you want? Is it fast, is it slow, is it loud, is it soft? What are the adjectives that you would use, and how long does it go on?'

"I eventually got her to say, 'Well, it opens in the following *kind* of spirit . . . and this might go on for two and a half minutes, at which point I might take it in such and such a direction.' "

"So," continued Mr. Schuman, "what I would get was not a specific story line, but rather the unfolding emotional climate. The one thing the audience can't be in doubt about is the emotional climate of the work.

"Being guided by what her needs were, I would then sit down and compose the music. Martha's system was, once she got the score, then she would set the ballet to it. In other words, the impetus came from her to the composer; then the composer would write his score; then she would proceed from the score."

Contrasting this experience with his collaboration for Antony Tudor's *Undertow,* Mr. Schuman rather cryptically remarked: "I had the great honor of being the first composer that he commissioned . . . and the dubious distinction of having been the last."

Tudor was more vague than Graham was when it came to supplying directions, reported the composer: "He would say, 'Now the opening of this should be the atmosphere of a damp night, and when you turn the corner and feel moisture on your hand, and you turn and look. There will be spasmodic outbursts, and finally, great calm, and you must write a beautiful melody.' "

Tudor had not told William Schuman there would be a birth depicted at the beginning of the ballet, nor what would happen at the end, for which he made only this request: "Can you write me a four-minute musical essay on fear? It will have to be music that would make the listener anxious."

Contrasting this to his collaborations with Martha Graham, Mr. Schuman observed: "Most of the music that I did for Martha, and most of the music that other composers have done for her, is abstract. Martha's style is so powerful that many composers start sounding like 'Martha Graham composers.' I can't write for Martha without seeing her in my mind: seeing her movements, seeing the techniques of her dance. So in that sense, you are writing for her particular characteristics. But those characteristics don't have much to do with the technique of how you write; they have to do with the desired impulses you have."

William Schuman also wrote the music for Graham's *Theater for a Voyage* and *Witch of Endor,* both of which he feels were perhaps not quite as strong. However, one dance that may never be done again, which he now labels "electric," was his score for *Judith.* Commissioned by the Louisville Orchestra and danced by the choreographer herself, *Judith* was considered by the composer as his "concerto for dancer and orchestra." Twenty-five minutes long, it is now lost, as Martha Graham herself could not remember the steps and never taught it to anyone else. The music, however, is preserved on a recording by the Louisville Symphony.

The premiere of Mr. Schuman's *Night Journey* was conducted for Martha Graham by Louis Horst. Recalled the composer: "I knew Louis very well. We got along fine. But nobody 'worked' with him. He was in his own way a tyrant, but a very interesting and creative man. He was very hard on the musicians. Those scores were very difficult to do the first time. He had men from the Boston Symphony, and I knew those men very well, and some of them said to me, 'If it weren't for you, we would have just walked out,' because he treated them as if they were in a vaudeville pit band or something. He was in a way a wonderful man. He did so much for dance and dance music. But he was a self-made person and didn't always have the finesse that one sometimes requires on the professional scene. But it didn't matter; he got what he wanted. He was a good functionary. He wasn't a brilliant conductor—but that wasn't his role."

When asked if he had any contact with the dancers after he had composed his pieces for Martha Graham's company, he replied: "No, only pleasantries. I would go in toward the end, and if I had some comment to make on the musical element, I would make it to Martha privately."

It was the same with Tudor's group. "You don't deal with the dancers," generalized the composer; "you deal with the choreographer. I would come in to the last few rehearsals and make my comments to Antony. Sometimes I would say that in such and such a place, it perhaps didn't go as well as another part of the score. Whatever it would be, it would just be minor comments. My job was always to be concerned with the musical element, not the others. Both Antony and Martha are extraordinarily musical people. They were both very sensitive to musical values, and both were very considerate of the composer's views, so I had no problems."

CARLOS SURINACH: THEATRICAL FLAIR WITH A CASTILIAN ACCENT

The scores that Carlos Surinach wrote for Martha Graham's works alone have had more than a thousand performances all over the world. Among the most well-known dances performed to his music are: *Embattled Garden, Acrobats of God,* and *The Owl and the Pussy Cat,* all for Graham; *Apasionada,* for Pearl Lang; *Feast of Ashes,* choreographed by Alvin Ailey; *Deep Rhythm,* as set by Doris Humphrey; *La Sibila* and *David and Bath-Sheba,* by John Butler; *Agathe's Tale,* commissioned by Paul Taylor; and *Bodas de sangre,* by Miguel Therekov. Sometimes these scores had complicated histories, which Mr. Surinach described in an interview at his home in Florida.[11]

Focusing on *Feast of Ashes,* the composer remarked: "People think that the music all goes together with the dance originally—and it doesn't."

"One day," he recalled, "Alvin Ailey was visiting me to find music. He had in mind *The House of Sorrow,* by Garcia Lorca, and he was speaking to me all the time about that work. So I said, 'Take *Ritmo Jondo* if you like. All you have to do is pay the rent—not to me; to the publisher. *Ritmo Jondo* is available. If someone wants to use it for a ballet, there is nothing a composer can do. Whatever you want: this is legal, you see.'

"So Alvin Ailey took *Ritmo Jondo.* He also took excerpts from another work of mine, *Doppio Concertino,* and I said that might not be good, to put those two works together, unless *I* did it, because I knew how to do it—and after all, it's my music.' He had all my records. All the choreographers in New York at one time had all my records. So he imagined what he wanted. All I had to do was tell him if something he had thought to put together didn't go musically. Then he would redo that little passage, according to what I had written. That's a cooperation!" smiled the composer.

This is just one example of why there is sometimes a bit of confusion about exactly where the music for dance works came from. Mr. Surinach clarified what had happened with this particular piece: "I made an arrangement of the two works. So now we have *Ritmo Jondo* as a concert piece; *Doppio Concertino* as a concert piece; and when they come together in that new version, the name is *Feast of Ashes.*" In addition, Doris Humphrey had originally set just the *Ritmo Jondo* score, for her dance called *Deep Rhythm.*

Certain other Surinach scores have been given several choreographic settings. For example, *La Sibila* was set by John Butler to the composer's *Concerto for Piano, Strings, and Cymbals;* this piece also became a ballet in Israel, under the name of *Celebrants,* performed by the Batsheva Dance Company. Two other ballets set to his music are *Hazaña* and *A Place in the Desert,* produced at Sadler's Wells. "I liked the choreography," Mr. Surinach said, "but I was surprised. That is a *dance,* and the dance is not like the ballet. If you do *Sleeping Beauty,* for example, it resembles other productions, and it's virtually the same piece; whereas in modern dance, the same music may have radically different themes and appearance, as set by various choreographers."

When asked how he likes seeing dances done to music he had already written in concert form, Mr. Surinach replied: "Well, at that moment, regardless of whether you do or don't like it, they can take it, by law. All they have to do is pay the performing rights, and also to hire the orchestra parts."

"Once a composer gives a piece of music to a publisher, he is exploited by the publisher," the composer went on to explain. "There's very little that the composer can forbid, or that he can stipulate. The only thing we can do is for a premiere: we have the right to choose the performers. But once this is done, then it goes to the hands of the publisher, and the publisher can give that to everyone who wishes it. All the person has to do is pay the publisher."

Working with Martha Graham, however, involved original collaboration on Mr. Surinach's part. When asked how this association all began, the composer intoned: "Martha Graham *summons* you!"

Before that, he recalled, he first met Miss Graham at a party given by Bethsabee de Rothschild. Mr. Surinach described the first moment he saw the choreographer there: "She was playing with one of those Chinese *papelinas moviles*. It was a beautiful one, and I said so. She replied, 'Yes, but never pay any attention to any of those things; symmetry is not good art; you must *cheat* the audience of knowing what to expect next!' "

"Mentally, that went very deep with me," reflected the composer. "I never forgot that—never in my life, even writing music. When I am about to do two things exactly the same way, I say, 'No! Don't fall into symmetry.' That's true. It's part of play-writing also: don't give the audiences—ever—in drama or in music or in a comedy, what they *expect* will follow. Deviate! And that, in music, is very important," emphasized Mr. Surinach, noting, "that's also done by Martha Graham, by John Butler, by many other choreographers: the unexpected."

Long a United States citizen, Carlos Surinach nevertheless retained a beautiful Castilian accent—in both his speech and his music—from his native Barcelona. Speaking of his heritage and how this manifests itself in his art, the composer mentioned what Martha Graham said to him once: "I don't want you to think it's the Spanish angle that makes me like you; it's the *theatricality*!" And the composer added: "She made me aware of this in my own work. Before, the theatricality had been unconscious. And from that moment, I knew more what to do."

There was a lot of good humor in the Graham-Surinach collaborations. For instance, when the choreographer called him and suggested a work based on Edward Lear's poem *The Owl and the Pussy Cat,* the composer had to admit: "You tell me that, but I don't know a word of what you mean," for he had never read children's tales in English.

"Finally," recalled the composer, "she gave me one of those books for children with the big print and the pictures of the owl and the cat; big, *big* letters for children to read," he laughed, "and she said, 'You read that, and then you come back, and I will tell you *my* way to do it.' "

Indeed, her way was not childlike. Mr. Surinach explained that it was his idea, however, to put in a Spanish tango for the pig. "Martha was hysterical about it," he recalled. "We had fun doing that piece."

Concerning the procedure they followed for this original collaboration, Mr. Surinach explained: "After she gave me the book, she arranged—as a sketch—a few scenes with the dancers. When you see that, you never pay too much attention, and you have to realize that if you would like a change for the convenience or for the benefit of both choreography and music, you can propose that to the choreographer equally as well as the choreographer may propose a change to you."

''So there were movements shown to me in a sketchy way, by the dancers. In the meantime, I was also sketching, with paper and pencil,'' continued Mr. Surinach. When asked what kind of directions Martha Graham gave him, he responded: ''Verbal or visible. She never gave me anything written.''

Even working closely together like this, a composer can still have some surprises when a dance is shown in the theater. For instance, Mr. Surinach recounted: ''In *Embattled Garden,* there are three minutes of music at the beginning. I put 'Prelude, with the curtain down.' And the first thing I see when I go to a rehearsal with Martha Graham, the curtain rose up in silence! She choreographed even those first three minutes. What can you say,'' he shrugged. ''It was *beautiful,* but my idea was that it would be. . . .''

The composer's voice trailed off, and then he picked up the thought: ''Other choreographers, particularly the Europeans, follow what you say. If you say this is going to be a prelude, they leave it alone; they don't touch it. But Martha Graham did!'' And in retrospect, he was able to laugh gently about it, with good humor.

Sometimes the composer's job is not over even after the first performance. For instance, Mr. Surinach related, ''the works of Martha Graham involved small pits. The most you can put there is twenty instruments. Then she would go to Vienna, and you find out that the pit is twice the size, and there's a whole symphony. So the orchestration has to be increased.

''*The Owl and the Pussy Cat,* for instance, has two orchestrations: one for the Met and Covent Garden and the San Francisco Opera House, among others; then a smaller orchestration to fit about 20–22 people in a Broadway theater that happens to be about the size as in the 'provinces.' ''

''It's a lot of work; a lot of paper,'' the composer continued to explain. ''I don't do the parts, but two scores—yes: from scratch. But then imagine the amount of sound; it changes everything. It may seem to be the same, but to get the same results, you must set the orchestra in another way. Therefore, the number of parts, and the amount of paper . . . !'' gasped the composer.

Mr. Surinach then took pointed out some of the manuscripts in progress lying on his workdesk. There were original pencil sketches in the process of being meticulously redone on separate paper in india ink—every note for every instrument in the orchestra carefully considered, transposed correctly, and then set down by hand. The composer pointed out that after his work is done, there still is no computer that can extract orchestra parts from a score, and so all that has to be done by hand also, by a professional copyist.

His ballet works are usually first written for piano alone. ''The choreographer will rehearse forever with that piano score,'' noted Mr. Surinach. ''So when you have that, and the choreographer has sketched out his movements, the ballet is roughly—but practically—finished. Then you go on and make the full score. If the choreographer wants to rearrange something while they are rehearsing on the piano, he does. But the music is not changed, usually. He may touch very little. A good choreographer generally doesn't make changes after the music is written," emphasized Mr. Surinach. "There is a moment you take the choreographer"—and here the composer gestured, as if by the lapel—"and you say, 'No changes from now on!' "

In working with various artists, Carlos Surinach has run into occasional disagreements when a choreographer will want to break into the structure of a musical composition. "Couldn't we put what went before a little later," one might ask him. "No! Because musically it won't work," the composer would declare, hoping to keep his piece intact.

Sometimes, in working with a piano reduction, problems of atmosphere, aura, or flavor may arise because of the lack of actual quality of sounds that the dancers will be hearing in performance. Mr. Surinach brought up, as an example, *Agathe's Tale,* which he did with Paul Taylor. "There was a problem there. Paul Taylor was very happy with the piece as played on the piano. He had a record with medieval music made with instruments from a museum in Switzerland, and he wanted an evocation of that. But I had to give him the instruments of today. It was the practical thing to do, so that the piece could be played everywhere."

Hearing the score with modern orchestral instruments, Paul Taylor was "a little disappointed," confided the composer, "because he wanted those ancient sounds. He even asked if the modern instruments could be made to sound like the old. But no, they can't. So he was very happy with the piece *until* he heard it with the orchestra. Usually, it's the contrary!"

VIRGIL THOMSON: A LONG LOOK AT BALLET IN THIS CENTURY

The viewpoint of composer Virgil Thomson is of particular interest because the choreographers who used his music include Lew Christensen, Erick Hawkins, Agnes de Mille, George Balanchine, Alvin Ailey, and Mark Morris. Equally noteworthy, as music critic for the *New York Herald Tribune* for many years, he gained a perspective that few could match in this century.

The author visited Virgil Thomson shortly after his ninetieth birthday, and was treated to some of his proverbial wit and incisive observation.[12] When asked if he ever had to review the musical part of a ballet or dance concert, the composer-critic responded: "I never had to do *anything* I didn't want to! I reviewed the ballet very often. You *can't* review the ballet without mentioning the music—though it's wiser now not to, because the music is disgraceful. Very few ballet companies even use an orchestra, and they are conducted by people who wait for the dancers, you know. They give no line. The music has sunk way down in the ballet business," he lamented, noting that twenty or thirty years ago, conductors of the stature of Bruno Walter and Sir Thomas Beecham would conduct for ballets. "They gave it a line, and the dancers jumped on time,'' observed Mr. Thomson. ''Now, they fiddle around sort of yawning with their legs.''

When asked what can be judged fairly in regard to the music of a ballet performance, Virgil Thomson replied: ''Why, whether it's any good! Is it music, or is it just jabber? The big companies usually use reputable music. They don't play it very well, and as I say, they wait for the dancers and all that. But they make ballets out of music either written especially for them or out of classical music that you can set a dance to.''

''The music of a ballet has to hold the thing together,'' he emphasized. ''So the best ballet music is that which is rather tightly constructed. That's why the Stravinsky ballets work, because they hold together as music. Lincoln Kirstein told me once that the life of any ballet is the life of the musical score. As soon as the score starts boring dancers, it's no good anymore,'' said the composer.

Apparently dancers are not yet getting bored with Virgil Thomson's own *Filling Station,* for it is still being presented in various cities around the country. First performed in 1937 by the San Francisco Ballet, it is now often cited as the first ballet created in this country with music by an American composer, choreography by an American choreographer (Lew Christensen), a storyline based on American life, and a premiere by a professional American ballet company and symphony.

Asked if he had any notion at the time of this ballet's creation that the collaborators were doing anything path-breaking, the composer indulgently scoffed, ''Oh, you don't sit around and criticize your work while you're writing it. You write it and make it work; you don't observe it. However, I *did* enjoy working with Lew Christensen on that.''

People who have never composed music often wonder how it is done, and dancers in particular wonder if their collaborators are conscious of movement when they are writing a score for ballet. Mr. Thomson clarified the process: ''Look, darling, you don't think about anything else while you are composing but what you are doing—not merely the sounds, but trying to make it work, making it hold together.''

''Lew would say, 'Here's a pas de deux, but it cannot possibly last longer than five minutes; I can't think of any more things to do beyond that, so you make it come out.' Five minutes is long anyway in a ballet,'' noted the composer.

''But,'' he continued, ''you don't think about things, except what you're doing. I mean, you don't whistle a tune while turning an omelette; you put your mind on doing that.''

''I've always worked in show business,'' Mr. Thomson commented. ''I've worked in theaters; I've worked in movies, operas, plays, oratorios. . . . I like show biz. I *don't* like the kind of dance music that is done after the choreography,'' he added. ''Martha used to work like that, you know,'' he pointed out, recalling how Miss Graham would originally mold her movement patterns and then have music made to order. "I don't like that," repeated Mr. Thomson. "I think it works better if you work together up to the point where the music has to be written. Then the music should be written, and the choreographer fits the dance to it."

"You *can* talk about it until you get each section in your mind, at least as to length, or as to the kind of music that you have to write in order to illustrate the kind of dancing that it is," suggested the composer. "After all, the music's got to move them around."

How did he feel about his concert works set to dance afterwards? "I never know how I feel about anything! If I say that they can do it, then they can do it. I wait until they do it . . . and then I don't *feel;* I *think*. I think that it works or it doesn't . . . and sometimes I'm not sure. But if they think they can sell it, I let them sell it. That means that their dancers and their audiences take it."

"You see, with a theatrical work," continued the composer, "it's not a matter of how you *feel* about anything; it's what you can *think* of to solve the emergency. The feeling is out front—not on the stage."

You can tell whether something works or not, according to Mr. Thomson, by noticing the audience's response. "They'll tell you, oh sure," he remarked. "Applause is always welcome, but tears are the real proof. If they cry, you've got 'em!"

Continuing to speak about emotion and meaning in music for the dance, Virgil Thomson noted the oft-quoted assertion by Igor Stravinsky that music doesn't "express" anything. In Mr. Thomson's opinion, "music recalls *other* music, a great deal, and how it happens that it stimulates or accompanies emotion, nobody knows how that works. You say, 'I think I'll try that'—and sometimes it works. But *having* emotion on the stage is the worst way to communicate," he advised. "Follow the story and pattern; the emotion will take place outside. This applies to the musical part, the dancing, everything."

Commenting further on the Stravinsky quote, Mr. Thomson remarked: "He loved to make deadpan jokes, and there was a little bit of that. You see, you mustn't take people literally in a domain which is not theirs. Stravinsky was not a literary artist; he was a musical artist, and when he talked about his music, he talked the same tommyrot that anybody else does. Sometimes it's suggestive, and sometimes it isn't. Beethoven and Mozart didn't talk too much about what they were up to!"

Another artist who apparently didn't feel a need to talk about what he was up to was George Balanchine, as he was setting Virgil Thomson's music for a ballet called *Bayou*. Did Balanchine talk to the composer about it? "Never!" replied the musician. "He was *at* it. He stood there, and he would say do this and do this—to the *dancers*. Then they would do it, or he would say, 'No, that doesn't work; do it this way.' He worked right with them, and the dancers imitated the movements that he was sketching with his legs and arms. Why should he talk to me?" asked the composer.

Elaborating further on the division of labor in the theater, Mr. Thomson noted: "Composers don't think about how dancers work; they think about how *they* work. They are just as amazed as anybody else when somebody takes a high leap and lights like a feather. But they wouldn't be able to tell the dancers just what muscles or leg positions to use in order to achieve that lightness. That happens among the *dancers*."

"Don't talk about ballet as though it were all full of emotions on everybody's part," he cautioned. "Ballet—particularly classical ballet—has a very limited vocabulary. The whole game is to make fifteen or so different things tell the story. It was Balanchine's rule—and this he used to tell everybody—that any movement on the stage which does not advance the story is useless. The movement composition must recount what it says it's recounting. And this works perfectly well too with ballets without a story—though there aren't that many. Though some are *said* to be without a story, they all tell *something*. They are always 'about' something, and we've only got some fifteen different 'words' with which to tell the story."

When asked what it is in music that can help to accomplish this, the composer was firm: "Nothing! Music walks down the street beside the dance. Music in a ballet, very much like music in a movie, makes a *structure*, which holds the whole thing together, and it goes on at the same time."

"Music which illustrates the dance is just as boring as dance which illustrates the music," he went on to observe. "They've got to get apart. Got to get the music away from the dancers, and the dancers away from the music. You're not illustrating the music; you're illustrating the *story*. And if the music helps you to do that, it's good music."

Virgil Thomson was asked if he felt there is some music that is more danceable than other pieces, and he replied: "Oh, there *is* music that is very hard to dance to: if the music is over-complex. You see, *The Rite of Spring* has foiled every choreographer—every single choreographer! No pattern has ever stuck to that music. It's too complex, too interesting. It's a concert piece. Nobody knows what to do with it that can hold the eye on the dancers."

"And nobody has ever really done a bit of choreography that has decently fitted to a Beethoven symphony," he added. "The progress of a Beethoven symphony is more interesting than what the dancers can do."

"Massine made a ballet to a Brahms symphony once, called *Choreartium*. They used to give it in Paris," recalled Mr. Thomson with a slight laugh. "Oh, he thought of all sorts of things to do: he picked up the girls like cannon shells and shot them across the stage—and it *still* wasn't as interesting as the music."

"When you take the music away from the classical ballet and play it as a concert piece, very little of it is as interesting as you think it's going to be," the composer-critic observed. "Nobody plays Adam's *Giselle*, for example. It works perfectly as a ballet, but by itself it's not interesting enough."

Reiterating his opinion that music for ballet should not be too complex, Mr. Thomson explained that in such collaborations, there is a great deal of personal taste involved, as well as artistic decision that cannot be formulated for others to follow.

"Nobody knows if it's good until you hear it," he suggested. "But in general, the music needs to be able to *move*. If it's constricted like machinery, or cogwheels, it tends to slow up the dance."

"See, dancers move all the time. They move *fast*. That doesn't mean that the *music* has to move fast, but that the music has to be flexible for movement; it has to *flow*. Or it has to have a kind of rhythm that whips the dancers around. And there is no describing exactly what that's going to be. You only know when you've got the wrong thing and it's *not* working," said Mr. Thomson ruefully.

How much awareness of the music is exhibited by audiences and critics nowadays? "In a ballet?" Mr. Thomson exploded. "They don't even mention the composer anymore! A ballet is 'by Balanchine' nowadays; it's not 'by Stravinsky.' It's ignorant," he chastised, adding: "In the days when ballet was still a serious mixture of the elements, they mentioned the people who had done the various elements."

What about the journalists who feel it is not appropriate to talk about the music for the dance because the orchestra is not giving a separate concert performance? The composer-critic had a curt reply: "If they're not giving a concert performance, they're lousy."

Are there standards by which you can judge the music for ballet? "Certainly," maintained Mr. Thomson. "You ought to be able to hear ballet music over the radio exactly as we hear opera music over the radio. The music should be able to sustain itself by *musical* means."

"But the ballet is in a strange state," he mused. "It's over-popular now. Too many people dancing. . . ." And, he suggested, too many people out front not interested in anything except how the dancers' bodies look.

"The perfect audiences," he went on to say, "were from, oh 1909 or 1910 until the death of Diaghilev in 1929. He kept the stuff interesting. He had interesting music; he had interesting decors; he had interesting dancers; and very often, there were interesting stories. But now, you have a worldwide public, and ballet quietly sinks of its own weight. You can't do anything about it; you have to let it run down. It will," he predicted, adding: "At the moment, it's running like mad. But it's not doing anything for dancing. And they're not even dancing that well. Nobody's leaping as high or landing as lightly as Nijinsky. No, nothing like that around."

When asked what it would take in this country to create the kind of situation that Diaghilev found in Europe, the composer could only suggest: "You can't *make* situations; they *grow*." And though funding is always welcome, he pointed out, pouring money into new commissions does not guarantee anything about the artistic quality of the production.

COMPOSER-ARRANGER FOR BROADWAY: TRUDE RITTMANN

What young composer doesn't occasionally daydream about having credits like these: *Carousel; Sound of Music; South Pacific; Gentlemen Prefer Blondes; Peter Pan; The King and I; Fanny; Paint Your Wagon; My Fair Lady; Camelot; Brigadoon; On a Clear Day You Can See Forever; Gigi;* and on and on for more than thirty years of top Broadway hits? These are, in fact, only a sampling of the show after show in which Trude Rittmann was responsible for the dance and incidental vocal musical arrangements.

A composer-arranger of unusual talent in a specialized area, she was in great demand for many years, working directly with choreographers and dancers, with directors and producers, and with composers of the songs, to arrange or paraphrase tunes in such a manner that they could be danced to. In addition, she often had to compose entirely new material for the dancers, always working on the spot. Then, before shows were opened on Broadway, she went along to the out-of-town tryouts, being on call for whatever musical first aid was needed as a production was being refined and polished.

When Trude Rittmann described her career in the theater, those former collaborations took on an ongoing life.[13] She commented that the friction and demands of the theater were in fact good for the composing process. For example, recalling her work on *Brigadoon* with Agnes de Mille, she mentioned: "Agnes didn't want anyone in her rehearsals—and especially not the authors! Her rehearsals were closed, and there were watchmen standing at doors, shooing everybody away who wanted to get in. I did the ballets, like a blueprint, for Frederick Loewe, who then rewrote after my blueprint. What I wrote were variations on his melodies, but according to choreographic demands."

Making the big musicals was always a team project, and after a piano score was completed by the composer, orchestrators would be called in. "The poor orchestrators are always, you know, chased to death for deadlines and need a helping hand sometimes," said Miss Rittmann. "Once in a while I helped Russell Bennett. I remember for *On a Clear Day* I sat *nights* working away because we had to get it done in time. He would give me a scene and explain to me what he wanted, and I'd do it."

The next step would be that still other people would take the orchestral score and extract individual parts for each instrument. "The copyists are in an even worse way," Miss Rittmann noted. "You see, I must always be ahead of the orchestrators. They depend on me as far as ballets are concerned, or choral arrangements, or incidental music—so I have to be ahead of them, and they have to be ahead of their copyists. It's a chain, and the chain is deadly."

"I always have been in the theater with a room of my own, with a piano—which was in my contract—and *away* from everybody," continued the composer. "Every once in a while, somebody would call, 'Trude, we need more bars here or there . . .' or 'Agnes or Jerry [Robbins] think you ought to change this scene.' Then I go and rewrite. But I'm always on call in the place. For the last fifteen years I didn't do any rehearsing anymore—only sat in my little cubicle and wrote, and checked back all the time."

When asked if her method of collaborating was the same with different choreographers, Trude Rittmann replied: "You could never—but really *never*—have one system for everybody. That didn't work. Because, in the case of Agnes de Mille, she has to always go before. She has to sort of get cooking. She has a few dancers, or she is just with me, and I say, 'Agnes, how would it be for such and such, music of that rhythm, or that form . . . or this?' And she would say, 'No, ummmmm, it's not right.' Or she would gasp, 'Oh yes! Go on!'

"I know I describe this in a primitive way," remarked the composer, "but it goes sometimes for hours and hours, and days and days. Meanwhile I am there improvising, and asking 'How do you feel about this? How do you feel about that?' That is Agnes's way."

"Now Jerry Robbins often goes independently of music, and we have an understanding of what meter we're going in. The very first one I did with him was *Look Ma I'm Dancing,* which has a lot of original scores of mine."

"But *he* usually has movement ideas," pointed out the composer. Then laughing, she recalled: "In the beginning when I met Jerry, I always knew he was *exceedingly* musical, and *rhythmically* talented. But he didn't play an instrument; he couldn't read music. And I said to him, 'It's out of the question that you are going on like that, and you *must* study music, and you *must* learn how to read, and you *must* play an instrument; I insist!' " Apparently the now-famous choreographer paid attention to his collaborator, who noticed: "He learned recorder, and learned how to read music. He studied . . . and all of a sudden, a whole new thing went on."

For their first show, however, this is how things went, from the composer's viewpoint: "He had an idea of a movement, and then I looked at it, and I started improvising. Then I started writing it down and calling out 'Hold it!' and 'Hold it!' He very often choreographed ahead of me, but not the whole dance—part, or an idea. But then, he would change his mind. *Every day* something was wiped out and something new was happening. You were always confronted with a new idea—he very much doubting himself, so always wiping out and starting all over because he felt it was all wrong."

Toward the end of a show's rehearsal period, Trude Rittmann would again come in handy, since she often did all the connections, or underscoring. For example, in *South Pacific,* director Joshua Logan would say: "Oh Trude, I need something very *explosive* there!" or "There has to be something that threatens." The composer particularly remembered that last remark for, she related, "that's when Mary Martin made a handstand in 'I'm gonna wash that man right out of my hair'—and fell into the pit, right on top of me." Dangerous business, being a composer; she was knocked out cold.

Another of the shows that Trude Rittmann collaborated on, and that also made theatrical history, was *My Fair Lady,* with choreography by Hanya Holm.

The composer contrasted the working habits of that artist with those of Robbins and de Mille: "Hanya is very different. Hanya is more methodical in how she develops her dances. I think we figured out how long something should be, what I should do, and what rhythms she wanted. And then at the same time—very often you do things at the very same time—I'd sit at the piano improvising, and they fiddle around also, and then we both stop and say 'That was good; let's repeat it.' If I can, I do it, and I write it down—quickly, like shorthand stenography: *very* quickly."

"Very often," emphasized the composer, "the dance and the music go absolutely at the same time. With Jerry, *very* often I did it absolutely simultaneously—when he would start bubbling, you know, and I would too."

Mentioning the time frame in which the big Broadway shows were put together, Trude Rittmann again emphasized that the planning stages took a long time. "First of all," she said, "there are creative meetings. Say, for a Rodgers show, he has already decided with the producer whom they want to have on the creative staff: the lighting person, for scenery, costumes . . . all these creative aspects are discussed in meetings. And you discuss back and forth what the exigencies are of their particular material, what has to be done, what is the time pressure, what are the problems—problems mostly as high as Mount Everest!

"And then, Agnes, for instance, and Jerry too, always worked ahead of time with me, and maybe with a dancer. Agnes usually had a couple of dancers. But she tries out certain things that strike her as important. She has certain plans, and very often I can write ahead of time. But *most* of the time, I am right at the piano, improvising from a certain thematic material from a song and the choreographic patterns. Or when it is a thing by itself, say 'The Small House of Uncle Thomas' in *The King and I,* this is a separate production."

That dance was among the many entirely original pieces composed by Trude Rittmann. She never got any credit for it. Why not? "Because Rodgers didn't want me to have credit," stated the composer quite bluntly.

Contracts at the time didn't specify credit for original work; one got a flat fee and a weekly salary that covered only the time a composer was actually with a production. For a long time, there was no such thing as a notice in the program or royalties. "Occasionally," said the composer somewhat ruefully, "my credits would be in the back of the program—along with the shoes and the ladies who dress the girls."

But things did change, and the usual way became a more fair procedure: the arranger-composers started to have agents and lawyers who secured contracts which specified program credits and royalty payments. So as her career progressed, Trude Rittmann did find that it was a good way to earn a living. But in earlier times on Broadway, she exclaimed vehemently, "pianists were just *milked.*"

When asked if the system had anything to do with the fact that many of the dance pianists in the theaters were women, she replied with a meaningful "Tsk!" followed by "Very much so."

Was there prejudice against women composers? "Absolutely!" declared Miss Rittmann, adding, "Also against women in the theater. I can tell you, I was usually the only one among all men. Agnes used to say—and she was absolutely right—that women have to be twice as good as men, to prove that they know their stuff."

Where did Trude Rittmann learn her stuff? She explained: "I loved the theater. I grew up in a time when Wigman and Dalcroze were active. As a child, I had lessons in eurhythmics." This included some physical experience of moving to music.

She was graduated from the Hochschüle für Musik in Mannheim, where her main composition teachers were Ernst Toch and Philipp Jarnach. By the age of 21, Trude Rittmann had already had a major orchestral work premiered in Zurich.

Her contact with dancers, however, was at that time limited to playing an occasional rehearsal—purely as a way to earn some extra money. Later, when she left Germany in 1933, such skill became her ticket to work in the free world. She did studio playing with the Kurt Jooss Ballet School in England, and upon arriving in America, she was engaged by Lincoln Kirstein to work with American Ballet Caravan.

In the course of her duties, Miss Rittmann often conducted orchestras for the ballet on tour. She also arranged all the repertoire for Ballet Caravan in two piano versions and often performed it, with fellow pianist Simon Sadoff.

The composer told the story of how her long collaboration with choreographer Agnes de Mille had begun: "She called me one night out of the blue; I didn't know her. Her accompanist fell ill, and the next day they had a concert in Cleveland. She had a tiny group and asked if I could jump into the breech. I said, 'But I don't know your program. How can I?'—'Oh, it's not difficult, except—' " At this point, the composer laughed heartily: "*Except* she was doing *Le Sacre du Printemps*. I said, 'Well, Miss de Mille, I have only one day to learn it; we cannot rehearse.' "

"Well!" continued the composer, "We met on the overnight train to Cleveland. The next morning it was raining cats and dogs. It was a women's something—possibly a matinee—and it was dreadful. We were in a little club or somewhere, and nobody was coming because it was raining so hard. The only thing they had provided was a second player to do the *Sacre du Printemps*—that difficult piece—four hands with me."

"I said everything was fine, but this young man they sent me—!" she sighed. "So it was half-empty because it rained so hard nobody came. It was a most dismal affair. But I accompanied everything fine, until there came this piece of Stravinsky, and this young man who had no time to rehearse. He was so impossible that I gave him a push," said the sedate-looking pianist, gleefully demonstrating with her elbow and wiping away tears of laughter, "and he was gone. Whoosh—out! I played by myself."

Subsequently, Miss Rittmann was called by Agnes de Mille very often for her concert tours, and gradually the choreographer began asking her to arrange things, and to compose new pieces. The composer related: "When Ballet Caravan folded because of the war, I started doing more and more work with Agnes de Mille. She did *Oklahoma!* while I was still with Caravan. But her second show was *One Touch of Venus,* with Kurt Weill, and *that* we did together. It was my first show on Broadway."

Looking back over her entire Broadway career, Miss Rittmann said that aside from the good pay, what she liked was "challenge! I *loved* working in the theater." She added: "This is still true of me. I love theater, and it had a great attraction for me, to create something that has a mood, has an atmosphere, has drama, and is still marvelous. I still adore it."

Part of Trude Rittmann's skill was her adroitness in researching traditional folk music of various nationalities, and then being able to compose fresh, entirely original music for the show dances that would be in the style of a particular time and place. She did this, for example, in the Siamese dance in *The King and I* and the Scottish-sounding funereal bagpipe music of *Brigadoon,* as well as in the settings of Western cowboy tunes for *Gold Rush.*

Citing Trude Rittmann's ability to convey an impression of authenticity, Agnes de Mille offered this tribute:

> This gift for arranging and developing popular songs into dances and for underscoring scenes, dialogue and business is unique. Her unparalleled help in infusing variety and dramatic effectiveness into shows as well as into accompaniments, is common knowledge on Broadway. . . . She is more than an arranger. I rely on her taste as on no one else's and in all departments of my work. I herewith make her my deepest reverance, and there are other choreographers, and the very best, bowing beside me. Several thousand dancers and all orchestrators and conductors rise to testify to the taste, good sense, musicality and creative force Trude Rittmann brings to every show she touches, and the cheer and decorum she maintains in rehearsal. . . .
>
> The sane musicianly counsel she supplies, the expert eye, the humor and the large background experience which reaches into the best Europe could teach and embraces all forms and styles. . . .
>
> Trude says quietly, "I had tonight in the theater a feeling about this work—"
>
> And Trude's feelings are like the needle on a ship's compass.[14]

3

The Partnership of Movement and Sound

RICHARD CAMERON-WOLFE: ON COLLABORATION

"In the world of modern dance generally," pointed out the composer Richard Cameron-Wolfe, "there is a more democratic relationship between musicians and dancers than there is in ballet. There is more drawing on the other arts for performance, and there is a more open discussion between musicians and dancers."[1]

Speaking about the different methods that he had used in working with a number of choreographers, this musician explained: "Sometimes you compose something out of inner necessity. It turns out to be appropriate for choreography, and you are willing to offer it to a choreographer. This can be satisfying if the dancer is sensitive to the inner music."

However, if a dance artist ignored the original nature of the music, this might offend some audience members. For instance, Mr. Cameron-Wolfe was upset by Antony Tudor's *Pillar of Fire* because it seemed to ignore the explicit program of the original score by Arnold Schoenberg.

A second method of collaborating is the way Tchaikovsky worked with Petipa, using a bar-to-bar scheme. Obviously, this worked splendidly for Tchaikovsky and Petipa. But when other teams try it, things don't always go so well. As Mr. Cameron-Wolfe noted, "sometimes the choreographer's expectations are very literal: for a big movement, you have a big sound; if the movement goes up, the music goes up."

For example, he related, once he was working with a group of dancers on an allegorical piece. When the choreographer objected to the composer's descending pitches accompanying her rising dancers, the composer finally asked: "What are you supposed to be when you are rising up?" "Like blades of grass growing,'' came the reply. ''Oh,'' said the musician quietly. The next day, however, when he played the same sounds and was similarly stopped, he added the rebuttal: ''But my music is like the rays of the sun coming down to meet your blades of grass in the dewy morning.'' The teacher was pleased to be thus enlightened, and exclaimed something to the effect of ''why didn't you tell me so in the first place?''

Many years afterwards, one of this composer's ''really happy'' collaborations came about during his residency with the José Limón Company. Working with the choreographer Fred Mathews on a repertoire piece for students, Richard Cameron-Wolfe found a structured work growing out of what was at first an informal improvisation on the piano. As they continued, Mathews would listen carefully. ''Oh yes, keep that,'' he would say encouragingly as some sounds were tried out with the movement. The composer later wrote everything down, with specific instructions for prepared piano, and *Solaris* became part of the Limón repertoire for several seasons.

Another of Richard Cameron-Wolfe's collaborations for dance was performed at the Guggenheim Museum in New York by the Multigravitational Aerodance Experiment Group, directed by Stephanie Evanitsky. The preparation for this unusual work (which involved scaffolding with ropes and saddles—''like an underwater ballet in the air,'' observed the composer), was also unusual. Mr. Cameron-Wolfe remembers that both he and the choreographer read essays by Leo Steinberg. Then the two discussed Picasso's art together, and then went their separate ways.

''All she gave me were general timings of four large sections of the piece, and the directions that the music and the choreography would be consistent with that element of Picasso's work that we had explored together: circus performers, lovers, drowners, and prevalent color,'' the composer said. He mentioned that drowners, for example, could be interpreted as people slipping from life to death, or people in a general state of crisis.

The final work was sixty-five minutes long, and was accompanied by live musicians playing on flute, clarinet, horn, and piano. The music had been fully written down, except for some short improvisatory episodic sections. The musicians became an exceptionally meshed part of the event, for they would walk around the ramp at the Guggenheim playing various places on the museum's spiral walk. A flute solo wafting a Spanish lullaby from the highest point of the walkway brought the work to a close.

NORMA REYNOLDS DALBY: INVENTIVE MUSIC FOR MODERN DANCE

The composer Norma Reynolds Dalby has been quite flexible in the ways she is willing to collaborate—which may help to account for the long list of over a hundred well-known choreographers and master teachers with whom she has worked on various projects. The list includes such names as Martha Graham, José Limón, Pearl Lang, Merce Cunningham, Todd Bolender, Alvin Ailey, Carolyn Adams, Glen Tetley, Lucas Hoving, Don Redlich, Bessie Schonberg, William Bales, Ze'eva Cohen, Virginia Tanner, Mary Hinkson, and Kei Takei.

"Music ideally does not just follow the dance," observed this artist, elaborating on the relationship of sound and movement. "There exists both a balance and a desire for independence between choreography and music." Furthermore, she pointed out how very exciting it can be to find out "what can happen in terms of enhancing both media if you do *not* follow the dancer precisely."[2]

"Certainly," she continued, "there is the supportive, accompanying element in music. As in a good song, the piano does not always function as wallpaper, but there are times when the singer is silent or supportive and the piano sings out. So too with good choreography: sometimes the music is less active than the dancing, or vice versa, or sometimes both are very active together."

From time to time, Norma Dalby has collaborated with choreographers who first work out their movement totally, to absolute metronomic beats. She feels that this inhibits the music—especially in terms of being tied "relentlessly" to a beat and in lacking the qualities of breathing.

It can be more satisfying, and more likely to get the best all-round combined piece, she suggested, if a composer and a choreographer feed and play off each other, first setting up a structure and discussing together what is desired, asking such questions as "What *kind* of piece do we want—and technically, how can we get it?"

Norma Dalby feels that there are a lot of musical things that can be explored with which choreographers may be unfamiliar, and which they might be delighted to use once they knew about the possibilities.

In her preferred way of working with a choreographer, there may at first be elements of improvisation in both the movement and the music, but as the choreography develops in set patterns, the composer develops notations to clarify what is finally set in her mind. Then she writes all the music out—and not necessarily according to traditional notation. Yet even when some improvisation is indicated, it is closely structured, often with notation of her own invention.

Something that Norma Reynolds Dalby seems to delight in is bringing the dancers themselves into the music-making. One collaboration which made such demands, which garnered rave reviews—and which the composer herself described as "pure joy"—was her work with Kei Takei for *Light 17, A Dreamcatcher's Diary*. It was premiered at the American Dance Festival in Durham and then presented in New York for a two-week stint by the choreographer's troupe, Moving Earth. The two creative artists subsequently collaborated on *Light, Part 24: Chanting Hills,* which was presented by the Juilliard Dance Ensemble.

The second piece had a formal chamber ensemble of musicians in the pit, complete with conductor. But for *A Dreamcatcher's Diary,* the composer explained, "whatever music was being played had to be taken care of by the dancers.'' There were no separate musicians on the sidelines, though one dancer, John Wilson, sang the solo vocal parts because the composer felt he had a magnificent, trained voice. In one section of the work, however, all the dancers were involved in a polyrhythmic percussion performance. To prepare for this, the composer had first to teach the performers basic physical techniques of stick-drumming.

The sounds of language are also fascinating to Norma Dalby. She confided that for *Light 17,* she was quite impressed with the dancers' ''thirst'' for clothes. So she took the sentence ''I want more clothes'' and reversed the phonetic sounds to invent a new and stately ''language.'' Some audience members—including this writer—assumed it was an ancient form of Japanese. In a similar spirit of playfulness and experimentation, Ms. Dalby selected steel bowls very carefully according to their pitches, and had Kei Takei's dancers play them with mallets.

Aside from her professional composing commitments, for many years Norma Reynolds Dalby has been the director of music for the dance at Sarah Lawrence College, which is well-known for its creative approach to collaboration. There, she works closely with students to help them develop their own unique scores for their own choreography, and she often contributes her specially tailored compositions for college performances.

As a teacher, she says she takes pleasure in so many interrelationships for good work. Picking just one from her memory, she mentioned *Stubborn Wood,* for which she collaborated with graduate student Tom Brown. ''We saw it as a piece for three people,'' explained the musician: ''a dancer, a clarinetist, and a pianist. We all accompanied each other; we all did solos; and the movement and the music came about simultaneously.''

Considering the different methods which musicians and dancers can use in working together, Ms. Dalby mentioned: ''Many composers might say, 'I want to write a piece that will stand on its own.' '' She would be pleased if that happened all the time, but she found more often that she frequently would not develop material intended for dance in the same ways that she might for independent concert pieces. ''When I am composing for the dance,'' she stressed, ''I want the music to be as complete as possible . . . but not in *combat* with the dance.''

Ms. Dalby has insisted that people in her trade be called ''musicians for the dance'' rather than ''accompanists.'' Yet she mentioned various ways that music can wreck a dance, most notably if the musician tries to show off his virtuosity at the expense of the dance—for instance by interrupting a mood or a quality in the movement. ''You have to learn the ways you can be a virtuoso,'' cautioned the composer-collaborator.

Although Norma Reynolds Dalby herself has become proficient as a pianist, organist, clarinetist, bassist and percussion player, she remembered that her first piano teacher looked down on improvisation and thought it was the worst thing she could do: ''a waste of time.'' But luckily, the composer did not pay attention to that teacher, for Ms. Dalby's first experience with the dance—with

Virginia Tanner at the Children's Dance Theater in Salt Lake City—called for improvisation. The musician quickly became so attuned to movement that the compositions which she recorded for Virginia Tanner are still in demand among dance educators.

Norma Dalby's experiments in music for the dance evolved to the point where she has not only composed a musical score, but also has directed the dancers by setting up parameters of movement and visual space. In her *Glyph II,* for example, the performers not only had to dance, they also had to perform on flute, mandolin, cello, violin, piano and percussion—and they had to sing, both solo and in choral combination. The composer taught the dancers techniques and limited their choices in order to have creative control over the final product.

If dancers can learn to make their own music, then does it help for the musicians to dance? The composer reflected upon this question a moment, noting that she herself had taken tap dance at the age of six and modern classes as an adult. But generally, she had a dim view of the notion that taking class will help either accompanying or composing for the dance. "It may be good for your body," she remarked, "but you are so concentrated on *how* to do something, that it doesn't really help you musically."

Instead, she felt that her own kinetic sense developed mostly as she was watching dance—and playing for it in studios. She found herself thinking, "I am doing the same thing they are doing, internally." The composer went on to observe: "There are expressive elements in music and dance . . . so although both are doing the same thing, the dancers do more about movement and the musicians more about sound."

Not surprisingly, Norma Reynolds Dalby is a strong advocate of live music for dance performances. She acknowledges that some choreographers seem to prefer to use taped sounds, but this to her sometimes seems like "frozen" music. She feels so strongly about this, that even when a tape must be made for extra-musical considerations, this composer tries to build a live element into the work. For instance, when she collaborated on *Metric Mix* with Kelly Hogan in Virginia, Ms. Dalby wrote an enormously difficult part for prepared piano. It involved having the performer read traditional notation and put the fingers on the keyboard accordingly. But the pitches that came bubbling out varied, depending on which pedals were depressed.

Because the composer herself couldn't be at all the performances to play the piano part, two tapes were made: one of the total work for piano and percussion, and one of just the prepared piano part, so that if a percussionist were available, he or she could at least play along with the tape and provide some live warmth and impetus with which the solo dancer could interact.

PACIFIC-ORIENTED COLLABORATOR: JEAN ERDMAN

Among the more exceptional dance artists in regard to her collaborations with contemporary composers is Jean Erdman. Initially a soloist in Martha

Graham's company, she subsequently toured with her own troupe and later became the director of the dance program at New York University's School of the Arts. In more recent years, she has explored a "total theater" approach to dance production.

Recalling her work with composer Lou Harrison, Miss Erdman told the author: "*Perilous Chapel* was our first collaboration, and it was also the first dance I ever composed. I was working *without* music, developing the structure and the rhythms. Lou came over and took down the counts, and then he made the music the way *he* wanted to, to fit."[3]

However, she emphasized, she did not bind the composer to fit his musical phrases to her dance phrases. One art did not have to mimic, or "Mickey Mouse," the other, she commented, adding: "You know, Balanchine choreographed every note of every piece, and all musicians love that because they can 'see' the music. But that's *not* the way I worked."

"It seemed to me that the dance structure and the musical structure should form a whole *between* them," explained Miss Erdman, "so the major parts and major phrases all coincide. There are certain accents that Lou picked up for certain moments of movement which were climactic, which went absolutely with the moment. But in between, he was building his music his way, and I was building the dance my way."

Creature on a Journey, also to music by Lou Harrison, had quite a different inception. It was inspired by the choreographer's trip to Bali when she was 19 years old. "When I came back and started to work on my own things," related Miss Erdman, "I was exploring in the studio. All of a sudden, I began to be 'danced' by something, and improvised an entire dance in one fell swoop. Usually I don't remember improvisations, but I didn't forget that one! It just seemed to come out whole. I almost didn't have to rehearse it."

At the time, related Miss Erdman, she and Merce Cunningham were planning a program together. "I showed John Cage this solo and said, 'Would you write music for it?' He said, 'I haven't got the time to do that, but I think I have a piece of Lou Harrison's that would fit it.' So he brought out Lou's *Counterdance in the Spring,* written for three players, each one in a different meter: 5/4, 4/4, and 3/4."

"For *my* rhythmic structure, I tended to keep a very slow underpulse and then make rhythms in between. I always felt that underlying pulse, and then the rhythmic patterns that the movement made could be within that. I had *my* rhythms, and the music had *its* counter-rhythms, and it all went together," beamed the choreographer.

Later, Jean Erdman commissioned Lou Harrison to write music for a number of her dances. Harrison shared an affinity for things Eastern, but the choreographer couldn't say how much that entered into her choice. "I just felt that his music was wonderful," she said. "I loved it, and he always seemed to understand what the dance was about. He's very sensitive to movement."

Her first important solo, *Transformations of Medusa,* had been worked out entirely in silent movement. Then her mentor, Louis Horst, wrote a score for it. That's how he intended new works to evolve, Miss Erdman emphasized. "A dancer could, if she had an idea, bring it into form, *then* have the composer come, see the form, and write the music for it."

"Some choreographer might choose music that I wouldn't think to dance to," Miss Erdman added. "But certainly, the music that was composed *for* the dances was written with the idea that it was *completed* by the combination. So the *dance* is completed by the combination, too."

"Where I started to work with movement and music together, was with John Cage," related the choreographer. "But even then, he used a metronome. He'd get the fundamental pulse and then make his measures wherever he wanted." Commenting on her collaboration with Cage for *Daughters of the Lonesome Isle,* Miss Erdman pointed out: "The dance structure has to hold its own, so that the musical pattern can go round it. But it fits very closely, even so."

Concerning the powers of perception needed by composers who first see the dance and then write the music, the choreographer noted: "There are very few composers who could do that! John Cage was one, and Lou Harrison was another. But when I met Alan Hovhaness, he couldn't do that. For *Upon Enchanted Ground,* I had to give him the idea of the piece, and then the minutes or seconds. Then I related my sections specifically to his music. But again, he had this fundamental pulse thing. So I showed him the first theme of the choreography and the idea of how I was going to build it. Then he made the music. Afterwards I built the dance on the music. That was very different from working with John or Lou."

Jean Erdman's collaborations with Lou Harrison have continued over the years. Recently, in the 1980s, they revised their *Io and Prometheus* for a production in Greece. For the new version, said the choreographer, "the performers helped to create what the actual final result was. Lou said he sent us a musical *kit.* He gave the singers parts without rhythms, except in certain sections. So the soloists could do whatever they wanted, like recitative, using those words and the melodic patterns that Lou had given them."

Solstice, another Erdman-Harrison collaboration, originally had a score by a Juilliard composition student. The choreographer had shown him some movements and indicated lengths of time. "So in a way," she noted, "he was composing to *my* score. But when he orchestrated it, it bore no relation to the underlying feeling of my piece. He was interested in orchestration. So he had a big orchestra and did a big thing. But he wasn't sensitive to *my* theme," complained the choreographer. "Maybe I'm spoiled, but since it was *my* idea . . ." she trailed off wistfully.

So Lou Harrison, never knowing whom or what he was replacing, wrote a score on a much smaller scale, one that fit better with the intention of the choreographer. It has the quality of a chamber ballet, and it very much complements the feelings of world mythology in the dance itself.

Another method of collaboration was employed by Jean Erdman in the making of her *Harlequinade.* She recalled: "Ezra Laderman wanted to compose the score to include rhythmic patterns for the dance part. I was intrigued by the idea, but it was a real sweat, reading a score for ten dancers and having them do exactly the rhythmic pattern of the *composer!* But that rhythmic pattern was in counterpoint to what he wrote for the instruments. This piece was very sophisticated. The score was for eight instruments and ten dancers: four men and four women were like a chorus, so the men had a line in the score, and the women had a line. Then the two soloists each had a rhythmic part in the score."

"I could read the rhythms, and we could get movements, but I found I had no idea how to choreograph it until the composer told me what *his* idea was in the music. So it was quite reversed," explained the choreographer. "At first he said, 'Oh, no, no: you do it.' But I said, 'Ezra, I *have* to know what was inside you when you did this; then I can take off from there.' So he finally told me what his idea was, and it was lovely. It had a lot of humor in it, having to do with how a man and a woman can relate to each other."

"So that was a completely different experience, and it came out very well," the choreographer said. "The main thing is that each composer whom I've enjoyed working with has been able to relate to the dance structure as in counterpoint—and still understand the underlying theme."

However, when the music occasionally didn't satisfy her, Jean Erdman felt no need to continue with it. This happened with her *Changing Woman.*

"The first composer was Morton Feldman," she related. "He was so full of theories and 'don't do this and don't do thats' because he had been trained by John Cage not to write 'nineteenth-century' music. So he insisted that he shouldn't do any, and he had *me* singing in the Earth Voice, a very simple tune. But I'm not a singer. I mean, I wasn't trained, and it would have sounded terrible. I *did* it once," she suddenly recalled, laughing. "But the music—well! He was so enamoured of John's 'silence' that he had *mostly* silence. He rejected, as John was doing by that time, the expressivity aspect."

"With John," she went on to explain, "you don't 'express' anything; you just 'do this.' This type of approach was just getting started when I did *Changing Woman.* To me, it was as though there were nothing there. So when I had a chance to go to the Orient to dance, I asked Henry Cowell if he would make a new piece for that dance. He came to my studio in New York and took down the counts, and watched the dancers, and made the music."

Recalling what it was like to perform such a piece herself, Miss Erdman noted: "The music is linked into the movement so closely, and I performed those pieces so much, that it's just part of the dance—absolutely part of the dance. And the dance is part of the music, the way the choices were made."

"You know," she concluded, "it isn't as if the dancer were a personality coming out on the stage. The dancer is part of the piece of dance and music. It is through the intricate details of dynamic and rhythm, that the meaning or expression comes through the dance. The dancer doesn't add anything with his or her personality; it's all in the choreography. Then, when they go together, part of what is being expressed is coming through the music as well. But it has to be at the moment for that particular movement, for the combination of music and movement to become the one meaning.''

A VISIT WITH LOU HARRISON

Lou Harrison's house looks out over the Pacific, which seems appropriate for a composer who not only has travelled and lived in the Orient, but who also has been particularly drawn to the gamelan styles of Java.

''I believe you can't be a very good composer unless you at least know what the neighbors are doing,'' said Mr. Harrison of his wide-ranging musical interests and styles.[4]

Earlier in his career, he composed a work for the Joffrey Ballet called *Gamelan,* using Western instruments. Shortly before Robert Joffrey's death, *Dance Magazine* asked the choreographer which of his works he would like to see in revival, and he replied; ''One is *Gamelan.* . . . For me, there remains a happiness in my heart when I think of *Gamelan.*''[5] That opinion is similar to the reaction of many audience members after seeing dances set to Lou Harrison's music—and to their feelings for the composer as a person.

Lou Harrison takes great delight in showing visitors his studio full of instruments of several gamelan tunings. In explaining the technique of traditional Javanese style, he emphasized: ''The music is all written out, but a gamelan piece has a basic shape which can be repeated or contracted. But *all* the music is composed.''

Relating such styles to his work for dance, Mr. Harrison observed: ''The ballet *Solstice* [for Jean Erdman] contains a lot of extracted gamelan music. It's pan-pentatonic. I just set out my tonality and designed two five-tone scales for each movement, and then simply committed the work. Of course, the things that were going through my mind at that time were gamelan. So there are two or three movements that very much *resemble* gamelan.''

Though Lou Harrison was quite active in the New York scene for some years, prior to that his varied life included working as a dance musician in San Francisco studios, and even performing as a dancer himself.

''There were few male leads,'' he recalled. ''So *I* often took the male lead. I danced in most of the major houses in San Francisco.''

When asked what kind of training he brought to this endeavor, he replied: ''After the kid folk dancing stuff that my mother insisted on, my brother and I both had dance training and music training. But I've always been very kinetic, so when I started working for dancers—beginning with Carol Beals—things went well.

''The first public dance work that I did as a musician was called *Strike.* It was right after the big general strike in San Francisco. We did it at the longshoreman's union headquarters on a boxing ring. It was quite exciting! I had all my instruments (mostly percussion) down below the boxing ring, so I'd see the dancers come out over me with a swing, and I thought, 'Uh-oh.' ''

The composer survived to work with Carol Beals for a number of years, as well as with other West coast dancers, such as Lenore Peters Job, Tina Flade, and Marion van Tuyl.

"Tina was lovely," recalled Mr. Harrison. "Being fresh from the Wigman school, she tended to improvise her dances, and so I, in self-defense, used a little Labanotation [written directions for movement], because I found that I couldn't compose when there was no fixed dance."

"And there's a tradition at Mills College from Marion van Tuyl," noted the composer. "She was the one who got dance out of the gymnasium circuit into the fine arts division. I worked with her for some time, using piano and percussion.

"Percussion was easiest, but I also improvised on the piano. Then later on I learned to play Chinese flutes and all sorts of other things, so I had quite a variety. During a class I could do the largos with a flute or some other sustained instrument; I could do the extremely exciting parts with percussion, then use piano too."

Very briefly, Lou Harrison even had a small dance group of his own in San Francisco. "I danced my own choreography to my own music, and I must say, I never understood why, but people liked it," he said. "Dancers seem to like to use my music, but when I did choreography and danced to it myself, I had a *terrible* time."

Speaking warmly of his later collaboration with Jean Erdman, the composer noted: "She was always very generous, very helpful—and saw to it that I got good musicians. She *still* is good to work with," he smiled, going on to give his version of the *Io and Prometheus* collaboration.

"Jean called up and said that she had been invited to dance in the Odeon of Herodus Atticus, which is just below the Parthenon. So she said she wanted to expand *Io and Prometheus,* which we had done 'several centuries ago,' in 1948. I said OK, but in the meantime I didn't have any notion of what the signs meant on the prepared piano score. This had been a mystery to me for years," laughed the musician.

"So she said, 'Well, please send me the score; I'll make a videocassette of the dance as it presently is, and I'll send you the words.' So what I did was a real rewrite, because what I had previously done, for the insides of pianos, would not carry in a large Greek theater. She also wanted to add words and make a small Greek tragedy."

"She sent me a videocassette, and before me on it came each of the four people who were going to sing what I would write, and they demonstrated their voices and their feeling. Then she sent me the words. So I did *for* them what I could see and hear *from* them, on the tape. It was very helpful, but I had never worked that way before," commented the composer.

"So I changed the piano part greatly, to be usable out-of-doors, and then I wrote all the voice parts. I think I did this in a week and sent it back to her, and it seems to have worked."

"As I recall," Mr. Harrison continued, "all—if not almost all—of the dances I did for Jean Erdman were already completed dances. What I did was to go in, take counts, make notes to myself of what was happening. I used to have a very vivid kinetic memory. I had only to look at a dance and put down the things. I actually could *do* parts of it in my house, just by looking, and by capturing the metrics. So I would do that, and then I'd go home and write."

Commenting further on this method of collaboration, Mr. Harrison said: "In some sense, that was easier for me [to have the dance movement completed first] because I could then, over a span of measures, get the music going and occupy the time musically—whereas chopping it out measure by measure is never very satisfactory musically."

Speaking of the way Jean Erdman essentially gave him free rein, the composer said: "She respected fellow artists all the way round. Every fellow artist was treated like a mature person. It was marvelous . . . and still is."

When asked how he felt about other choreographers using his existing pieces for dance purposes, Lou Harrison was enthusiastic: "I'd just say, 'Go and do it. I'd love it. I'd love to see it if you're going to do it somewhere I can attend.' I prefer live performances, of course, and there is that problem: dancers so often just use tapes now."

Concerning the business end of composing music, Mr. Harrison realistically conceded: "I have never thought of earning a living by composing. You have to support your 'vice.' Composing is pleasure, and if you like it enough, you will learn to support it one way or another. But it certainly is not going to make a living for you; that's out of the question. In the United States, most of the arts are 'amateur' in that sense, because nobody can earn a living at them. So I've long ago decided that as long as music is a pleasure for me, I will continue to earn money one way or another to afford it."

One of the ways Lou Harrison afforded his composition was by working in the dance studios at Mills College and other places. "Modern dance studios were hospitable to new musical procedures," he pointed out. "On the West coast, it was under the aegis and mentorship of Henry Cowell that John Cage, myself, Ray Green, Gerald Strang, and oodles of others began exploring percussion music as a viable concert idiom. It was no trouble at all to work in a dance studio, because most dancers at that time had large percussion collections. And remember, then there was the connection with the Wigman school, which used a lot of percussion in the studio too."

"But when John and I and the others here began giving concerts, we wrote a *lot,*" said Mr. Harrison. "We were the ones who wrote the main body of percussion literature that is still done."

"*None* of it was improvised," he emphasized. "Oh no! Improvisation is something that happened after the war. We occasionally used structured improvisation, but the realm of improvisation then was the ability to keep a class going, with whatever the dancer wanted. It certainly wasn't to approach the public! That's a whole development later. When *we* presented things to the public, they were *formal.*''

It seems that Lou Harrison continues to prepare his musical collaborations with dancers very carefully. Indeed, on the day of his interview with the author, he was expecting the dancer-choreographer Remy Charlip to come and work out timings for a new piece to be done with an entire gamelan ensemble. And in a letter to the author, written several months later, the composer mentioned:

I just last week completed a ballet for Erick Hawkins, and it was a great pleasure to do. I have yet, of course, many hours of putting black spots on paper to complete the final orchestral score, but the composition is done, and I must say that I am very pleased with it. Because he suggested no specific subject—though he did specify length—I simply composed out of my vivid memories of his choreographies and his visual stage presence. I look forward to hearing it and hope, too, to be able to see it as well. It is in five connected movements and scored for that combination that he asks everybody to use. I do understand his wish to keep order in the pit and am happy that he, like Jean Erdman, always uses live music.

MAXIMUM EXCITEMENT FROM MINIMALIST MUSIC: LAURA DEAN AND STEVE REICH

It seemed appropriate that a recent private showing of Laura Dean's *Sky Light, Tympani,* and *Magnetic* took place in a building that was formerly a mosque—hence the large dance space, so that the dervishes could whirl! And among the continual surprises in Laura Dean's works is the most amazing spinning dancing that anyone—dervish or not—could ever hope to see, whipped up by the ongoing intensity of live musicians who closely interact with the dancers.

Indeed, the proper name of the company is Laura Dean Dancers and Musicians, and it is an unusual showcase for the creativity of one person, since the choreographer has more and more taken to writing her own music. Laura Dean said: ''When I think of scoring choreography, I think of scoring music; in a sense they are one and the same.''[6]

Among the works for which she has created both movement and music are *Music* (for six dancers, synthesizer, piano and violin); *In a Circle* (for six dancers, synthesizer, and two sets of rock drums); *Spiral* (for eight dancers, cello, two grand pianos, and singer); *Sky Light* (for two drummers); *Magnetic* (with two keyboard synthesizer players); and *Tympani* (which lives up to the promise of its name, employing three kettledrums and two pianos).

When she created her group, Laura Dean had not composed much music before. Her first foray into this was for her dance *Song,* and two works for the Joffrey Ballet: *Night* (for two pianos) and *Fire* (for two sets of drums, Indian harmonium, tambourines, two bamboo flutes and double flutes). Both were considered controversial by audiences who were essentially ballet aficionados. Nevertheless, *Night* continued to be in the Joffrey repertoire.

Among the musicians at the private showing mentioned above were Eleanor Sandresky and Phillip Bush, who explained how they had been rehearsing with the dancers for about ten days, two to three hours per day. Their working material consisted of only a few raggedy sheets of music written out by Laura Dean. This was a "shorthand" method, the musicians explained, for in this style, the composer makes patterns and then repeats and repeats and repeats. However, Mr. Bush had to write out one tricky permutation for himself, because while the pattern of pitches kept repeating exactly, the rhythmic organization kept shifting over the bar line.

In this kind of music—which can be very generally labelled "minimalist"—there was also a hypnotic use of a drone, in the manner of bagpipes, for instance. This is not essentially harmonic music, in the sense of having a pitch-oriented tension and progression; rather, it is driving, relentless music due mostly to the rhythmic insistence in it. Such music might not be very safe to drive a car to, but for driving dancers to whirling movement, it seems to work just fine.

During preliminary rehearsals, the musicians at first used a metronome to keep themselves pegged accurately to a rigid beat. After a while, they could put away the metronome. There is always a danger of musicians speeding up when they are set to continuing rhythmic patterns unabated for long periods of time. But these instrumentalists seemed to minimize this possibility. They felt that after a while, the ensemble itself got so strong that neither the dancers nor the musicians threw off the beat. (It should be noted that there was no conductor for these pieces.)

When Laura Dean's dancers are not performing to her own music, they have from time to time performed to the music of Steve Reich. As with *Impact,* premiered at the Brooklyn Academy of Music, the composer is often on hand with his instrumentalists, helping to provide a sparkly percussion companion to the dance.

Steve Reich's system of working with sound does complement Laura Dean's choreographic methods. Tracing the collaborations of these artists, Deborah Jowitt noted in the *Village Voice:*

> Dean's dances are always clearly structured, elegantly patterned. And Dean's structures have none of the frequent climaxes and big contrast of dances made to conventional Western music. Like the scores she writes herself, her dances tend to repeat patterns over and over. Long sections of spinning are a feature of her style; so are geometric patterns and an emphasis on precise rhythms. No princesses. No soloists. No stunts. . . . .
>
> When she returned to New York in 1970 with a big arsenal of steps she believed in, she started looking for a musician to collaborate with, someone who was also interested in repetition, in simplicity of means, in doing things for a long time. A friend put her in touch with composer-percussionist Steve Reich, who had just returned from studying in Africa with a master drummer and was beginning to make highly polished, sophisticated compositions utilizing techniques and rhythms he had learned. From the beginning, Reich and Dean had what she terms "fantastic communication" and the ensuing

several-year stretch of intense artistic and personal interchange must have been fruitful for both of them. . . . Now that Dean, who studied piano and composition herself, is creating her own scores, she's bucking inevitable comparisons with Reich, who is, after all, an important person in contemporary music. On the one hand, she makes no bones about acknowledging Reich's influence; on the other, she seems to find it healthier . . . to think in terms of correspondences and common concerns. She never phases, because that's a Reich thing; and her ringing, unabashedly human vocal harmonies are unlike anything of Reich's.[7]

Speaking more recently about the current scene, Laura Dean cited a new excitement in the field as more and more dancers are discovering for themselves how to make their own music, or how to work effectively with other live composers and live musicians. When she first chose Steve Reich's music for some of her own dances, she pointed out, she did not simply put the needle on some of his recordings, but rather brought Mr. Reich and his whole ensemble of musicians right up there on the stage. For these collaborations, the two creators sat down with the musical scores and discussed the structure of the pieces. Miss Dean emphasized: "Any good dancer is not dancing to the melodic quality; they dance to the *structure* first."

Laura Dean likes to point out that she was one of the first dancers of her generation to put so much effort into providing live music for the dance. Her advice about working with live composers is that "the most important thing is mutual respect. You should first establish a dialogue, mainly about structure. Otherwise, the choreographer is using the composer's music as wallpaper background."

Just what is so bad about working with tape, after all? Miss Dean feels that it doesn't encourage dancers to have a physical concept of sound. She suggested that the abundant use of taped sound by so many companies is probably essentially a budgeting consideration. Yet that had been no deterrent for her. "It's because I *made* it happen, that I have live music," she declared proudly. "When you have a live dance performance, it is partly a responsibility of a live performing artist to have live music too."

In her own development, Laura Dean took twelve years of classical piano lessons and also studied musical theory. As a teenager, she played lots of Bach, and also loved the Bartok pieces based on Hungarian folk tunes.

Even though she has forged ahead to different musical idioms, she has nevertheless retained her love of live sounds, in all styles. "There is such a *joy* in listening to live music," she said, "that I have never in my life *not* had live music for my dances!" Turning to questions of taste and style for dance, she added, "Steve Reich is the best composer for dance today."

For his part, Steve Reich was equally enthusiastic about his former collaborations with this choreographer. "Laura Dean is the only choreographer that I feel technically and artistically in tune with, because her use of repetition and variation is akin to my method of working as a composer," he remarked.[8]

Yet Reich's recorded music has been used often—and quite successfully—by a number of other choreographers. For example, his *Music for 18 Musicians* has been set by Alvin Ailey, Pearl Lang, a company in Munich, and one in Israel. Because the performances are so far-flung, the composer regretted that he could not attend most of them.

One thing he did see and enjoy was Lar Lubovitch's setting of *Music for Mallet Instruments, Voices, and Organ.* The composer considered that "a good job was done with the relationship" in that dance. In addition, one might note, Mr. Lubovitch has had audiences literally leaping out of their seats and cheering both for his *Tabernacle* (set to Reich's score *Tellim*) and the pink-and-grey-streamered *Cavalcade* (which uses the composer's *Octet*). Both of these musical works reflect the composer's long-standing interest in Hebrew traditions. Mr. Lubovitch successfully picked up on this aura, managing at the same time to create a work directly accessible and meaningful to contemporary audiences.

In addition to his interest in minimalist procedures and ritualistic methods drawn from Jewish music, Steve Reich brings to his composing and performing a background in African drumming. He went to Ghana and studied this music, imbibing not only the physical techniques of drumming, but also an understanding of non-Western methods of combining various polyrhythmic patterns. However, he is swift to point out that he does not use either the scales or tunes of non-Western traditions such as the African or Balinese, though he has investigated both rather thoroughly. "That would be like trespassing," he commented.

Expressing his thoughts in a radio interview with Terry Gross of WNYC, the composer elaborated on the influence of one's own national roots:

> The sounds that surrounded America from 1950 through 1980—jazz and rock and roll—cannot be ignored. They can be refined, filtered, or rejected. But to ape another culture of another time has to have a certain sterility as a result. It's like taking a plant that grows in another very different environment; you have to build a hothouse, a miniature tropical environment, to keep it alive. That's what museums are for, and that's why it's important to have orchestras that play the music that they do. But in terms of living composers, I don't think that you can pretend you are someone who is completely divorced from this time and place. And that's been very much how I've dealt with non-Western music. I avoid sounding like it, because I think that would be absurd.[9]

Reich's own studies of the jazz and popular musical styles of America included playing the snare drum as a teenager, and playing for social dances on weekends when he was a student at Cornell University. The teachers whom he felt influenced him most were William Austin and Hall Overton. He also was deeply touched by the recordings of such great jazz artists as Miles Davis, Charlie Parker, and John Coltrane.

Among the important ingredients in Reich's artistry are the discoveries he made while using electronic tape. For instance, he found that if you take a loop of tape, it will drift gradually out of sync and gradually accelerate. This type of cumulative, out-of-kilter relationship can be achieved electronically, or it can actually be planned and written into a score for acoustical instruments, with interesting mathematical and aural results.

All these explorations are what Reich brought to his musical partnering of Laura Dean's dancers. Speaking of his collaborations with her, the composer said: "It is a wonderful way to work, if the composer also participates as a performer and is responding to and aware of the dancers."

In his *Writings about Music,* Steve Reich made many comments that are pertinent to dance. For instance:

> Serious dancers who now perform with pulseless music or with no music at all will be replaced by young musicians and dancers who will re-unite rhythmic music and dance as a high art form. . . . For a long time during the 1960s one would go to the dance concert where no one danced, followed by the party where everyone danced. This was not a healthy situation. Using rock and roll in a dance concert is not the answer. The real answer is to create a genuinely new dance with roots that go back thousands of years to the basic impulse at the foundation of all dance: the human desire for regular rhythmic movement, usually done to music."[10]

Finally, he reminds us: "Obviously, music should put all within listening range into a state of ecstasy."[11]

4

Composer-Conductor-Instrumentalists

One fertile source of new music for the dance is the talent of many composer-arrangers who also collaborate with choreographers as conductors and instrumental performers.

STANLEY SUSSMAN: MULTITALENTED MUSICIAN

The multiple titles of Stanley Sussman are an indication of the varied musical services that the dance world needs and welcomes. For openers, he is associate music director and composer-in-residence for the Cleveland–San Jose Ballet, as well as principal conductor for the Martha Graham Company and for the New Mexico Ballet.

Mr. Sussman came to his dance affiliations initially through his activities as a studio pianist, and through his arranging of music for dance bands when he was in the service.

Speaking with the author, Mr. Sussman described his first assignment as composer-in-residence in Cleveland: it was for a ballet choreographed by Dennis Nahat, titled *Wu T'ai Shih.*[1]

''The translation that was given to me is 'Five Dance Poems,' '' explained the composer. ''It had something to do with five; it had something to do with dance; but it also had to do with some form of movement—*not* of dance form, rather of *spiritual* movement.''

''I was new to the entire situation,'' he continued. ''I had been writing music all my life, so I picked up whatever atmospheric feelings I would feel—and just wrote. The choreographer and I went for a five-movement suite. It was a *form* dance, not a story ballet. The choreography portrayed ideas relating to the elements: Earth, Water, Fire, Air, and People.''

Subsequently, the composer reset his music as a concert suite titled *Orchestral Episodes,* which was premiered by the Cleveland Philharmonic. After that, he wrote two more original works for the Cleveland Ballet and orchestrated a fourth, all for Dennis Nahat's choreography.

Their second work was *Last Act,* a serious narrative ballet subtitled *Mr. and Mrs.* "For this," related the composer, "we got the story line, the order of events, the action, the psychological involvement—everything was worked out. Then I wrote the piece; then Nahat choreographed it. It has to do with a marriage in very serious trouble, ending in catastrophe. The scenario for this one was a joint effort between choreographer and composer."

When asked if director Nahat ever specified certain rhythmic or metric aspects, Mr. Sussman replied: "No, I think he was primarily concerned with the order of events and the length of the piece. I think he left the other things up to me. So the only parameters I had were the story and the length, the sequence of events, and what was going on. Then I *played* for all of the rehearsals, on the piano, and I would orchestrate at night." Later, of course, he would also conduct orchestral rehearsals and the full performances.

Such total involvement on the part of some musicians like Stanley Sussman sometimes brings public notice in the form of program notes, bowing time onstage, subsequent audience applause, and press coverage. Sometimes not—as suggested by one of Stanley Sussman's counterparts, the late John Herbert McDowell.

OVER 140 DANCE SCORES: JOHN HERBERT MCDOWELL

John Herbert McDowell was music director for the Paul Taylor Dance Company, he choreographed some works himself, and he composed extensively both for film and live theater. He was a success. Yet, speaking to Beth Tyler in an interview for *Ballet Review* shortly before his death, this composer-conductor voiced some of the mixed feelings that are not unusual among musical collaborators for the dance in America. He said:

> Collaboration is very hard. To begin with, for instance, there are a great many very good composers who cannot collaborate, they're so tuned in to what their thing is. In collaboration, automatically, you give up things. . . . you have to be very accepting of what happens and cut things or sometimes add things at the very last moment under great duress, and maybe you're not very happy, but at least it gets through opening night. Collaboration is very difficult, but I've had some wonderful times collaborating, obviously, or I wouldn't have been doing it—one hundred and forty dance scores, eighty theater scores, and eighteen film scores.[2]

Touching upon one of the most sensitive aspects of collaboration, Beth Tyler brought up the question of the lack of press coverage for dance music in general. The composer told of his experience in writing *Phantom of the Opera* as a major, forty-minute ballet for James Waring, with full orchestral score. Simultaneously, he was working on *Public Domain,* a pastiche of taped popular music for Paul Taylor. He noted what the professional newspaper critics wrote about the two pieces:

> I think Clive Barnes said that *Phantom*'s music was by John Herbert McDowell. Walter Terry, writing in the *Tribune,* mentioned every other composer on the program, all of whom were dead—Prokofiev, Tchaikovsky—and never even mentioned there was a world premiere of a forty-minute orchestra score—much less said anything about it.
>
> *Public Domain* opened a week later, and Barnes gave the first two paragraphs of his review to the music, an absolute rave, that it was the best tape score he'd ever heard. . . . Everyone wrote at great length about this piece. Now, I'm not ashamed of *Public Domain,* it's a very nice piece, but it was very E-A-S-Y, very facile. And it was fun, so I sort of tossed it off. At the same time, I'd been working on *Phantom* practically to the point of extinction, just giving my all, and I knew and still think that *Phantom* is an extraordinary piece. Critics didn't even mention the music, or at the most they said it was there.[3]

Finally, in a comment that has been heard from many other musicians for the dance, McDowell remarked: "One of the few frustrations about writing for dance, people really pay very little attention to the music, and in certain cases the music has been much longer and more painful gestating than the dance itself has."[4]

DONALD YORK: VERSATILE MUSICIAN FOR PAUL TAYLOR

During a recent theater season, one could read ecstatic reviews of Paul Taylor's *Snow White* in all the newspapers, and sure enough, there would usually be a sentence that indicated merely that "the music was by Donald York." Who is he? And how did he come to compose for one of the most outstanding choreographers of our time?

A meeting with the composer revealed him to be a genial man still in his prime, with a modest manner that was refreshing, given his substantial professional credits.[5] A Juilliard graduate and member of the American Society of Composers, Arrangers, and Producers (ASCAP), Mr. York has a lengthy list of manuscript compositions and private recordings. Along the way to his post as music director of the Paul Taylor Dance Company were some impressive grants for composition: one from the National Endowment for the Arts, a Fromm Prize, a Mellon grant, and funding from Meet the Composer.

As a keyboardist, he performed on piano, organ, and many electronic instruments. He toured with Hall and Oates and as part of the First Moog Quartet. He performed with the Detroit and Boston Pops Symphonies and made four U.S. tours. At one point, he was pianist with such jazz luminaries as Clark Terry and Chet Baker.

In the theater world, Donald York was music director for singer-comedienne Bette Midler's show *Clams on the Half Shell,* for both her U.S. tour and the CBS-TV presentation. On Broadway, he was music director of *Little One*. For a Broadway revival of *Can Cans and Cakewalks,* choreographed and directed by Roland Petit, Mr. York did musical arrangements for the dances—as he also did for Michel LeGrand's *A Christmas Carol*. In addition, his credits included three film scores. All in all, a most unusual versatility in output before one even touches upon his modern dance work.

Formerly married to Lila York (then one of Paul Taylor's dancers), the composer first came to Taylor's attention when the choreographer saw his work with Bette Midler. Hearing some tapes convinced Mr. Taylor that he had found a collaborator for his work-in-progress, *Polaris*.

Mr. Taylor offered the composer a fascinating proposition: the piece was to be the same dance done twice, with different cast, lighting, and music for the repeat. As a framework, Taylor gave York a diagrammed structure and indicated that he wanted a contrast of light and dark feelings. Mr. York had to duplicate the counts exactly for the second version—which even he admits was not always easy, because he had gotten into some tricky metric changes the first time around.

Out of this initial collaboration grew a continuing partnership. Donald York became music director for the Paul Taylor Dance Company, not only composing new works, but conducting the New York City seasons as well as some tour engagements. In addition, he sometimes serves as concert pianist—for instance, in *Le Sacre du Printemps*.

Donald York was exuberant about his composing for Paul Taylor, saying: "He is not 'on' the music, but 'is' the music! He lets me go . . . trusts me to give him something."

When they were beginning their collaborative work for *Diggity,* Mr. Taylor merely said, "Write me some popular jazzy-sounding music," recalled the composer. When it came to *Snow White,* Mr. York said Paul Taylor gave him an outline of general happenings—a découpage or scenario, with this kind of direction: "For one minute, Snow White dances in the forest and finds the house." York wrote music in the time frame specified, and then Taylor would choreograph.

Paul Taylor left much of the musical decision-making to the composer. Donald York welcomed this, in contrast to his experience of Broadway work, where, he says, "choreographers tend to be more specific about beats and tend to have made up the dance first in movement and then try to put it to the music." But with Paul Taylor, when there were sections that did not seem to work—for instance, in the original opening of *Snow White*—both choreographer and composer worked together to rearrange some entrances and to switch some music around as needed to support the evolving dance.

Mr. York felt that this method of collaboration does work best. And about Paul Taylor's musicality, the composer is effusive, pointing to the choreographer's "extraordinary sense: he feels the structure of the music and phrases and plays with them in such a way that they are not literal. He likes to let music breathe independently of the dance."

The composer said that personally he feels it is boring if the dance is literal. "But if the music and dance breathe independently and not exactly hand in glove, it is exciting."

Mr. York mentioned that on the road as Paul Taylor's conductor, he would occasionally take company class with the dancers. "It did not help!" lamented the musician. But being *around* the dance helped: being married to a dancer, having friends and associates who were dancers, conducting for the company's performances—all of these experiences seemed to help his composition for the dance.

"Dancers *feel* music," observed Donald York enthusiastically. "They're always bopping to it! It helps for a conductor to *feel* music like a dancer."

If all that sounds a bit like love, the economic figures would probably reinforce that impression. The practical financial aspects of composing for modern dance are such that not only Donald York but other composers as well, mention in passing that they have sometimes lost money by doing music for the dance. Consider, for example, that the cost of copying and duplicating parts alone can easily run upwards of $5,000 for an orchestral work. Mr. York said that composing had only recently become a way for him to earn an adequate living. Earlier in his career, grants accounted for every commissioned score, though Broadway was more commercially rewarding.

But Donald York's collaborations have begun to attract more notice from the public. There is now a commercial record devoted to his music for Paul Taylor's *Snow White* and *Diggity,* with expert performances that are attractive to the listener even removed from the theatrical experience.

Critics, too, are beginning to notice York's collaborative composition more. For example, in *Dance Magazine,* Susan Reiter wrote about the Taylor-York collaboration for *Syzygy:*

> York was interested in composing a really loud, violent piece, with lots of percussion, and was working with synthesizers and a computer. "That actually took me in another direction that is very specific—a very rhythmic, more minimal style," York says.
>
> "It's so different from other music he's done," Taylor explained. "I was surprised." But surprise seems to be the mainstay of the collaboration. "We just don't know what's going to happen; that's what makes the fun," the choreographer notes cheerfully.[6]

A more somber Taylor-York work, *Last Look,* was televised on PBS. At the previous live premiere, the author had the curious experience of seeing the conductor-composer reflected onstage in the mylar panels which serve as a backdrop for this macabre piece. So for that performance, at least, the multifaceted musician was not only in the pit conducting his own composition, but also onstage with the dancers—or at least his reflection gave the illusion that this was so. An odd occurrence, but it emphasized once again the versatile involvement often demanded of musicians who work with dancers.

TANIA LEON: COLLABORATING WITH THE DANCE THEATRE OF HARLEM AND THE ALVIN AILEY AMERICAN DANCE THEATER

"I did a tango once with Leonard Bernstein," said composer-conductor Tania Leon, expressing admiration for one of her musical mentors.[7] Miss Leon herself is in the prime of an equally varied career that has included collaboration with some of the best dancers in the world.

She was asked if she had, deep down, a true preference for any part of her activities: whether for conducting symphony concerts, performing on the piano, improvising, composing, or collaborating for dance. "I love it all," she replied. "I eat music."

Surely one of the major musical talents to be collaborating with American dancers at this time, Tania Leon has also managed to juggle many other responsibilities: she is the conductor of the Brooklyn Philharmonic's community series; an associate professor of composition and conducting at Brooklyn College—where she also leads a contemporary music ensemble; the artistic director of the Composer's Forum in New York City; and a generous proponent of new music by her colleagues through various professional organizations.

Her own compositions are published, recorded, and increasingly heard in live performances. At the time of our conversation, she was embarking on a major work commissioned by the American Composer's Orchestra—a full-length piece for piano and orchestra, to be premiered only eight months later at Carnegie Hall.

Her abilities span many styles. Expert at putting together performances of avant-garde symphonic works for appearances in Kennedy Center or other great theaters both here and abroad, she seems equally at home in Broadway pits—where, among other things, she conducted the hit show *The Wiz* for an entire year.

In the dance world, she was formerly music director of the Dance Theatre of Harlem and more recently, was acting music director for the Alvin Ailey American Dance Theater. With the latter company, she prepared the musical reconstructions and conducted for the full-evening program of "The Magic of Katherine Dunham." That entire evening was charged with magic—and it seemed obvious that a considerable portion of that electricity was generated by Tania Leon.

Indeed, she remarked: "When I do a show, I know everything, from the costumes the dancers must have, to the scenery, to the props. If something is missing on the stage, I notice it right away, because sometimes the entire picture changes, and there is a rapport that I have to keep going between people down here in the pit and the people on the stage. So I am the conductor of energy from one place to the other, and I have to be careful with *everything* I do. If there is a lighting plot and one light doesn't lead properly . . . or if something blows up, or whatever, it immediately changes my perception—'' and thus, she implied, what she might have to do.

The conductor was asked if there were disasters during performances that she could look back upon with a bit of humor. ''Of course,'' she replied. ''Somebody might get an injury, and you're expecting someone to go onstage, and another face comes out and looks at you like 'Here I am!' You're expecting one ballerina, and you know the tempos of that ballerina, everything. All of a sudden they send someone else out there . . . and you look at the face and say to yourself 'What?' '' she laughed.

Since her long-term affiliations with the dance have included the Dance Theatre of Harlem and Alvin Ailey American Dance Theater, it seemed as if Tania Leon believed in going to the top immediately. ''I did!'' she affirmed without hesitation. ''The point is that I have been very proud of *myself.* I don't knock on people's doors and say I need a job. Everything I do, people call me for.''

Describing the artistic desires she had as a child growing up in Cuba, Tania Leon said: ''Let me tell you something. I've always wanted to be a dancer. I've always wanted to be many things. I like painting. I like mathematics. I wanted to be a surgeon. An astronaut. A pilot. A dancer. I like everything with passion. And that's one of the things that I have to do in my life: focus and discipline myself; if not, I would be all over the place.''

''But there was an attempt at dance,'' she recalled. ''When I was about twelve, my grandmother took me to have some ballet lessons, because I liked dancing. I wanted to learn Spanish dancing, and flamenco and ballet. So I passed the audition and everything, but the academy didn't accept me. It's part of one of the secrets of my life. I was not accepted in the ballet school—but not because of my abilities. The thing is that at the time, the excuse that they gave my grandmother was that I was 'black.' ''

''Years later,'' she pointed out with pride, ''I came to the United States and I became a founder of the first black ballet company in the world!''

''It's a mystery to me. My grandmother told me, you see. And it was as if I could never touch anything. I used to go to the ballet and see Alicia Alonso, and I was in love with dancing, but I wouldn't touch it. And *ballet* is what I liked!'' she emphasized. ''I loved all that sophistication.''

May 29, 1967 is a date deeply imprinted on Tania Leon's mind. That is when she came to the United States to study with Leonard Bernstein, Sejii Ozawa, and other masters.

How did she get into her dance work? ''Coincidence,'' she said. While she was studying at New York University, a friend asked her to cover studio classes at the Harlem School of the Arts. ''While I had to wait between classes, I used to improvise on the piano,'' she explained. ''One day I was doing this, and a very handsome man walked into the room. I followed him with my eyes and said 'Wow! Who is that?' ''

"I kept playing, and about an hour after that, he approached me and asked if I would be interested in playing, because he was going to open a school, and he needed a pianist. He liked my playing, and he thought it would be interesting. That was Arthur Mitchell!" beamed the musician. "So two weeks afterwards, I got a call from him that a gentleman had arrived from Europe, and that he was going to have his first class. I was the first one to play there for Karel Shook. So that's how the whole thing began. Then Arthur Mitchell talked to me about what his dream was, about forming his company, and so forth, and . . . I *loved* the idea. That's how everything happened."

Miss Leon started playing for classes initially, then soon became composer-in-residence. Her first ballet was a score for piano and orchestra, *Tones,* which was initially performed in 1971. This work was Arthur Mitchell's first choreography for Dance Theatre of Harlem, and it continues to be a staple of the company's lecture-demonstrations.

For *Tones,* Tania Leon not only composed the music; she also played the piano part and conducted the recording. Then, for the first performance with live orchestra—which was at the Spoleto Festival in Italy—she performed the piano part.

As music director for Dance Theatre of Harlem, Tania Leon went on to compose more original music, and also to do special arrangements, such as *The Beloved* and *Dougla.* Elaborating on how *Dougla* came into being, Miss Leon explained that choreographer Geoffrey Holder came up with the idea and gave her actual tunes, plus the structure that he wanted for his dance. "From there," she explained, "I departed and did the arrangements." She watched the choreography as it developed, and she began putting various percussion and wind instruments together—including many African and Latin American ones. For this particular work, she said, "The main melodies and the basic rhythms were written. After that, you encourage improvisation, without losing the basic rhythm."

Since she had grown up steeped in the out-of-doors *comparsas* (carnivals) and music-making of Cuba, Tania Leon was probably the perfect collaborator for such a work. She plays congas and other drums herself, and is most effective in eliciting from other musicians the kinds of sounds she wants. "You can do it!" one hears her say many times during rehearsals. And the musicians seem to respond by giving her what she wants.

For the Katherine Dunham programs danced by the Alvin Ailey company, the music had to be considerably reconstructed, and Tania Leon spent an entire summer working up the musical input for the dances. She recalled, "Katherine Dunham told me all the nuances, and then she talked to me about the story behind the dance. You know, the printed music at that time didn't have any kind of details, so we had to sort of sensitize everything."

The audiences were delighted not only by the energetic music provided by the orchestra in the pit, but also by the little group of musicians that would wander around onstage with the dancers at various points in the different pieces. Miss Leon explained how this was accomplished: "The beat has to be steady, particularly in the bomba (bass drum). And we have something called the claves that never changes. This is in the structure of the rhythm and stays the same throughout, and all the improvisation is done around that."

All the parts of the orchestral instrumentalists in the pit, however, were entirely written out. "The specific pattern of the drumming was also written out," explained Miss Leon. "One of the drummers had to always keep a specified pattern going for each dance."

Speaking further about the intriguing process of including improvised music for dance performances, Tania Leon pointed out that included in the Ailey repertoire are works by Duke Ellington. "But with the Ellington works," she noted, "everything is written out."

Concerning the question of musical improvisation for dance performances, the musician pointed out that in her experience, "every improvised thing has been very structured. In other words, we know for how long the improvisation was going to be done. The cues have to be worked out very well."

This issue seemed particularly intriguing, for one could imagine that if a particular, well-known jazz artist performed something with his or her particular stylistic stamp, then it would be very difficult—if not impossible—for another musician to duplicate it for performance with dancers. Miss Leon agreed that this is so, and said that in such instances, it may be preferable to use tapes so that the dancers will always have the true flavor of an artist's distinctive style.

With Tania Leon's compositions and arrangements, even for the ones that are written out, it has happened at times that for various reasons Dance Theatre of Harlem or Alvin Ailey's company have performed to tapes of her music. But even then, one can sense a very special musical personality.

JACQUES D'AMBOISE, LEE NORRIS, 1,500 CHILDREN, AND THE EVENT OF THE YEAR

On one side of Madison Square Garden, the circus was setting up for its annual spring visit to New York City. On the other side of the building, at the Felt Forum, a second show was being readied. Fifteen hundred children were gathering to perform in a preview of "The Event of the Year," sponsored by the National Dance Institute (NDI). The students came from Brooklyn, New Jersey, Harlem, Westchester, Massachusetts, Maine; some attended a school for the deaf; and fifty-six young dancers and musicians came from the People's Republic of China to participate in the show. Inside the theater were representatives of the press with cameras, as well as a benefit committee that included a baroness. The printed program included letters of good will from the mayor and the governor of the state.

The show that was the focus of all this activity was the brainchild of Jacques d'Amboise, who for over thirty years was a principal dancer of the New York City Ballet. His music director since the inception of NDI had been Lee Norris.

Just before show time, d'Amboise conferred with the conductor, and the two parted with a bear hug. The band applauded for d'Amboise, and then let loose with a joyful burst of upbeat music. A stream of children came flowing across the stage: Afro-American children, Hispanic children, Caucasian children, Indian children, Chinese-American children, fat, skinny, short and tall children, in all manner of costumes, along with some guest adult stars and a few dancing police officers. At the intermission, the musicians—all old pros—admitted that they found it "very inspiring" to play for these dancers.

A few weeks before, the children and the musicians had had their first run-through together at Lincoln Center's Alice Tully Hall. It was an interesting experience for the parents and other onlookers to see all manner of percussion being brought in: cymbals, gongs, drum sets, congas, bell trees, wind chimes—as well as several electronic keyboards and an electronic marimba. A sax player entered, then a baritone player, a trombonist, and a clarinetist. There was a rather cozy cramming together of the piano and the synthesizers: the classic and the modern co-existing in a little combo of only a dozen players. Quite different from the symphony orchestras that used to accompany d'Amboise in all his celebrated solo ballet roles!

The composer Chou Wen-chung entered. It was he who made the arrangements for the Chinese children to come to New York, and he also contributed one of his own compositions, *Beijing in the Mist.* At the rehearsal, Mr. Chou proceeded to unpack a little bag of delicate Chinese cymbals and bells and to pass them out to the commercial musicians in the pit.

Soon the product of months of planning and preliminary collaboration began to take form, both musically and aurally. Onstage, Jacques d'Amboise and his staff ran the children through their dances: *The Great Wall, Dumplings, Pieces of China, Phoenix Nest, Chopsticks, Peking Duck, A Recipe for Sweet and Sour Sauce,* and so on.

Far below, from the deep pit, one of the musicians called up: "We've got our own private gulag down here." Although they couldn't see the children perform, they played with concentration and gusto the music by Virgil Thomson, Morton Gould, Chick Corea, Jed Distler, David Amram, Dick Hyman, and Lee Norris. Onstage several hours later, Jacques d'Amboise thanked the students personally for their efforts, and down below, Lee Norris exited, mopping his brow mightily.

* * *

Lee Norris is a musician whose versatility and enthusiasm are well-matched to the talents of Jacques d'Amboise. Working together on the National Dance Institute programs for over a decade, these two weathered differences of opinion, collaboration by telephone from one coast to the other, budgetary constraints, and the annual miracle of putting on a polished show danced by over a thousand young students.

The composer-conductor-arranger explained in an interview a little about how these mammoth programs are put together.[8] For the first decade of NDI, Norris composed or arranged most of the music himself. But for the special Chinese project, it was decided that other composers would be asked to contribute too.

"It becomes a little more difficult with a composer to write a piece for a specific theatrical situation," noted Mr. Norris. "The parameters are more defined with a story line, whereas if you go to a composer and say 'Write me a four-minute piece,' you're not limited stylistically or with certain bars or 'slow here; fast there,' or whatever is needed for a particular plot."

Nevertheless, a number of well-known composers did lend their talents to the endeavor. For example, Virgil Thomson took out some pieces that he had written fifty years ago and allowed Lee Norris to orchestrate them. Morton Gould wrote a whole new suite, originally for piano but subsequently orchestrated by the NDI conductor.

"The music was very good, but it was also very difficult," said Lee Norris concerning the suite. "My musicians sweated on one movement called *The Great Wall.* Morton has such a natural sense of time—like interspersing 2/4, 5/8, 3/8, 7/8 bar to bar changes." Mr. Norris couldn't explain exactly how the children managed, but for his own part, he said: "I was amazed. As a matter of fact, we all were. *We* were counting like crazy. But Morton wrote some wonderful things, and it was dynamite."

An entirely different experience involved the piece written for NDI by Chou Wen-chung. He had done all his own scoring, and when the music was heard at the first rehearsal in piano reduction, it was almost impossible for the musician to give a reasonable facsimile, since the instrumentation envisioned was so atmospheric and involved many special percussion effects.

Mr. Chou's piece was danced by students from the School of American Ballet, who had more training in classical technique than most of the other children on the program. "But in general," noted Mr. Norris, "one thing about Jacques is that he challenges these kids. He doesn't play down just because something is for children. He's just creative—for *dancers.*"

Somehow, though he had varied experiences in the field of commercial music-making, Lee Norris never worked with dancers before he came to NDI. The background he brought to these collaborations included shows with Carol Channing, Skitch Henderson and the New York Pops, the concert spinoffs with "Bob" of *Sesame Street,* composing many film scores, and conducting major symphony orchestras in classical concerts.

Speaking about his collaborations for NDI, Mr. Norris explained: "In the conceptual process, Jacques comes to me and paints pictures. I use the tape recorder as we talk, and it would be hard for me to go wrong, because he's so graphic in what he wants. I take his counts . . . he sings in his off-key voice what he wants. I tape our conversation and let it run for two hours. I may not use it all, but after ten years, at least I knew where his head is. Our 'wave length' is just incredible. Sometimes he's amazed at how we get it together, but I guess that's what happens when you work with someone. It only happens with time, right?

"The first years, Jacques would call and say, 'Can you come on Tuesday morning? I want you to see such and such a number at such and such a school.' Then two weeks later: 'Can you come Thursday to Westchester? I'd like you to see something.' I did, and it was important, but in the last couple of years, because of my schedule, there have been some numbers that I haven't seen at all until we get down to the Felt Forum. But I'm not surprised when I do see them, because he has described them to me exactly the way they would be—he's very graphic! As a matter of fact, he dances it in my room. in my office. When we're working, he goes through the whole thing. I've kept my old tapes, and they're wonderful: he's dancing, and he's talking, and he's singing it, and I live with that. So the picture starts forming. But then, he never hems me in in terms of what to write.

"Then I'll call him and say, 'I've got an idea. Remember you were talking about a tango? I got an idea to do an eccentric tango.' And I'll sit at the piano and play him the melody—over the phone—from California sometimes. I can't see him moving over the phone, but I can hear his reaction. We work like that. It's been a joy!"

Then the conductor-composer paused, and added: "We battle a lot. We don't as much now, though. That's become a big thing, too. In the first years, people used to come in and wait for the big blow-up between Jacques and Lee. Now if you talk to other people, they say 'Boy, you two guys are mellowing; you must be getting older!' But it used to be that—once I walked out; once he walked out. Something he would do would upset me, or something I would do would upset him. It would build on a Saturday or Sunday rehearsal, and there's probably been one major blowup. But that's part of it, I suppose."

"You're not surprised to hear that, are you?" asked the conductor-composer suddenly. One shouldn't be surprised; such emotional eruptions are a common experience among theatrical collaborators who must work under the pressure of time and irritatingly close quarters.

MORTON GOULD: PROBING FOR THE SOURCE OF CREATIVITY

During the New York City Ballet's American Music Festival, audiences had the pleasure of witnessing Morton Gould as a musical collaborator in several capacities. First, he was in the pit conducting the orchestra in two of his *Apple Waltzes* from an unfinished ballet by George Balanchine. Then he slipped onto the piano bench under the stage and played the featured solo for *Interplay,* while the current crop of young dancers re-created Jerome Robbins' choreography onstage.

Finally, the evening ended with *I'm Old Fashioned.* This piece began with a film clip of Fred Astaire and Rita Hayworth dancing together. It then continued live onstage through a number of Morton Gould's ingenious orchestral variations upon the Jerome Kern tune, matched with Jerome Robbins' choreographic variations on the film's dance.

The composer subsequently met with the author to discuss his various experiences with ballet, spanning more than four decades of work.[9]

"I wasn't even a ballet fan, believe it or not, though I have the image of writing a lot of balletic music," remarked Mr. Gould. Sitting in his presidential suite at the ASCAP offices overlooking Lincoln Center, the composer put his remark into perspective. "Remember, that when you are talking about the late thirties, early forties, ballet was not popular the way it is today. So when I say that I was not a ballet fan, it's in the context of the time, a period when one didn't casually say, 'Well, why don't we go to a ballet?' because there were not that many ballets to go to!"

"Now why I have taken on that image?" pondered the composer as he recalled his association with ballet. "First of all," he said, "I was so busy when I was in my teens and early twenties. I was always on deadlines with radio programs. It ate you up alive, because you had to do seven or eight numbers every week. So I didn't go much to ballet. Now there *are* people who spent a great deal of time when they were growing up, going to ballet and opera and so on. I did very little of that."

What Morton Gould did do was to begin improvising, composing, and arranging at a young age. By his middle teens, during the Depression, he left school and became a professional musician. At the age of 18, he was a staff pianist at Radio City Music Hall, where he sometimes had to don various costumes and play onstage.

When questioned about his early collaborations with dancers, he could remember only two instances. One was a week of playing the piano for the ballerina Tamara Geva. The other experience consisted of a single summer in Woodstock, New York, when he was only 15. Recalling his visit with some artist friends to that upstate colony, Mr. Gould said: "There was a dancer-choreographer there, Don Oscar Becque, and I played for his classes." These were not exactly formal dance classes, apparently, but rather training sessions for actors who wanted to learn how to move onstage. "For instance," said Mr. Gould, "Burgess Meredith was in that class; Alfred Korn; Olive Deering; and Eddie Albert. I would improvise."

The composer claimed that he did not even do much ballroom dancing. "I remember vaguely dancing with girls when I was 15 or 16," said the cordial Mr. Gould. "But for some reason or other I stopped—not the girls, but the dancing."

Unlike some musical collaborators for the dance, Morton Gould did not trace his success to deep immersion with the ballet world. To what, then, could he attribute his wonderful feel for the dance? "I don't know!" replied the composer. "My music has always had a rhythmic impulse. I think there are composers who write relatively abstract works, but I'm the kind of composer who has written a wide gamut of idioms like ballet, stage, TV, and movies."

When asked what he felt was different about writing ballets, in contrast to writing concert music, Mr. Gould replied, "I think, for me, that you accommodate to your choreographer colleague. He or she has to accommodate to you too. It's a give and take."

"Different choreographers work different ways," he continued. "In the case of Balanchine, we would talk about a certain atmosphere. There were never really any programmatic things; his ballets were basically abstract. But then, I would write movements, sections of things, and he would say, 'That's good.' Or sometimes—I cannot imitate him—but if he said 'Good concert music,' I would know he didn't like it as ballet music," remarked Mr. Gould with amusement. "But there was very little of that," he added hastily. "I think almost all of my music can be done balletically."

In fact, it has happened a number of times that Morton Gould learned only secondhand about choreographic settings of his compositions. For example, once some friends told him how much they enjoyed his new ballet at La Scala Opera House in Italy. "What ballet of mine?" inquired Mr. Gould. "I never wrote a ballet for them."

"Well," the composer recounted, "I finally put it together, and it turns out that somebody choreographed my *Spirituals for Orchestra*. I wrote this in 1940. If you said to me, 'Well, what works of yours do you think would be balletic?' I would never have mentioned this piece *Spirituals*. Yet apparently it was in the repertoire of La Scala Opera Ballet Company for years. I don't even know the name of the choreographer."

Addressing again the question of what there is in his compositions that is so attractive to choreographers and dancers, Morton Gould ventured to comment: "I think that my music has a kind of built-in rhythmic vitality that people feel. Even a nondancer feels the impulse to move, and I think that's the beginning of it."

However, considering the current profusion of ballet companies and dance styles, the composer noted: "Now there is a choreographic approach that uses just the opposite: it *doesn't* want that kind of pulse; it wants a carpet where music doesn't intrude, where the music doesn't direct the action—where the action directs the music. The choreographers *I've* worked with all depend on the music to trigger them—certainly in the case of Balanchine, of Jerry [Robbins], of Agnes [de Mille], and Eliot Feld."

Speaking of his collaborations with Jerome Robbins, the composer touched upon *Interplay,* the piece in which he had so recently performed as piano soloist. "That goes way back," said Mr. Gould. "That's 1943, a wonderful ballet by Jerry set to my music. That was a piece already written. Jerry heard it, reacted to it, and did this ballet which became a classic.''

Had Robbins talked to him about the choreography when he was creating the piece? ''No,'' said Mr. Gould. ''We're talking about the days when I was musical director of a weekly live radio program, with a large orchestra and famous artists—for which I supplied all the music (both composing and arranging), decided on the soloists, and so forth. In the course of this particular radio series, I had written a work for José Iturbi, who at that time was a very famous pianist. I called the piece *American Concertette.''*

''Anyway,'' he continued, ''Jerry heard it, and like all great choreographers have to be, Jerry has always been very responsive to music. He was a dancer with American Ballet Theatre at the time, and he came to see me and said he would love to use the piece. So what happened with my piece was that Jerry heard it and *then* did a ballet to it, originally for Billy Rose's Concert Varieties at the Ziegfeld Theater. Oddly enough, I didn't see it for a while. I think Billy Rose called me to come over and look at it. I was very impressed when I saw it. Jerry called it *Interplay,* which is a terrific title, and it has become known as *Interplay.*'' (Robbins himself danced in the premiere performances.)

Many years later, *I'm Old Fashioned* was a direct collaboration between Robbins and Gould. The composer recalled that first the choreographer had shown him the movie clip of Fred Astaire dancing with Rita Hayworth. ''Then we started. We had conferences. We spoke. We walked around this. We tried out different things. I would try out ideas on the piano, and Jerry would either react or not. He'd say, 'How about this approach?' '' Sometimes Robbins would show the composer movement.

''Basically,'' explained Mr. Gould, ''what he was doing was to try and feed me enough ideas—enough imagery verbally—to trigger off musical themes that I might come up with. These on the other hand would trigger off certain things on his part. So it was a give and take. We went back and forth. As a matter of fact, we scrapped a number of different approaches. I had written a *tremendous* amount of music. What's in the ballet now is about a third or one-quarter of what I wrote.''

''Jerry, as I said before, is very sensitive to the music,'' emphasized the composer. ''But you know, it's a creative process: something that both Jerry and I thought very positively about on Tuesday, by Wednesday both of us might have changed our minds about and said, 'Well, you know, maybe that's not the way to go; maybe we should do it this way.'

''And now what happens is that the deadline approaches: the pressure mounts up. Jerry works a great deal with the bodies, with people. So something that was originally loud turns out to be something that you want soft, or the other way around; something fast gets slow; something slower gets faster . . . and bit by bit you put this together. We had our disagreements; we had our agreements . . . and finally the whole thing gels. It is an effective audience piece, and I am making a concert suite from it.''

Turning to the subject of how audiences react to the music for ballets, Mr. Gould commented: "For me, the important thing is for them to react to the *totality*. For instance, if the music works but the ballet doesn't, you'll end up with no ballet. No company will keep a ballet in the repertory that doesn't work. I don't know how my colleagues feel, but I would also hope that my musical score could stand on its own outside of the ballet. I think my scores do."

"You know," he added, "all art, all music, is really Russian roulette. You never know, even for a simple concert. A performer walks out onstage, or an orchestra comes out, and there is no way of knowing whether it's going to be a disaster or a triumph. It could be a terrible performance or a great performance. It's all variable. Whether the new piece is something that's powerful or that has vitality and durability, or whether it's going to be something that's a passing aberration—who knows?"

Noting that in the coming concert season, the 75–year-old Morton Gould was scheduled to have three major premieres at Carnegie Hall alone, the author asked him: "What is your next ballet?"

"I don't know," replied this prolific composer. "But if somebody comes to me with an idea I like and a commission to do it, I'm available!"

PERFORMANCE

5

Free-Lancers in the Pits

Playing for ballet and modern dance is not a full-time occupation for orchestral musicians in the United States. But despite their part-time and often half-hidden association with dancers, many musicians in the theater pits still display an artistic sympathy for the performances to which they contribute.

"There is a certain excitement that gets transferred," said cellist Michael Rudiakov, "and you can always *sense* whether what the dancers are doing is good or not. You can *sense* whether this is a real winner or not."[1]

As one of New York's busiest free-lancers, Mr. Rudiakov has played for some of the world's best-known ballet companies when they visit. How does he like being down in the pit, in contrast to performing chamber music and solo concerts, when he is the focus of attention onstage? "I find the ballet solos just as beautiful and sometimes more enjoyable than playing a sonata, because the tunes are so glorious, and the orchestra around you gives a wonderful support," remarked the cellist.

"Some of this ballet music is just first class—the best!" he went on to say. "It's a great pleasure to play. I can't think of any score that I've played that is not interesting. If you think of Tchaikovsky and all that he has written: *Sleeping Beauty, Swan Lake, Nutcracker;* and *Coppélia* [by Delibes] is a wonderful score; *Petrushka* [by Stravinsky] is of course a masterpiece. This is all wonderful music, and it's good to play. It's good to the player, and good to the dancer. This is a wonderful combination."

Yet asked if he can see the dancers from his normal position in the pit, Mr. Rudiakov responded, "Hardly ever. That's one of the things that's not so good."

Indeed, cellists normally have to sit with their backs to the stage—if they are not in fact under it. Sometimes they try to compensate for their unfortunate deprivation. For instance, the late Richard Merewether, a well-known horn player in London, enjoyed telling the author about his Sadler's Wells days, when it was absolutely forbidden for the musicians to look at the stage. But they always tried to anyway. One cellist in the company simply attached a rear-view mirror to his music stand in order to get a glimpse of all the attractive ballerinas. The management suspended him. In retaliation, the entire cello section walked out. The management re-retaliated by replacing them all with eager newcomers seeking employment. Eventually, the original cellists were reinstated to their regular seats with Sadler's Wells—but unfortunately, minus their mirrors, a term written into their contracts.

Yet, even deprived of such visual apparatus, many musicians are still elated to know that they are accompanying stars of the ballet world. Bassoonist Myrna Gynsky, for example, would remember for decades that she once played for Edward Villella when he appeared with the Bergen County, New Jersey, Symphony. And a surprisingly wistful look would come into the eyes of old pro Artie Chanken as he recalled playing oboe for Maria Tallchief and Andre Eglevsky—and how disappointed he was to realize that he would be sitting underneath the stars as they danced. His only awareness that he was playing for ballet came from the thumping on the stage above him, and amusingly, from seeing the heads of the audience bob back and forth as they followed the movements of the dancers.

A MUSICIAN'S LIFE AT RADIO CITY MUSIC HALL

One theater where the musicians legitimately have gotten a lot more than a peek at the dancers is New York's Radio City Music Hall. There, the pit section can be lifted up and transported across the stage—until the entire orchestra is deposited behind the dancers.

Horn player Gregory Squires, who performed at the Music Hall for over a decade, enjoyed pointing out all the mechanical wonders of that theater—though he complained mildly that the bumpy rides were a little hard on the professional "chops."[2] However, he did say that the orchestra members naturally enjoyed being able to watch the dancers.

Before the reorganization of the Music Hall a few years ago, Mr. Squires recalled, playing there was full-time, year-round work—one of only three secure orchestral positions in all of New York City (the Metropolitan Opera and the New York Philharmonic being the other two coveted posts). The instrumentalists would perform four shows, five days a week, with varying gaps of waiting time in between.

The architects of the theater took the performers into consideration, for there are club-like quarters in the building, where waiting violinists and clarinetists can read, rest, talk—or, not having to watch their figures, perhaps indulge in pastrami sandwiches. The musicians were sympathetic to the more rigorous rules that applied to the dancers, who had to weigh in, and who could be fined money from their modest pay if they did not smile while kicking up those famous legs during a show.

In that tight little world, Mr. Squires found that the dancers and the musicians did become friendly. They even had a between-shows bowling league, and it was claimed that some of the performers had one card game continuing for twenty years, interrupted only by shows. Another way that Gregory Squires and other musicians used their interim time was to duck out and teach private students.

Understandably, for most free-lancers, such a schedule could become wearing after a number of years—especially after weeks and weeks of playing Christmas carols. Mr. Squires, for one, retired early, starting his own recording studio, in which he specializes in classical music, including some for dance purposes. Now he limits his horn playing to special occasions in Kennedy Center and tours in Europe.

EDWARD BIRDWELL: FROM LOW HORN TO CULTURAL CHIEF

Another horn player, one who used to specialize in low parts but who has progressively lifted himself out of the pits to ever-increasing responsibilities, is Edward Birdwell. As music director of the National Endowment for the Arts (NEA), for some years he enjoyed an office high in one of Washington's landmark buildings, the beautiful Old Post Office, or the Nancy Hanks Center, as it is now called.

But from 1964 to 1976, Mr. Birdwell was a regular member of the New York City Ballet Orchestra. In addition, he played with American Ballet Theatre occasionally on tour, as well as with the Joffrey Ballet and other groups.

A visit to his Washington offices was an aesthetic experience in itself; for with its bell tower above and its performances of music in the stylish and sunny atrium below, the building seemed a stunningly appropriate setting in which to survey the cultural life of the entire nation.

Looking out of his office windows, Edward Birdwell could nevertheless keep in touch with his past, and as he spoke with the author, he vividly recalled his dozen years as one of New York City's top free-lance musicians.[3]

Mr. Birdwell's path to Washington started out at the Houston Conservatory. After earning advanced degrees in music education, this Texan began his performing career with the Houston Symphony. Moving to New York, he chose to specialize in second horn parts, which often involve considerable difficulty, particularly in jumping from high to low registers. Much in demand, he not only performed in theater pits for ballet and Broadway shows, but also appeared regularly on concert stages with such outstanding orchestras as the American Symphony Orchestra, Musica Aeterna, and the Brooklyn Philharmonic. In addition, as a managing partner of the American Brass Quintet, he toured all over the country.

Early on, Mr. Birdwell was marked with a flair for management: he served as assistant dean of the Aspen School and Festival, as director of the Los Angeles Chamber Orchestra, as manager of the Boston Symphony Orchestra, and later, as concert manager of Carnegie Hall.

But looking back on his days as a pit musician for ballet, Mr. Birdwell mentioned, "At that time, New York City Ballet had annually about twenty-four weeks of work; two ten- to fourteen-week seasons—roughly like it is now. They had to jiggle it around a little because of the operas, but during those times the ballet was—and still is—very loose about allowing us to sub and do other things. I think Mr. Irving [the conductor] and Mr. Balanchine realized that if they wanted to get high quality musicians but could only guarantee them twenty-four or twenty-five weeks of work, they'd have to be flexible in letting them come and go to things that may overlap."

When asked if his colleagues agreed with audience members who consider the New York City Ballet Orchestra the finest one in the country, Mr. Birdwell replied, "Yes, I think we were proud of the orchestra. We knew we were not the New York Philharmonic; we didn't have the rehearsal time, and we had a huge repertoire. We tended to play a large portion of the same repertoire year in and year out, so we didn't need four rehearsals for some performances. The Philharmonic would normally have four rehearsals per concert, but the ballet orchestra was one chosen for its ability to read and work quickly. That's the nature of the free-lance business in New York. And Mr. Irving was careful when he was auditioning to get people who were very quick. I'm not going to say that we ever gave the most profound performances of any of the music we did, but we generally gave very good and creditable performances of most of the works. It was a good job, and there were good colleagues. I enjoyed working with Irving—and Balanchine had an appreciation of the music that was more than you normally find in a dance company," Mr. Birdwell remarked.

As with most musicians, however, Edward Birdwell's contact with the choreographer was through the funnel of the conductors and the artistic material itself. Balanchine would come to orchestra rehearsals, but if he had a comment, it would be made to Mr. Irving. "I don't think Balanchine ever said anything directly to me in those twelve years," commented Mr. Birdwell. "But he would publicly make statements to the effect that if the orchestra played good music, then if people came and they didn't like the dance, they could close their eyes and listen to the music!"

"So that's unusual," observed the NEA director. "Plus the fact that he was dealing with a better repertoire than some of the other companies did. You know, those were some great pieces of music: Tchaikovsky *Suite,* Bizet *Symphony in C,* and all the Stravinsky music and the French music like *Jeux* that we did. So you were playing decent music. You weren't doing oom-pah-pah that some of the other companies do."

Like a number of cultural leaders whose practical experience has given them a broad perspective, Mr. Birdwell voiced pleasure in noting the country's "dance explosion.'' But he quickly added his concern for the explosion in musical training, in regard to the unrealistic expectations on the part of thousands of young people taught in our conservatories and universities—all of whom assume that they can earn their living as professional concert artists. ''There are just not enough orchestra jobs to go around,'' he pointed out realistically. Indeed, many of these young graduates would be only too happy to follow in Edward Birdwell's footsteps down into the pit of the New York State Theater, to play for the ballet there.

THE PENNSYLVANIA BALLET ORCHESTRA ON TOUR

''We *all* started out as soloists—naturally!'' said Marion Head, personnel director of the Pennsylvania Ballet Orchestra.[4] ''Once you graduate from school, you think you are ready for the concert life. The reality is that people can do lots of chamber music or branch out into opera and ballet and other pit work and hope to be as versatile as possible.''

As personnel manager for the ballet orchestra, her job includes finding, hiring, and occasionally firing musicians. Being a free-lancer herself, she knows everybody in the Philadelphia area and is familiar with who is available. She does her duties by direct contact, mostly by getting on the phone to work out schedules.

When new players have to be recruited, the most important attribute she seeks in musicians is their ability to play attentively in the orchestral ensemble. Though some instrumentalists might have wide-ranging styles when they perform as soloists, when they join the orchestra, their personal interpretations must of course be subordinated, and rhythmical accuracy is a top priority. However, Miss Head also listens for good technique, intonation, and a basically good sound on an instrument. About 98 percent of the ballet musicians are regular players from season to season. When asked if these musicians had to know anything about the dance, the manager laughed: ''I am sure we would all fall on our faces as dancers!''

The ability she most values is flexibility. To achieve this, musicians have to be constantly watching the conductor. ''One of my jobs,'' said Marion Head, ''is to glare at musicians if their gaze wanders to the stage during performance.'' Otherwise, she has to hustle people into rehearsals and the pit on time, make sure they are at the bus stop or airport, and generally be a ''den mother.''

Just a few years ago, Pennsylvania Ballet was one of the last hold-outs of ballet companies to tour with its own orchestra. The situation at the time was rather special: they had thirty-two dancers and thirty-one musicians. The resident company orchestra had been an integral part of performances both in Philadelphia and on tour for over twenty years, except for some festivals like the Blossom, where the Cleveland Orchestra was the sponsoring organization. Of course, having such a resident orchestra was an expensive undertaking, but while other ballet companies performed with tape on tour, Pennsylvania Ballet patrons and dancers were very supportive of having live music.

''The main problem with tape,'' pointed out Maurice Kaplow, the conductor of the orchestra, ''is that the dancers are stuck with the same timing, and in *this* company, the dancers are used to dancing to the music. We agree about the parameters. Most dancers know what they can do . . . and we know. This is tested in performances. Music is for setting the stage for what they have to do. They are dancing to whatever sounds *we* make.''

Mr. Kaplow found a different attitude in the European and Russian traditions, where, he felt, the music was apt to be ''painted'' on the dancers. And right down the line, all the Pennsylvania musicians felt that ''accompanying'' was a misplaced word. Indeed, Mr. Kaplow emphasized that as he is conducting, the music should not be absolutely metronomic, but should breathe. He noted that in this company the dancers do listen and bend to the music.

The founder of Pennsylvania Ballet, Barbara Weisberger, placed enormous value upon the contribution that music can make to a company's performance. Among the decisions she made was to have live orchestra from the company's beginning. ''It was very important to me,'' she said, ''even though it was very difficult economically, to have live musicians, and to tour with a live orchestra. We used to have our own group initially that went with us *everywhere*.''[5]

''My idea was to have—I won't say a 'great' company, but as Mr. Balanchine said, when you do a piece of choreography, don't think of making a masterpiece; just do it. But one thing I felt very strongly about,'' continued Mrs. Weisberger, ''is that if a company was going to have a standard of quality that I envisioned, then live music was essential.''

Asked if the expense was resented, she replied quite candidly, ''Oh yes! But generally not by the dancers. There might be moments in which they did, because they were always struggling financially. You know, salaries were very low, but I really don't think they were being resentful about that. In the long run, had I not had the live music and had it not been the esteemed—the *quality* company that I think it was, I don't think they would have been happy. And I think that the music had a great deal to do with that.''

''I don't say that *all* companies need live music,'' she added. ''But you start out with a vision of what that company is. This was a ballet company that was not going to be one of the large companies, but it was going to be of a certain size and budget. And there were going to have to be a lot of people who would come and buy tickets to see it. So you start out with certain expectations, and in the case of the Pennsylvania Ballet, taped music would definitely have affected those expectations.''

The musicians with that company found that the ballet repertoire was often very demanding—but also that in many cases, they enjoyed unusual opportunities to perform a larger variety of repertoire than they would have experienced in the more competitive life of a solo concert instrumentalist.

For example, Pennsylvania's pianist, Martha Koeneman, was recently called upon to play five performances in just one weekend, including the lengthy *Symphonic Etudes* of Schumann, as a piano solo (with choreography by Richard Tanner); Stravinsky's *Capriccio for Piano and Orchestra* (the "Rubies" section from Balanchine's *Jewels*); a Khachaturian *Piano Concerto* (for *Underlight,* with choreography by Dane LaFontsee); and an extremely demanding new work specially commissioned by the ballet: *Ordinary Rhythms,* with music by Carson Kievman for percussion, piano, and small orchestra. In addition, Miss Koeneman played the piano parts within the orchestral texture for other works, as well as many hours of rehearsals for the dancers. Artistically, she in effect had an advantage few concert pianists enjoy: touring with "her own" orchestra and conductor, so that the performances could become quite finely honed over time.

Another unusual satisfaction for some of the orchestral musicians was the responsibility they felt toward their contributions to the performances. For example, the percussionist Susan Jones mentioned that she personally had to arrange many parts to accommodate what was possible for the reduced personnel of a small chamber orchestra. So she often went to dancers' rehearsals in order to become aware of where they might need extra accents or particular coloration. Ms. Jones feels that "live dancers respond and blend more with live music. Tape takes away the sparkle and magic."

But it must be noted that despite their enjoyment of playing for the ballet, the Pennsylvania musicians all seemed to look forward to getting out of the pits for a while. In summers, many of them would disperse to places like Santa Fe, Lake George, Chatauqua, and other resorts that offered opportunities to play concerts outdoors under the spotlight of the sun.

In the United States today, ballet must depend on fluctuating box office receipts and contributions, and upon the choices of boards of directors, arts panels and politicians. Consequently, there have recently been tremendous upheavals in the organization of professional companies. The Pennsylvania Ballet is one that has experienced some of this turmoil and change, and for the time being it has a dual identity as the Pennsylvania-Milwaukee Ballet. Musically what has happened under this format is that there are two separate orchestras. Maurice Kaplow has been appointed music director of the two groups, and only he and a second conductor travel back and forth. The orchestra's touring is virtually a thing of the past, for when the dancers visit additional cities, the host theaters' orchestras are engaged for the performances.

Talking about these changes, Mr. Kaplow acknowledged that the current musical arrangements are "not as good as the way things used to be. But you have to deal with finances," he emphasized. And while he had nothing but compliments for such orchestras as the Kennedy Center ensemble, he mourned, "It's still not the same as having your own wherever you go."

CYNTHIA JERSEY: FREE-LANCING FOR BALLET DE SANTIAGO

In today's competitive marketplace, many young instrumentalists welcome opportunities to play in the pits as a good way to break into professional life. Especially in New York City, they will frequently obtain employment playing for visiting ballet companies from all over the world.

The North American debut of the Ballet de Santiago from Chile was a good example. The full orchestra playing for their production of *Rosalinda* (using John Lanchbery's arrangement of the Johann Strauss opera *Die Fledermaus*) was listed as "The New York Opera Repertory Theater Orchestra." This group was engaged for the Chilean company's run at City Center. Double-bass player Judy Sugarman had to double as contractor and fill in all the seats that were necessary, all in a matter of three weeks.[6]

The first time that conductor Michel Patron Marchand and the instrumentalists faced each other was for the run-through just before the performances. Ivan Nagy, then artistic director of the ballet, came along to listen—and so did the dancers themselves. They seemed pleased by what they heard. And by performance time, some audience members were overheard remarking: "It's a rather young orchestra—so refreshing to see instead of the same old dead wood! It's a pick-up orchestra, you know; they give them no credit on the program—just hire them. But aren't they good?"

One of the young musicians in the pit, originally from Ipsilanti, Michigan, was Cynthia Jersey. A French horn player, she was just embarking on a full-time career. She had previously played solo horn in the highly competitive Juilliard Orchestra and had toured both Europe and Latin American playing with various orchestras. Yet despite her top-notch background, she confided that during her first year as a "pro" she had earned only six thousand dollars.[7] In her second year, she figured she was clearing just about as much as a secretary might. But artistically, Miss Jersey was fairly bubbling over about her work with the dancers.

"I love them," she said. "It's as if they were fairy people to me. I have no understanding of dance. I have never had a dance lesson. But I *feel* like a dancer, and I love to watch the dance. So when I'm not playing, I sit with my eyes glued to the stage, watching these people."

However, it must be noted that the musician was also glad to have the money. "A week of ballet for most people is a lot. In this case, there are several rehearsals and eight performances. Without steady work, it's hard to survive."

The horn player also spoke highly of the conductor. "He was good in that he really loved music. With a lot of conductors, you actually get the feeling that they don't love music, or that they hate the musicians. One of the two, you know. They might love the music, but they hate us."

"But *he* was positive," she beamed. "He didn't get in the way. He didn't tell you how to play your horn . . . and he was very appreciative of the work.

Everyone was a little desperate for gigs at this time, and the whole atmosphere was really friendly among the musicians. Everyone was saying, 'How come it's not always like this?' " What the audience heard that was unusual was the stomping of the instrumentalists' feet every time the conductor mounted the podium for his bows. That is the ultimate way for orchestral players to show their esteem.

"Perhaps contractors don't usually hire people because they're nice people," pondered Cynthia Jersey, turning her mind to the instrumentalists. "You have to hire the best players . . . but sometimes, contractors may continue hiring people who are past their prime, and there are a lot of pit musicians who have bad attitudes. They just play for money, you know. But this—the ambience was just wonderful."

The musician pointed out that the pay for ballet work was often higher than the union scale for some other orchestral work. "Perhaps we don't get the ego boost of being onstage," said Miss Jersey. "And it's hard work, believe me, when we do two services a day: that's six hours of playing. Most other people also had things going on between the ballet services. I had fifteen services in nine days."

For a horn player, a lot of ballet music is "oom-pah-pah." "Pretty boring," acknowledged Miss Jersey. "But," she added, "if you like playing in an orchestra, it's still fun to be a cog in that great machine. So I don't mind doing that. I support the business of live music. When I see an audience thrilled by live music, that makes my day. It probably makes my year! That's what it's all about."

Asked if she ever attended ballet performances herself, Cynthia Jersey hesitated. "No. I wish I would. I don't have money to buy tickets; it's very expensive, you know. And . . . I don't get *tired* of music, but if I have a night off, I'm not going to dress up and go out. I'm probably going to stay home and cook—which I don't get to do very often. Kind of a backwards life, compared to most people. But what we're doing is taking live music to *other* people. You might not think that the music part is that important in ballet, but it is. Because it is some *person* making a vibration on an instrument. All you have to be is superb!"

MUSICIANS DANCING

Recently some musicians have been drawn into the visual aspects of dance performance. In New York City, for instance, there is a little artists' cooperative called Gathering Wood made up of choreographers, dancers, performing musicians, visual artists, and composers. Typical of their efforts was Elizabeth Brown's flute playing in *Orpheo I* by the British composer Thea Musgrave. Reviewing a performance of this piece, Jennifer Dunning of *The New York Times* said: "Moving as persuasively as she played the flute, Miss Brown wove those strands of music into a potent suggestion of Orpheo's dark voyage after Euridice.''[8]

Privately, the flutist liked to emphasize, ''I am not a dancer who plays the flute; I am a flutist who is studying dancing—a *little!*'' In any case, what she did seemed quite attractive. And in the *Duet for Flute and Dancer,* composed by Ezra Laderman and choreographed and danced by Nancy Allison, the musician was no longer in the dark obscurity of the pit. Miss Allison had Miss Brown dressed in pink to be color-coordinated with the dancer, who had a feathered costume herself. The flutist, barefoot, had to play entirely from memory, and was brought into the dance itself as Miss Allison summoned her to the middle of the floor during the work.

One cannot say if such collaborations are the wave of the future, or if musicians will eventually climb out of the pits en masse and begin dancing onstage. This is a possibility for which some of Miss Brown's more portly colleagues would probably feel quite unprepared. And while many of these explorations are certainly interesting to hear and see, it seems a fair prediction that most musicians for dance are going to continue to be seated—and usually hidden.

EDWARD CARROLL: A TRUMPETER'S ARTISTIC TASTES

When Rudolf Nureyev and the Paris Opera Ballet danced onstage, the clear tone of virtuoso trumpet player Edward Carroll rang out to the far reaches of the Metropolitan Opera House. As one of New York's top free-lancers in ballet and modern dance orchestras, Mr. Carroll is frequently heard performing solos on the risky and specialized baroque trumpet in addition to playing his regular instrument in less stratospheric ranges. He is one of those ruddy-cheeked, perennially young-looking types whose age is impossible to guess. But artistically speaking, he is an old pro.

The author met with him one day after a run-through of Bach's *Brandenburg Concerto No. 2,* as choreographed by Murray Louis for his *Bach Suite* and performed by the Rondo Dance Company, with the entire Philharmonia Virtuosi, under Richard Kapp. Speaking during his break, the trumpeter had some hesitations about the use of the second Brandenburg concerto for a dance performance.[9] ''For this type of music—music that was *not* written just for dance—you usually try *not* to perform it twice in the same way,'' he explained. ''Every time you're performing in concert, you try to find a bit different tempo, a bit different balance. But when you perform it with a dance company, everything has to be exactly the same. Kapp's job here is to listen to the rehearsal tape and then try to match it. That's terribly frustrating!''

Was it difficult for him to alter the speed of his solo? ''It's not that it's difficult,'' he explained. ''You feel like you're just a computer chip, imitating somebody else's performance. I can't stand doing that! So there's some frustration playing music for the dance. Certainly, you understand that they have to meet their rehearsal tempo. But. . . ."

"I have played for years with the Paul Taylor Company, and for all the ballets that come into the Metropolitan Opera House in the summer," he went on to say. "For example, in two seasons I performed *Romeo and Juliet* around forty times. Every company comes in and does that score. And you know, you don't *feel* the same as a musician: sometimes you're more intense, other times more relaxed." Nevertheless, he pointed out, "If the dancers are accustomed to a certain tempo, you *have* to meet it. We're cast in a role as accompanist."

It seemed regrettable that Mr. Carroll was playing so beautifully and couldn't see a thing going on behind him onstage. "Oh, but sometimes you can," he was quick to answer. Did it change his feeling about a performance if he could see the dancers and the performance to which he is contributing? "It changes my feelings about the *evening,"* he replied. "It doesn't change my feelings about the way the music is being handled."

If the trumpeter's feelings are strong about tempos in the use of concert music for dance performances, they are equally strong in regard to concert performances of ballet music without the dancers.

"I find it difficult now to do excerpts from Prokofiev's *Romeo and Juliet* or Stravinsky's *Rite of Spring* and *Petrushka* without the dance," he remarked. "But on the other hand, that was music that was *built* for dance. It makes very little sense to me without the essential ingredient.

"It's a bittersweet relationship for me, because so much of the ballet music I *care* about so deeply. I love Stravinsky. I like Prokofiev. There are tremendous scores written just for dance that work beautifully. For example, *Appalachian Spring* [by Aaron Copland, for Martha Graham] is one of the worst concert pieces I've heard—and it's thrilling on the stage. It was designed for this . . . but I'm not so sure the second Brandenburg is; I *know* it's not designed for it!"

Yet having said that, when it came curtain time that evening, Edward Carroll went on to give another stunning performance on his baroque trumpet.

A VISIT WITH PAUL TAYLOR'S MUSICIANS

Wearing earphones so he could communicate with Paul Taylor, music director Donald York was readying things in the pit for one of the season's first rehearsals with the company's dancers and orchestra at New York City Center.[10]

It was 3:15 P.M. on the dot. The theater was dark; the curtain was down. An engineer's voice from nowhere discernible queried: "Ready, Mr. Taylor? . . . Maestro?"

The concertmistress, Jean Ingraham, put rosin on her bow in readiness for her featured violin solo, and in a few moments, *Esplanade* began, to the radiant strains of Bach. After it was over, the orchestra members thumped their feet loudly in enthusiastic tribute to their colleague's performance. Mr. Taylor himself walked onstage, looked down and said simply, "Gee, that was beautiful!" as he clapped for the concertmistress and all the instrumentalists.

Later, during a union break, Donald York chatted with his players and the author underneath the stage, which is the location of the musicians' locker room at City Center. The conductor corroborated the fact that standard textbooks and coursework do not cover the specifics of what he has to do today. One orchestra member chimed in and complimented York on his stick technique—something important to the instrumentalists who must depend upon him for their exact entrances. He is their only funnel to the dancers.

As a conductor, Donald York said he is leading a personal crusade to make the pit music better, and he noted that it is especially helpful to be able to work with the same musicians year after year. To try to achieve this for the Taylor seasons in New York, he has a contractor round up thirty-five musicians, including instrumentation for chamber orchestra, piano solo, and quartets. With his assembled musicians, Mr. York has about four days to rehearse—a total of twenty hours or so to whip up an entire month-long New York season, including a run-through with dancers on the stage, and fifteen or sixteen different pieces.

The very programming of the company, as pointed out by company manager Robert Yesselman, takes instrumental requirements into major consideration. For instance, the company might save money by having some pieces that do not require full orchestra programmed for the same evening. Rehearsals too, must be structured so that the company does not have union musicians sitting around waiting.

Mr. Yesselman noted further that if the Taylor company schedules three performances or fewer of one piece, the union fees to musicians are based on individual performance scale; if they schedule more performances, the fees are on a weekly basis. And while underscoring his delight in having their superb orchestra for the New York seasons, the manager also noted realistically that out of town, most of their touring performances have to be accompanied by taped music.

Commenting further about this aspect of touring life, former lead dancer (now rehearsal mistress) Bettie De Jong said that the dancers do pick up on the orchestra's energy. While touring with the company, she personally found that tapes can get to be deadening precisely because you know what to expect. "Having live music wakes you up!" she said.

Beneath the stage again, the author spoke with violinist Tim Baker and with John Taylor (no relation to the choreographer; this one is a trombonist and contractor for the orchestra). Other musicians passing by overheard the conversation and kept putting in their two cents' worth on the subject of playing in the pits for dance.

They were asked if there is such a thing as stage fright for those in the pit. Emphatic "Yeahs" came from several directions. The musicians feel pressure to play well, even in the pit. A lot of this emotion is not because of the audience, it seems, but is rather self-generated, "because you want your colleagues to hear you play well."

The musicians milling around the tight little area were eager to learn that the author was giving them prime attention. They deplored especially the kind of notice given so frequently in newspaper reviews of many dance companies: " 'The orchestra could have been better.' Period. Now what does *that* mean?" asked one musician in bewilderment.

"Nobody else is really aware of the orchestra—except when there's a mistake," is a sentiment that seemed to float around. "Yes, but you see, when it's going along perfectly fine, then everybody just sits back in the audience, and you enjoy the entire experience," suggested someone else, adding, "When I go to ballets, when something happens in the orchestra and there's a mistake, your ear *is* jarred."

Another musician said: "Let me tell you what happened to me when I played recently with the China Ballet. There was a change in the program, and they told the stagehands; they told the lighting people; they told the dancers; they told the conductor—who didn't speak a word of English—but they never told the orchestra! The conductor gives a downbeat, to *Don Quixote,* and we're all playing *Giselle!* He cuts us off after four bars, and we're all sort of looking at each other. He doesn't speak English. Finally, he looked at the concertmaster's music and says about the only two words that he knew: *'Don Quixote.'* So we started over again, and there were giggles in the audience. I don't know if I should be quoted on this," continued the musician, "but it shows something about the management's view of the ballet—that they told the stagehands and the lighting technicians, but they didn't tell the musicians."

"One of *my* pet peeves," added another voice, "is that a number of times I've attended ballets, or read about performances where I know they are using tapes and not live music, and it's not even mentioned that there's no orchestra . . . yet they may even discuss the scores. You often can't tell from a review whether there was a live orchestra or not—and *that's* something we certainly care about! We would at least like to see it mentioned if it was a live orchestra."

Unfortunately, a live musical element is relatively rare in dance performances. A quality orchestra is an even more precious commodity. Many of the musicians realize this. "The thing is," commented one of Taylor's players, "this is probably one of the very best orchestras in New York. Even if you had the musicians from the New York Philharmonic in here, I daresay you'd probably get a much better performance with *us* just because it seems as if everybody really cares about the job that they do. Night in and night out, you hear wonderful performances."

Everyone in the locker room applauded that remark. "This is my second year," another violinist said, "and as I was listening to rehearsal the other day, it seemed as if the sound coming out of the nine violins of this orchestra was close to the sound of the full-sized orchestras that I play in elsewhere."

"Yeah," agreed one of his colleagues, "that's because everybody pulls their weight." Then there came a rapid melange of voices: "Part of it is that the management here, starting with Paul Taylor on the top—They love the orchestra!—They love live music! They respect the music! They respect the players!"

"Don't musicians find that in other companies?" enquired the author. "Well, it's very unusual," came the reply. "There's *no one* that treats the music and the musicians with more respect than this company!" "I agree with you," said another member of the orchestra.

"So this company and situation is sort of a model for what musicians like?" "Certainly, as far as playing in a pit," agreed the instrumentalists. "However, probably everyone would prefer to be sitting *onstage* playing," ventured one voice, and this opinion was seconded by a chorus.

The personnel manager clapped, which meant it was time for the musicians to climb the short staircase back up into the pit, and so the rehearsal continued.

* * *

In a private interview, Paul Taylor was asked what it felt like when he himself had been dancing on the stage: did he feel emotionally different when he had live music? "Yes," he replied, "I was always very grateful for live music rather than tapes—though tapes are *accurate;* you can count on having the same tempos. But it's more important to me to have the live music. It may vary from night to night, perhaps in tempo and feeling, and certainly from city to city as you dance with different orchestras."

Why did he prefer the live orchestra? "Simply because they *are* live," he explained. "It's a presence there, and no machine is ever going to replace that. They are participating with the audience and the performers live—they're breathing, living human beings, and even with mistakes and flaws and everything, it's much more vital and *beautiful* to have that in the pit than to have some microphone that you know is trumped up in a way. It just adds to the splendor of the whole evening."

Then, Mr. Taylor continued: "As a performer, too, a dancer, you'd have an extra 'tuning in' because you knew you just couldn't depend on the rote of what you usually did to a tape. It puts you 'on your toes' so to speak. You really have to listen to hear what those musicians are doing, because if you go on in your same old way, at your same old tempo, you're going to get left behind or get ahead. That's just one very practical aspect."

Turning to his present collaborations with Donald York as music director, Mr. Taylor paid him this compliment: "Don is the best conductor I have ever worked with. His sense of timing is absolutely marvelous; it's a miracle. The whole thing about his music and being able to play it is remarkable. He has a God-given sense for what is right. He knows what our tempos should be; we've decided on that. He doesn't usually vary his tempos unintentionally. But for some evenings, just for the night, it might be better to move things along more, not drag or take time here, because it's working for the audience, or for the dancer. With Don, there are *intentional* variations.''

Questioned about about possible disasters with music, Mr. Taylor thought a minute: ''Well, they were very far removed from what we think of as art. One time in City Center, we were in the midst of a Beethoven last quartet, and it was a very quiet and lovely thing.''

''I was onstage,'' the choreographer laughed, ''and I heard the most God-awful racket going on in the pit. I happened to look over, and there was a fistfight going on! What had happened was that the stagehands were very strong union men and misunderstood and thought that one of the musicians was taping the performance—and this is against the *stagehands'* union rules, if you can believe it. The stagehands had gone down and tried to remove a microphone, but the microphone wasn't hooked up to a recorder; it was simply amplifying the sound of a harpsichord, something that couldn't project in a large auditorium. So there had been this misunderstanding, and there was a regular brawl going on, *during* the performance!''

Normally, things are more civilized down in the pit.

A DAY WITH THE NEW YORK CITY BALLET ORCHESTRA

An April morning, in the conductors' lounge at the New York State Theater: it is the day after New York City Ballet's opening night for their spring season, and conductor Hugo Fiorato is already back studying his scores.[11] He leaves off doing that and leads a visitor past the lights backstage and into the theater, which is totally empty except for two people in the rear observation booth. The visitor sits in the front row for what is to be in effect a private showing. There is an exceptional hush, an air of anticipation. It is a very special thing to be in a great theater so early in the morning.

On the music stands are the parts for *Kirkohotaus (Valse Triste)* by Sibelius, to be danced by Patricia McBride and Ib Andersen, as choreographed by Peter Martins; and *Antique Epigraphs* of Debussy, for the choreography by Jerome Robbins.

The harpist enters the pit and uncovers her gold instrument. She has an electric tuner, which she plugs in. Someone flicks a switch, and the lights over all the music stands turn on simultaneously. The first note of the day sounds as the harpist tries a single string, then the octave, then triads, then on up the instrument. A violinist enters and chats with her.

Next on deck is the oboist, with his little box of reeds—a source of constant occupation. The stagehand population has multiplied, and they assist in carrying in a second harp. Nobody pays any attention to the lone observer, as if she has a magic cloak of invisibility allowing her to follow all the proceedings undetected.

Now more musicians start coming in. Mr. Fiorato returns, and the librarian queries the order of the day: *La Source* is to be the first piece. The clarinetist seats himself under the lip of the stage. The oboist plays the first real melody of the day. A very formal-looking percussionist enters dressed in jacket and tie, and the stagehands are coming along in dressing up the stage. The silver-haired tuba player enters, wearing silver shirt and silver tie, and carrying his color-coordinated silver instrument.

The first tuning of a violin is heard. As more musicians walk into the pit, their manner spells experience. This is not just a pickup group of young players fresh out of a conservatory; these are seasoned experts.

Next come the first dancers across the stage, one carrying toe shoes in her arms, and one wrapped in a colorful flowered shawl. The librarian formally delivers the baton, and Hugo Fiorato, like the captain of a ship checking his crew, surveys the orchestra, then goes through a curtained gateway from the theater to the pit. The concertmaster taps his bow. The observer's watch has stopped precisely at 10 seconds after 10:00 o'clock—and with it, any consciousness of life outside this theater. ''Good morning. *La Source,* please.'' And so commences the day's rehearsal, with the Romantic music of Delibes and Minkus.

There is no way, whether through laser recording or anything else, that the lovely quality of these strings can be captured and reproduced through electronic speakers. Nor can any synthesizer give us the richness and variety of wind tones as played by artists such as these musicians of the New York City Ballet Orchestra.

There is also something about the aura and the sounds of a morning rehearsal that are distinct and special in comparison to a formal public performance, despite all the starts and stops. Perhaps it is the concentration of the players; perhaps it is that their frame of mind is different in the morning than it is in the evening; perhaps it is the totally musical nature of the endeavor, uncomplicated for the moment by any action onstage or audience in the theater. It seems actually more pure than a performance.

''*Very* staccato,'' directs Mr. Fiorato. ''As nice and crisp as we can make it.'' And the musicians continue the ''Ethiopian March.'' A trumpet solo is joined by the dramatic sounds of the other brasses, and one can easily imagine some big classical lift onstage. A cymbal crash ends the section.

Next comes the fast mazurka. It sounded pretty good, but the conductor says: ''Keep it short. That part at letter F sounds sort of like ground glass.'' The string players are able to take such criticism with good humor, for Mr. Fiorato generally gives his suggestions in a good-natured way; he wastes no time and gets right to the point. These musicians have mostly played this work before, and their rehearsal time is quite limited nowadays for any older repertoire that the dancers have been doing for years.

Finally, at the sound of the well-known *Naïla Waltz,* the inner curtain goes up. All is pristine white onstage. Music director Robert Irving is looking over a score, seated in the theater. Meanwhile, the orchestra finishes up with the Romantic music and gets ready to play *Glass Pieces,* for which Mr. Irving takes the podium. Several new musicians must enter, and a synthesizer has to be tested for volume. "These things have invaded us lately," the conductor confides later.

The music by Philip Glass is sectional, with distinct repetitive material. The texture and perpetual motion seem exceptionally appropriate for the kind of dance that Robbins has set to it. The scoring is unusual for a ballet orchestra, too: the first movement is for synthesizer, horns, flute, and saxes; the second has strings (viola and cello only); and then a clear, nonvibrato, nonjazzy sound of the saxophone is heard, very eerie and beautiful. The third movement features percussion, saxes, and winds, which echo off the walls of the empty theater. The bassoons and horns and violins soon offer more motion. Then the bass trombone gives a blast that is doubly eerie, reinforced by the synthesizer and bounding around this large open space. Audiences will never hear the music quite this way, since multitudes of people and clothing modify the sound waves during a public performance.

And so the morning goes, until it is noon. Mr. Fiorato simply says to the orchestra: "Fantastic. Good bye." The musicians pack up, and one violinist ventures to give his opinion of *Glass Pieces:* "The music says the same thing the dance does. Both are very impersonal. You know, many young people have a heavy problem with alienation—and that's what the piece is about, both in the dance and the music." Asked further if he ever got lost, with all the repetition in his part, he says quite candidly: "Doesn't make much difference if you do!"

Solo horn player Paul Ingraham spots the observer and sees through her cloak of invisibility. "So you're writing about unsung heroes—us!" he beams. "Well, sometimes you do it for the money, sometimes because you enjoy it." It seemed as if this morning was one time he enjoyed it.

Until the evening performance, the instrumentalists' day is free—that is, if they are not teaching or making a commercial recording or going to another rehearsal for a chamber concert, as Paul Ingraham, for example, does so often. Mr. Fiorato, however, stays in the theater. His day is not even half over, and noon is not the time for lunch; it is the time to go up on the stage and sit at the side of the pianist and conduct the tempo some more, while co-ballet master in chief Peter Martins watches the dancers from his perch on a high stool by the edge of the stage.

The fire curtain has been raised now, to reveal the dancers of the New York City Ballet in rehearsal clothes, with a pas de deux in progress. Mr. Fiorato observes the dancers and conducts the music of *La Source,* which the orchestra had just rehearsed—this time for the pianist alone to follow.

Dancers now enter in costume. The rehearsal mistress says: "No faster than that." Martins pipes up: "No slower, either." Mr. Fiorato occasionally makes suggestions to the pianist by singing. At one point, he gets up and walks right next to the dancers so that he can see the exact timing of a fish-dive.

Meanwhile, back in the pit, the harps are covered and the musicians leave, but the lights are still on over the stands, and the lone librarian puts parts in order for the evening performance, which starts eight hours from now. Eventually he too goes out, and the pit is again empty, waiting, ready.

In a little while, Patricia McBride has the stage to herself for the Sibelius piece. It is a poignant solo. Mr. Fiorato likes it too and observes that he agrees with Balanchine's approach that "you don't disturb the music." Mr. Martins seems to be following that tradition too.

That evening, the musicians are all formality, dressed in tuxedos and gowns. Some children from the audience come forward and peer over the railing into the percussion section. The variations are wonderfully danced; the fish-dive is good, and the musical cutoff for it perfect. Now there comes a sound not present earlier during the day: thunderous applause for all the performers—dancers and musicians alike.

Toward the end of the intermission, a child asks his parents, upon seeing the musicians return to their places, "Do they take attendance?"

"No," replies his father. "They just all show up."

6

The Orchestra for American Ballet Theatre

If you ask members of ballet audiences if they like to have live orchestral music going on while the dancers do all those breathtaking turns and lifting of beautiful partners, the answer is always an enthusiastic "Oh yes!" This is true whether the speaker is a sparkly-eyed three-year-old being introduced to the art, a poised damsel of twelve, a gentleman connoisseur, or a greying grandmother who has loved the dance ever since she was a little girl in some *Nutcracker* production herself.

Yet as Dennis Cleveland, concertmaster of American Ballet Theatre, put it, "our goal is to enhance the dance. We want people to notice the music but not get preoccupied."[1] Because theater pits are built purposely to hide all the bowing and blowing of instruments so the audience is not distracted from the action onstage, most ballet-goers are also insulated from much contact with the musicians of large companies like American Ballet Theatre (ABT).

MEETING A VIOLIST

One day after a matinee, however, the author caught up with the attractive ABT violist Joan Kalisch. What was a zoology major from Vassar College, who also had earned an MBA at Fordham University, doing in the pit at the Metropolitan Opera House?

Like many of the musicians there, she was, if anything, overqualified for playing theater music. Originally a violin student of Boris Koutzen, she was awarded a full scholarship at Yale University, where she earned a Master of Music degree. After a year of living in Europe, mostly playing contemporary works and chamber music in Rome, she came to New York in 1965.

At that time, she explained, a number of ballet companies—both those based in New York and those from abroad—would "pick up" musicians from Local 802 (the New York chapter of the American Federation of Musicians). They would do their New York engagement, and then travel around the country with such a free-lance orchestra. It was one very good way for young musicians to get work for periods of eight or even twelve weeks at a time.

Our violist (then still a violinist) toured three years with both American Ballet Theatre and the Harkness Ballet. Then marriage and motherhood made touring unwelcome, and other opportunities opened up to her through accumulated contacts and recommendations—such as playing with the American Symphony Orchestra under Leopold Stokowski. She learned to relish that special excitement which seems to come only to musicians who perform on the stage of Carnegie Hall, where they feel the audience is really listening. Joan Kalisch also developed as a chamber music player and switched to the viola as an artistic preference, "because in quartet music it has its own more recognizable solo part."

American Ballet Theatre offers one of the most attractive seasons for musicians, with an eleven- or twelve-week spring and summer season at the Metropolitan Opera House in New York. Even though this is greatly truncated from the days of touring, the instrumentalists nevertheless welcome the fact that with ABT they can secure tenured positions and count on returning from year to year.

ONE CONDUCTOR'S VIEW: KENNETH SCHERMERHORN

Speaking about what he had wanted from his pit musicians while he was conductor at ABT, Kenneth Schermerhorn mentioned that there should be no difference between a fine orchestral musician for symphony concerts and one playing for ballet. However, he did note that "ballet music is pervaded with violin solos." Because of this strong predilection, there are apt to be five or six major extended solos for the concertmaster during the course of every performance. To be assured that these would go well, Mr. Schermerhorn always liked to take his concertmaster on tour.

By the mid-1980s, only the concertmaster, the librarian, and the three conductors went along regularly on ABT tours. By then, economics had already dictated that the company could use its regular orchestra only for its New York season. For every other location, either the host city's orchestra was employed, or an entirely new pickup group was hired by the sponsoring hall just for the ballet's engagement. More recently, not even the concertmaster has been touring.

Putting aside the issue of finances, Mr. Schermerhorn was asked about his artistic preferences in regard to music for ballet. He said he favored the sound of a large orchestra, since that is what most of the nineteenth-century literature called for. He felt that touring with a small orchestra was not always musically satisfying. But the alternative—working with new musicians constantly, all over the world—can create its own special artistic problems too. For example, when ABT went to Eastern Europe, Mr. Schermerhorn opted to also take along his resident pianist, percussionist, and trumpet player, just to be assured of an American sound for such works as *Fancy Free,* with its jazzy score by Leonard Bernstein.

When asked about what it is like to be conducting shifting personnel on tour, Mr. Schermerhorn conveyed an inkling of what must be at times a tiring and pressured way of life. "Some of the music is difficult," he said. "Tempo alterations are frequent, and you have to work fast in the corpuscular atmosphere of the pit."

Mr. Schermerhorn considers the primary question of setting the tempo to be a "group effort that involves the ballet master, choreographer, musicians, dancers, and the conductor—not necessarily in that order! In addition, if there is a solo for violin, cello, or piano, for instance, then that player has to be involved in such decisions too. You try to please as many people as possible," he suggested, while emphasizing that dance is mainly a visual phenomenon.

LIFESTYLES OF THE INSTRUMENTALISTS

For the musician in the pit, dance work provides "a good job that pays well," as violist Joan Kalisch noted. Furthermore, she pointed out, it was something she could do and usually be able to keep up her other professional commitments. In addition, she found that free-lancing allowed her to be home quite a bit when her children were young. Living on the West Side of Manhattan, she could even bicycle home for supper in between matinees and evening performances.

Nevertheless, after several decades of the free-lance life in Manhattan, shared with her husband, flutist Karl Kreber of the Dorian Quintet, this musician felt pressures of financial uncertainties. She began going across the street from Lincoln Center for 6 P.M. business classes at Fordham University, which let out in time for her evening performances at the Met. Several years later, she emerged with an MBA, and the entire family moved to Texas in search of a different lifestyle and a different kind of artistic fulfillment.

But after a stint of working as an accountant in the oil state, Joan Kalisch found herself—like a migrating bird—back north in the pit at the Met for the annual spring season of ABT. Moreover, she and her husband were starting a new chamber group with other New York musicians, were planning new concerts, and even were looking at small apartments in hope of having a permanent second home in Manhattan.

Such interest in chamber music is typical of many orchestral players at ABT. Trios, quartets, quintets, and other ensembles seem to provide an emotional and artistic outlet that is lacking in the pit. Unfortunately, there seems to be a vague feeling among string players that when they are down there working away, the audience is not paying much attention. Yet, they point out, the conductor will grimace if they make the least mistake. There is also a ripple of sympathy through the string section when the audience starts clapping in the middle of a solo by one of their colleagues. At those moments, they feel as if they are merely providing background sounds for a sporting event.

At Carnegie Hall and elsewhere, these same top-caliber instrumentalists perk up when their music is the focus of attention. Many are substitutes, for example, with the New York Philharmonic. They wistfully notice such small differences as the fact that "there is coffee in the lounge for the Philharmonic musicians," as if the latter are real people, and the musicians in the pit are somehow less worthy.

The business arrangements for all of ABT's live musical performances are the responsibility of James Stubbs, principal trumpet player and contractor acting on behalf of ABT management. In recent seasons, he noted, the company regularly employed fifty-six musicians by contract, but usually had to have sixty-two to sixty-five, including extra string players, a third oboe, a third flute, and a third trumpet. For jazz works such as *Ebony Concerto* and *N.Y. Export: Op. Jazz,* Mr. Stubbs would also hire free-lancers who were good jazz players on saxophones or other instruments.

Since tenure was instituted a few years ago, positions in the ABT orchestra are not often available. When they are, Mr. Stubbs looks for people who are "good sight readers and alert to tempo changes on the podium. For instance at the ends of phrases, the 'punctuation chord' might come earlier—or later—than you might expect, depending upon what the particular dancer was doing at that moment."

The instrumentalists rarely audition, though in one recent season the concertmaster seat was won that way. Placement is more usually in consultation with people already in the orchestra—by word of mouth or personal recommendation.

THE SOLO CELLIST

For many years now, if you were to lean over the Met rail during an intermission, you would be very likely to see principal cellist Daniel Morganstern catching a few minutes' extra practice—perhaps for another of his solo recitals at Alice Tully Hall or in other theaters around the world.

Like other ABT orchestra members, Mr. Morganstern is a fine concert artist who has had rigorous conservatory training. A student of the late Leonard Rose and a graduate of the Juilliard School, he auditioned for ABT in 1963; he has been with the company ever since, except for one year with the Joffrey Ballet.

But to adjust to the economic realities of life in the pits in the eighties, Mr. Morganstern and his wife, June de Forest (a first violinist with ABT), evolved a split year, both for financial reasons and to assure that they could dedicate substantial time to their great love of chamber music. They play the ABT season in New York, then for four months the two hold parallel positions with the Chicago Lyric Opera. In between, they go on tours: "to a lot of the same sorts of places we *used* to tour with ABT," the cellist observed, specifying "convention halls, universities, and in smaller concert series of cities and towns all across the country." In one recent season, Mr. Morganstern had given around twenty solo recitals, in addition to touring the Far East as a trio with his wife and a pianist.

Giving her viewpoint, June de Forest recalled what it was like to tour with ballet companies in the sixties, when she finished her training at the Manhattan School of Music. She travelled with the Royal Ballet seventeen weeks to the west coast; with the Joffrey and Harkness ballets; and from 1967 to 1971, with all outstanding ballet companies that Sol Hurok brought over, including the Bolshoi.

Although some musicians think that such touring was not a very great way to make a living—partly because they were expected to cover their own meals, hotel rooms, and other expenses—others remember the camaraderie with a note of poignancy.

Musicians in ballet are aware of an unspoken traditional hierarchy, in which the musicians are on the bottom. So when the newest fledgling dancers (next up on the totem) could not fit on the bus that held the principal dancers and soloists, some young corps members got to share rides and Scrabble games with the "untouchables." Daniel Morganstern recalled particularly that Cynthia Gregory, Eliot Feld, and Sallie Wilson were among the then-young dancers who were not only good traveling companions, but also very aware musically of what they heard coming from the pit during performances.

But time has jaded the feelings of even the most dedicated players. "The audience doesn't consider us at all," some say; or, "even when we play something exceptionally difficult in an exceptionally good performance, the press doesn't mention the orchestra." There is also some consternation about the musical distortions that are necessary—for instance in the big Tchaikovsky solos—to accommodate for different choreographers' ideas or different dancers' capacities and preferences.

And yet some musicians mention that they learn artistic lessons from dancers. For instance, Daniel Morganstern related that when he was on tour with the Bolshoi, he would occasionally be able to watch. He felt he learned something important about pacing, from the experience of seeing the Russians do their "adagios extra slow and their codas top-notch speed." He transferred this type of pacing quite consciously, for example, when he performed in concert the Tchaikovsky *Rococo Variations* for cello and orchestra, trying to change the flow markedly between the sections. "It brought the house down," he recalled gleefully. He also suggested that there is in ballet "a certain gracefulness that one can do well to emulate" in instrumental performance.

THE CONCERTMASTER

One person who often gets lots of applause from audiences is Dennis Cleveland, who as concertmaster of ABT plays all the solo violin melodies. Coming directly from the Atlanta and Houston symphonies, he said that "it is very gratifying to be able to play so many solos . . . but the frequency is sometimes hair-raising." Since he was entirely fresh to ballet work, he suddenly had to learn over forty new works in one season.

Mr. Cleveland made a point of having separate rehearsals with the dancers from time to time, so that in the solo sections they would mutually know what to expect. He found at times that such playing was very stressful because the changes would be quite unexpected in an actual performance.

The concertmaster noted that he is not usually consulted about tempo. "My job is not really to dictate to the dancer. Yet I have not been forced to distort much musically," he said. In his initial stint with the ballet, he came to realize that "a work can go many ways, and much of the time, the dancers' ideas are 'right on' in connection with musical tempo."

THE LIBRARIAN

The only other ABT musician who has regularly travelled on tour recently is Harold Themmen. He has served as the third clarinetist in New York, as first clarinetist on tour, and as the orchestra's librarian forty-six weeks a year.

As librarian, Mr. Themmen's tasks have included arranging to rent or buy the music from publishers for some forty ballets. Surprisingly, most of these must be rented, and the fee for a full-length ballet like Prokofiev's *Cinderella,* for example, might run up to $1,500 per performance.

Mr. Themmen's duties also include making cuts and inserts while preparing all the parts. This has to be done both before the season's rehearsals and on tour, when some of the choreography might have to be changed for a particular stage, necessitating musical changes as well. There is an enormous amount of paper work, and Mr. Themmen employs copyists to assist him.

Two sets of parts are kept for each ballet. When playing in one city, the librarian sends the second set ahead so that the new pickup musicians can look over their parts before coming to rehearsal. With a new group of musicians in each location, that means wall-to-wall rehearsals for about two days. Then they continue to rehearse all week up until the final day. After the last performance in a city is over, Mr. Themmen flies ahead, on the dancers' day off, so that he can get the next batch of parts in order one program ahead.

Harold Themmen is typical of the versatility of ABT's musicians. A product of New England Conservatory in Boston, he played first clarinet with the Boston Pops under Arthur Fiedler. But in those days, Boston lacked a ballet. So when this musician came to ABT over twenty years ago under the baton of his conservatory colleague Kenneth Schermerhorn, that was his first exposure to the art. As a conductor himself, Mr. Themmen has worked with Broadway shows, as well as in summer stock productions of such favorites as *South Pacific* and *Camelot.* As a performer, he also played with Sol Hurok's regal tours featuring the Royal Danish Ballet, Ballet Marseilles, the Royal Ballet, and other companies.

The world of ballet musicians is close-knit in many respects. When there are little jobs to be done, it does seem to help to know somebody. For instance, when conductor John Lanchbery was leaving and there were still bits and pieces of *Les Sylphides* and *Giselle* that needed to be arranged for ABT's production, the librarian's wife, Ivana Themmen, was called upon, since she is a highly skilled composer. (PBS recently aired an entire TV program devoted to a profile of her and her work.) For *Les Sylphides,* she had to arrange a new male variation: one of Chopin's melodies was given to her, and she orchestrated it for Mikhail Baryshnikov. In *Giselle,* she arranged a girls' variation and did some reconstruction to match John Lanchbery's orchestration.

Ivana Themmen had also been commissioned by ABT and others to do the reverse of orchestration: piano reductions for rehearsal pianists, including versions of *Pillar of Fire* (Schoenberg); Verdi's *Variations;* Handel's *Airs;* Stravinsky's *Les Noces;* Brahms' *Serenade;* and the *Aubade* by Richard Rodney Bennett.

SECOND FIDDLE

Another talented family connection turned up in a conversation with Lucy Morganstern, who is a second violinist at ABT and the sister of the principal cellist. Her credits again reveal the variety typical of New York free-lance careers. She studied privately at the Mannes and Manhattan schools of music. Though she earned a degree from New York University in early childhood studies, she never stopped playing the violin seriously in recitals, borough symphonies, and so on. She was regularly a member of the American Symphony Orchestra, Musica Sacra, the Queens Symphony, the Long Island Philharmonic, and the Joffrey Ballet Orchestra.

Second violin parts in some of the older classical ballets are particularly prone to having a lot of offbeats and "filler" material—inner harmonic figurations which are nevertheless important to maintaining the overall texture of the music. However, Miss Morganstern said she particularly enjoys playing such works as Prokofiev's ballet *The Prodigal Son,* because she finds that even the inner parts were written in an interesting fashion.

Another source of challenge is that a gifted second violinist may be called upon to play a more difficult role in another ballet company. For instance, once for a tour with the Pennsylvania Ballet, Lucy Morganstern served as assistant concertmaster.

HEADING THE ORCHESTRA COMMITTEE

One person whom the audience can barely see during performances is nevertheless important for the smooth running of things in the pit, namely the head of the orchestra committee. Recently violist Olivia Koppell has been acting chairperson.

Aside from her concern with business operations, Ms. Koppell has also been involved in ocasional auditions for new players. She is present just to make sure that things run smoothly, along with a review committee consisting of the leaders of the various sections of the orchestra. Though the ABT seasons now stretch from spring into summer, the orchestra committee meets throughout the year, especially when a contract is about to be renegotiated.

Ms. Koppell likes the long-term relationships within the orchestra. "Everybody has played the repertoire and is used to playing with each other," she noted. "It feels like family."

Concerning how the musicians feel about the *dancers* in general, she commented: "We all admire their physical accomplishments and discipline. We know how hard they work. We admire most of the dancers—mainly the soloists—who show special feeling for the music, like Cynthia Gregory. You can tell some really feel the music. We are partial to those who seem to know the music. Martine von Hamel is another one," she added, "and Kevin McKenzie . . . and obviously, Baryshnikov. We are all totally spellbound by him! When he gets on the stage, he *becomes* whatever role he is playing so intensely. He does the steps so well, but on top of that, he does *become* whoever he is portraying, and he is very musical in his phrasing, in tune with the subtleties."

When questioned about how much the dancers and musicians meet informally nowadays, the violist said: "We would like to have more contact with them. We might see them at the cafeteria and so forth. It would be nice if there were more interaction, but our schedules are different . . . and we are in different places in the theater," she observed realistically. Though she felt that there seem to be dancers who fit the stereotype of the "15-year-old with the chirpy voice," by and large, the orchestra's committee head had high regard for the dancers as intelligent artists.

Concerning the economics of the company, Ms. Koppell ventured this opinion: "I don't think the dancers begrudge us what we get. We also support whatever they want to do."

Another group the musicians seem to appreciate is the audience. For example, Olivia Koppell remarked with a smile that they stare at the audience often. She added: "The audience puts on a real show for *us*—especially on a gala or other important evening. Mrs. Reagan was there at one gala, and on opening nights of previous seasons, Jacqueline Kennedy Onassis used to come." Obviously such theater-goers are a stimulus to the musicians' flow of adrenalin.

CONDUCTOR ALAN BARKER'S EXPERIENCES

When he was on the ABT roster, Australian conductor Alan Barker invited the author to follow him around during rehearsals one week, and even to sit in the pit of the Met among the musicians during a dress rehearsal.

Speaking about what working in the pit was like for him, Mr. Barker commented: "Sometimes we feel slightly separated from the dancers and the other action, because there's that physical wall, and we're on a different level. Of course, it's all right for *me,* but the musicians can't see what's happening on the stage. I try and explain to them so it will help them understand the dramatic and musical effects we're trying to make. But it would be an ideal situation if they could work in rotation and all have a chance to sit in the house and actually see what's going on, so they would understand. However, they don't have time off. They always play during the season for every performance."

Maybe the conductor should have said the orchestra members are *supposed* to play for every performance. For when asked what it feels like for him to begin an evening's performance, Mr. Barker acknowledged: "I used to face it with a fair amount of trepidation. Now I guess I've had many years and a fair amount of experience. The principal anxieties one has, I suppose, are in the case of an orchestra such as ours here, when one is likely to have some substitute players in. That happens quite often. Oh yes!" he sighed. "We had five 'ill' string players one evening for a *Romeo and Juliet* performance that I conducted. So there were five subs in, and some of them hadn't played it before."

"These sorts of things can cause some anxiety," he confided. "One just always hopes that the orchestra will be paying sufficient attention to be flexible enough to go with us if we want to adjust the tempo or even drastically change gear to accommodate a dancer who may be either in extremely good form and wanting to sustain, or who may be having a hard evening and may be needing some help. This can happen, because dancers are not machines; they are human beings and need support."

"Ballet poses many problems which are not found in either opera or on the concert platform," Mr. Barker noted. "I like that set of problems, and I love doing it." He himself posed the question of what are the prerequisites of a ballet conductor. "You know," he reflected, "some people think that if you just get up and play the music the way Tchaikovsky wrote it, it will work. Well, it's not so. The way I learnt about it was that I joined a ballet company, and even though I joined the Australian Ballet in Melbourne as an assistant conductor, I was made to spend many hours playing the piano for class."

"I used to hate playing for class," Mr. Barker acknowledged. "But I learned to know all the steps. For class every morning, I played some printed music, and I improvised. But it was essential to find out the rhythm that's implied in the basic steps of the dancers' vocabulary, and then to find out the velocity—as opposed to the rhythm—that was needed to execute the steps.

''Then the next thing was to play the piano for repertoire rehearsals, where—especially in the classical repertoire—these steps which were covered in an hour-and-a-half class at the beginning of each day were used in a piece of classical choreography, and even in a piece of contemporary choreography. For example, one can take the works of John Butler or Glen Tetley or Ashton or Kenneth MacMillan and find in all of them a very strong classical ballet foundation. *Then,* when one started to deal with an orchestra, one had that background to understand where adjustments needed to be made.''

In Australia, Alan Barker had continued with his piano playing for about four years. Simultaneously, he was conducting performances as well. But he is among those conductors who don't think that one has to become *too* involved with ballet. When asked if he ever took a ballet class, he laughed, and sputtered: ''Good heavens, no!'' However, he went on to point out that his ABT colleague Paul Connelly had worked with the Bejart company and knew personally ''the agony that ballet class is'' from having taken it himself. But Mr. Barker didn't consider this a necessary prerequisite for conducting ballet scores. ''I think one can learn from *visually* working with dancers and also hearing their complaints when the music is too fast or too slow, in the classroom. Knowing *how* to make it work is important,'' he advised.

''Now this is the next thing,'' outlined the conductor. ''When one has learned all these technical things about dealing with steps and choreography and dancers, there is a tendency—and I went through this period as well—to overcompensate towards the dancers' needs, till one finds that the rhythmic structure of the music starts to disintegrate. I think it's only in the last ten years that I've found the road to follow which says 'I can accommodate you this far in your requests for indulgence with the music, but beyond that I can't go because the music starts to lose its shape.' I think this is one of the greatest problems to solve. But it's also one of the greatest joys to make it work: to make music out of the constrictions that are placed upon us sometimes by the dancers' needs.''

7

La Bayadère: From Rehearsals to Curtain Calls

A DAY WITH THE PIANIST

As one waits at the security desk of the Metropolitan Opera House, a hall door opens to reveal several people intently studying posted rehearsal schedules. Martha Johnson, ABT's pianist of long standing, finds out what she is supposed to play in a few minutes—having had no advance warning—and leads the way to a large subterranean studio.

The pianist is greeted in a friendly manner on all sides. Natalia Makarova walks in wearing one of her legendary bandanas, and the rehearsal for the "Shades" section of *La Bayadère* begins.[1]

This is the *prima ballerina assoluta*'s own staging, and so she seems to care deeply that the corps do everything right. Her comments to the pianist mostly have to do with tempo and where to begin. "Not so slow," she requests. The musician must have a fine sensitivity to tempo: exactly what is a little faster than "so" slow?

The music is by Ludwig Minkus, a French composer who worked with the choreographer Petipa in the Czar's court. Martha Johnson mentions that she tried to do research on Minkus and could find out relatively little. Unfortunately for the ballet world in the West, most of the more than twenty full-length works he composed are apparently lost.

Conductor Alan Barker offered this view of the composer: "It's popular in musicological circles to denigrate Minkus as being a bit circusy or rumty-tum and so on. I suppose that is understandable when one considers that he was just about contemporaneous with Tchaikovsky, who was working in such a different extreme, writing such wonderful big symphonic scores (which incidentally were often criticized by the choreographers of the day as being 'unchoreographicable' because they were *too* symphonic). But the Minkus scores are loaded with lovely melodies. It's not the *greatest* music, but it is readily accessible. People can still hum the melodies as they come out of the theater.''

''Minkus's own powers of orchestration were not terribly inspired,'' the conductor observed. ''When John Lanchbery takes one of the scores, he adds some harmonic interest and lovely orchestral color, and puts them together so that they have a great *flow* to them and a more symphonic quality than they would have had otherwise.''

''In the case of *Bayadère* there are all sorts of exotic little Oriental touches: the use of triangles and little cymbals and things to make Oriental Indian sounds,'' noted Mr. Barker. ''I think especially beautiful is the orchestration of the candle dance in Act 3, which is done so simply with some string accompaniment, and the harp making little glissandos up and down, and occasionally a solo violin or solo flute. It's very lush and very simple, and really very beautifully orchestrated.''[2]

In the rehearsal studio, part of Martha Johnson's job is to suggest such coloration—with only the piano to aid her. So here she is, once more spinning out the lovely adagio where all the Shades (spirits of the departed maidens) come in, disembarking from a boat in a miraculous series of arabesques. Miss Makarova corrects the coordination of arms and the inclination of heads. ''A little pick up in tempo,'' she requests. Then a few seconds later: ''It's too fast.''

It has been, the musician says, four years since this full-length ballet has been presented in its entirety by ABT. Martha Johnson deplores the fact that in the interim, her personal copy of the piano reduction has disappeared—despite the company precautions of lock and key. So she is today having to mark a new score freshly with all the dramatic and movement cues, entrances of characters, cuts in the music, and any special reminders from the conductors and directors.

Sitting behind Martha Johnson like a quiet shadow, one derives pleasure from watching these young women forming a corps of such remarkable accomplishment. Miss Makarova makes mostly slight corrections, in the nature of ''take your arms away from your body; make the hands long,'' and so forth, in trying to make a uniform final pose after the last of the Shades has entered. She also demonstrates how the flow of movement should continue in the arms—with no jerks and stops, no extra accents as they reach the various points in space. One is reminded of the ballerina's autobiography, in which she describes the concept of cantilena: ''singing'' with the body. Today she imparts that style onto other dancers.

Next comes the waltz, and Martha Johnson plays it in a simple, clear version. Susan Jones, who had taught the dance to the corps, aids in putting it together now for polishing.

Miss Makarova intervenes to explain the differences in executing a certain little jump: the feeling is to be up, not accenting the down. ''The down is the release,'' she explains. She doesn't use many words: a brief demonstration here and there is enough. Yet one can see the difference when the muscles are controlled and positions are changed, even slightly: in the way a foot is presented, the degree of tension as a dancer is holding the chest, the inclination of the hand or head, or the extension of the flow of movement into the entire limb in relation to a musical phrase. It is quite beautiful to behold. A great deal of the musicality of the corps dancers seems to lie in the full use of a musical phrase, with the effort of the entire body.

The pianist also has to be attuned to the implications of these terse directions from the dance director. She can help by slight changes in musical accent and in dynamic, and by being deeply aware of the nature of the movement being executed at the moment.

After an hour of working with the corps, Martha Johnson moves to another studio where the soloists are to practice their parts. The pianist mentions that ABT does over forty ballets, and that things can get difficult. The last thing in the world she needs today, working with Natalia Makarova, is to have to edit her piano score all over again.

Alan Barker walks in. ''Thank God we have a conductor!'' sighs Miss Johnson. The next two hours reveal the reason for her relief, for Mr. Barker sings, conducts, and occasionally comes to the piano to double a few melodies with one hand. Most importantly, he sets the tempos for the pianist and runs back and forth from his full orchestral score on a music stand to help erase pencilled ''cut'' marks on sections that have just this week been reinstated, or to indicate how he will be conducting: ''in two; you count four, but I conduct in two; then in one for four bars. . . .''

For the soloists, a video monitor has been rolled in. The principals study the tape of a previous ABT performance and try to duplicate the steps. At moments, one is actually seeing triplicate: Makarova will be leading, and then two casts of soloists will shadow what she is doing. ''It's fabulous that we have the video tapes to refer to,'' comments Miss Johnson, while her hands follow along silently on the keyboard.

It's getting to be a long rehearsal. ''Is she dead yet?'' pipes up Martha Johnson at one point. The snake in the dance has delivered its poison, but it takes a few more musical bars to see the temple dancer expire completely. ''OK,'' says Miss Makarova. ''Last time, and do something nice!'' The artists do—and the three hours of rehearsal are over for Martha Johnson.

Where does she go on her break? Surprisingly, it's up to the ticket office, just like a balletomane, to check on reservations for her friends and herself.

''You mean you actually attend performances?'' the observer queries.

''Of course,'' responds the musician enthusiastically. Martha Johnson seems never to tire of the ballet world and work. And even though she claims to have been ''screamed at by the best of them,'' she manages to keep her cool and be very well respected by her colleagues. She has been doing this at ABT for over twenty years.

ORCHESTRA REHEARSAL

The next day, the kind of prerehearsal hubbub heard when any orchestra gathers together is going on as usual in another windowless subterranean studio at the Met—a room built for something other than good sound. Then James Stubbs, the personnel manager, stands up in front: the traditional sign among union orchestras for all to quiet down. The concertmaster taps with his bow so that in turn the oboist can sound an A for everybody else to tune to.

Alan Barker ensconces the author behind the harp, flanked on the right by four contrabasses, and on the left by thirty drumsticks and mallets. The conductor steps up to his music stand. "OK. From the top of number one." The harpist gives a finishing turn to his tuning pegs and sees that he must count these sections of rests: eight bars, then nine bars, then ten bars, then eight bars, then ten again, before coming in with his first notes.

"Trumpets, slightly too bright. Don't forget it will be a three-hour blow," cautions the conductor. The percussionists mention that since a scrim was placed on the edge of the stage, they can't see the dancers at all; so the whole orchestra has to be told the plot of the ballet, about a Brahmin who wanted the temple dancer to marry him—or else!

They finally make it to the waltz section, and the harpist can do his plink-plunks. The sticks to the left get changed. Triangle beaters on the gong produce an unexpected pleasant sound, and the percussionist smiles to the harpist. Both are pleased with the effect of this little detail.

To the right, one notes the care that the contrabass players take with their pizzicato notes and their bowing. It is a pleasure for musicians to be able to play what they are supposed to. One begins to understand why violist Joan Kalisch keeps coming back from Texas for ballet seasons.

Barker stops. "Something's wrong. Maybe a bass note." The conductor adds, "I felt the 'and' eighth note on the second half of the third beat was a little late." And so on through the morning; such little details are the musical parallel of what is going on in the other studios with Natalia Makarova putting a little finger here and an elbow there to change the whole tension and feeling.

"What we have to do is enjoy the eighth note of silence," urges the conductor at this point. Then follow some delightful combinations: oboe solo with harp arpeggios; contrabasses and celli plucked, against a viola countermelody. Then all the strings enter, then a triangle, then a flute.

Suddenly there is a big blast from muted brasses in a minor mode, and the huge gong is struck with a four-inch, yarn-wrapped mallet that is faintly reminiscent of caveman equipment. One can easily imagine something melodramatic happening onstage.

At last, we come to a lovely solo that Lanchbery had scored for harp. Alan Barker folds his arms and lets Robert Barlow go it alone. All the miniscule notes on the page run up to heaven.

When it is over, the harpist comments, "Jack Lanchbery was cuckoo for harp!" as he demonstrates how he has to mark pedalings and fingerings into his part. In addition, there are places that he has to edit actual notes, sometimes just changing the register. He made little charts of how the pedaling must be for of his particular harp, which has forty-seven strings. He leaves a little message to other harpists, asking that they not change these carefully thought out markings. The part may be used by many people in different countries for years to come, with each person adding their autograph with a flourish for posterity. Fred Eckler, the nearby percussionist, adds this opinion: "Eighty percent of composers don't know how to write for percussion. Lanchbery did!"

Jack Everly, one of the three conductors at ABT this season, comes in to observe. He can never be quite sure when he will have to conduct a ballet for the first time, sometimes even without a rehearsal, so he has to know the scores well. He is slated to do *La Bayadère* next week, and he has never even seen the ballet before.

Meanwhile, at this rehearsal, we're into a broad march. The bass drum comes in wrong—all alone. The seasoned pros are not above laughing all around. Mr. Barker remarks: "This music moves between elegance and the ludicrous if the slightest thing goes wrong. Anyway, I needed an excuse to stop, and if you're going to make a mistake, that's good: make it with conviction."

Then with a seriousness that belies the sounds, the musicians set to again, this time with cymbals clashing, and the full orchestra bowing and blowing away in the kind of commotion common to circuses and large masculine leaps in ballets. Then the rhythm changes to triplets at a helter-skelter pace, and one can imagine the dancers heading offstage in fast chainé turns—to much applause, of course.

Before leaving the scene, the observer shakes the personnel director's hand and promises to come back the next day to see what happens in the second act. "Good," he comments. "Tell me if anything interesting happens."

Down the hall, one of the musicians is asked: "Is Alan Barker always this nice as a conductor?" A disembodied voice from around the corner pipes up, "No!" and another one adds, "Either nice or awful. No in-between." One is reminded that orchestras frequently seem to consist of "us" instrumentalists pitted against any conductor.

TO THE PIT!

It is ten o'clock on Thursday morning during this week of rehearsals for *La Bayadère*. The orchestra is in its place in the pit. The back of the usual stage is opened up, and the stagehands are busy with scenery. There are more lights than one can count. The fire curtain is lowered; there is tuning; then all is quiet with anticipation.

Alan Barker takes the podium. ''After our triumphant reading of Act 1, we will have a go at Act 2. I suspect that 80 percent of you can play the 'Shades' section from memory, blindfolded, and standing on your heads.'' They go through it anyway. The house lights go out. ''If you think we're having a bad trip playing this act, well, he's having an even more terrible time on the stage,'' remarks the conductor as the musicians come to the ''opium dream'' section, in which the prince is confused as to what is real and who is who.

Concertmaster Dennis Cleveland sounds as sweet and lovely as one could ask for in his violin solos, despite his declaration in front of the Lincoln Center fountain the previous night, that it was sometimes difficult to keep up his interest in the Minkus melodies early in the morning. The last note of the high violin solo ends, and the orchestra members applaud heartily for Cleveland. They apparently do not get tired of the melodies.

There is a union break, and the musicians disappear swiftly down and around the hallways. At the end of a tunnel, most unexpectedly, is a nice cafeteria, where the author chats a few minutes with the oboist. He mentions that the oboe itself was invented in India, perhaps as early as 4,000 B.C. So it was natural for arranger Lanchbery to use a lot of oboe in trying to evoke the Orient for this ballet.

After the break, the author achieves what must be for many instrumentalists a hidden ambition: to enter the pit of the Metropolitan Opera House for an orchestra rehearsal. Just like those who are there to work, she stoops under the stage and wends her way to an allotted seat, right under the stage and behind the violas. It is interesting to find that one cannot see players on the other side of the orchestra because of the construction of the stage supports.

But what is most surprising down here is the brightness of the sound. Even in comparison to what one hears while sitting in the very first row of the audience's seating, there is no comparison to the exciting live quality of sounds that are coming from all around—albeit from around a post.

''Welcome to the dungeon!'' is a cordial greeting echoed by several players. Dungeon or no, this is the spot where probably thousands of music students practicing their hearts out would give their eye teeth to play. But today, one musician, at least, is content to sit with no instrument, and simply listen and look.

The viola players are not too enthusiastic about their parts. They remember Tchaikovsky and Prokofiev ballet parts, and are spoiled by those masterpieces. There are, in the Minkus ballet score, and even in Lanchbery's arrangement, a lot of oom-pahs for brass and violas, but even these must be crisp and exact. They can impart or mar the overall style, depending on the instant of attack, the instant of release, the kind of accent, and the precision of the tempo. Even ''vamps'' (introductory repetitions) of just the accompaniment figures are extremely important for the dancers to get going in the correct tempos—probably more so than the melodies. The audience may listen to the melodies, but the dancers' feet pay attention to the bass and accompaniment patterns for their impetus.

The usual first cellist is not here today, so the solos are played by the instrumentalist next in line. "Lovely, Ellie," compliments Mr. Barker, and there follow whistles and foot scuffles in approbation from all her colleagues. And so they proceed to play the second act.

DRESS REHEARSAL

Ten minutes before the scheduled rehearsal time, trumpeter–personnel manager Jim Stubbs escorts the author into the Met theater for an afternoon run-through that is open to the Friends of American Ballet Theatre.

But first, he has to find a carpenter to nail his music stand down; he cannot, perhaps because it might infringe on union rules. In following him, the author suddenly finds herself onstage confronting the Buddha-like statue used in the last act of *La Bayadère*. The audience is already seated; for the curtains are up. Onstage, the scenic events of the ballet are happening in reverse: the rubble of the temple destroyed goes up; the statue goes down and is then uprighted. The cast is gently practicing pirouettes, but the stage crew keeps practicing the destruction of the temple.

Pausing for reflection under the eyes of the Buddha, it is hard to believe that a few minutes ago, out in the sunshine, the well-dressed women of this New York audience were indulging in last-minute ice-cream cones to fortify themselves for watching the performance. There are a few older gentlemen present, but this is primarily a gathering of feminine patrons.

Mikhail Baryshnikov, artistic director of ABT, leaps over the bridge connecting the theater and the stage. The Friends' announcer welcomes the guests and announces that Susan Jaffe, Martine von Hamel, Patrick Bissel, Cynthia Harvey, Cynthia Gregory and others will be seen this afternoon. It is going to be a treat.

Alan Barker will be conducting at the evening performance, so Paul Connelly is doing the dress rehearsal, with his wife, principal dancer Susan Jaffe, onstage in the lead role. The audience can see the second cast rehearsing behind the main one, either marking their steps or, in some cases, doing some sections full out. Yet another cast is in the wings going through the parts, just as they had practiced in the studio earlier this week, except now there is the full orchestra instead of a solo piano.

The Brahmin, portrayed by Alexander Minz, enters in rehearsal clothes. Other dancers enter in costume to the brass march that the orchestra had practiced so vigorously down below in the studios.

Accompanying the tragic events brought on by the Brahmin, the brass and timpani effectively evoke the chaos of the toppling of the temple at the moment of the ill-fated wedding. The statue topples too. Smoke comes up from the floor. This time the rubble comes down. All the while, the trumpets are blowing their brains out; the snare drums and cymbals are banging away; and finally, as things subside a bit, the high violin and oboe are heard, as the onstage couple performs their scarf-holding walk to paradise together. The curtain comes down, and there is a short break.

The peacock chair for the opium dream sequence is brought out. Susan Jaffe is practicing. Paul Connelly watches from below; the dancer smiles at her conductor-husband. Mr. Baryshnikov comes onstage to talk to the Brahmin. People in the audience chat while the orchestra practices a section alone; after all, they came mostly to *watch* a rehearsal, not to listen to wrong sounds being righted.

PERFORMANCE AT LAST

And now comes the moment everyone has been waiting for. The front doors are opened; the ushers unhook the velvet ropes. The audience eagerly files in. Programs are handed out; seats are located. And there they are: the elegant orchestra in the pit, busy with their usual hubbub of warming up. One would think they had not played for several weeks, let alone for a three-hour rehearsal that ended late that afternoon.

Fernando Bujones, former principal dancer at ABT, walks in to take his seat, and the audience applauds for him. Later the fans also spot Cuban ballerina Alicia Alonso sitting in a box seat, and they pay their respects with another round of applause, which she acknowledges.

Alan Barker seems to take brighter tempos than conductor Connelly did at the dress rehearsal. The fakirs seem more frenzied; there is yet another Brahmin; von Hamel has a different Oriental use of the hands than Jaffe did earlier. Every dancer does different things with each part, and one can see such a work many times and still find it both interesting and touching.

The famous "Shades" scene begins, and one man in the audience cannot help saying out loud: "Isn't this something!" And so it is. Maybe the best seat after all is not the one under the stage, but rather the one out in the theater.

POSTSCRIPT: MAKAROVA ONSTAGE

For *La Bayadère,* Natalia Makarova's work took place behind the scenes. Later the same week, she is in the spotlight herself, in the lead role of *Romeo and Juliet.* At the end of the performance, it rains whole gardens of bouquets over the Met stage as the ballerina takes her final bows.

It has been a long night, and one of the violists wants to go home. She keeps being detained by souvenir-seekers from the audience who lean over the pit railing and beg for just one more sprig as a remembrance of a wonderful evening at the ballet.

"OK," gives in the violist. "But this is the *very very* last!" It is past eleven o'clock. "This is a rose that fell on my chair," says the violist, offering it to a fan. So the last of the musicians and the last of the audience finally depart, carrying not only the roses but also their own memories of the evening's performance.

8

Maestro, Please. . . .

What difference does it make to a dancer onstage whether the music is piped over a loudspeaker or emerges from the orchestra pit, directed by the hands or baton of a live conductor?

One reply to this question was given by Victoria Pasquale, a gifted young soloist with the Joffrey Ballet.[1] She said: "There is nothing like dancing with a live orchestra! You do have problems, with tempo and so on, for it seems that no matter how much you rehearse, you never know what the music is going to be like until you actually hear it in performance. So you've always got to be prepared to change your tempo, to be quicker or slower. You have to have that little bit of anticipation of what's going to come next.

"But there is really nothing like it as far as the music 'bringing it into you.' You get a tremendous feeling of being *part* of the music when you are dancing to live orchestra, rather than just dancing *to* the music. If you haven't danced, it's kind of a hard thing to understand. But when you have orchestra, you're definitely more a *part* of the music."

"If you have a tape, you know the tape will be playing no matter what, until someone stops it," Miss Pasquale continued. "But the orchestra has so many parts that it creates a whole different feeling. It's not just one stream of sound; there are all *different* kinds of sounds coming up from the pit. And so, each time there will be some slight variation: maybe the clarinet will be stronger one night, or maybe the violins will be a little stronger on another. This can affect our dance performance, because we really depend a lot on the music as we hear it," she emphasized. "You can't dance without the music, and I think an orchestra really gives you a lot more inspiration and a lot more *freedom*. It has such a richer sound coming up to you. It certainly has more feeling in it than a tape that is being broadcast from speakers. It's just nice when you go out there and there's that rich full-bodied sound of a full orchestra that knows what it's doing."

Working with the Joffrey Ballet, Miss Pasquale was fortunate always to dance with live orchestra in performance. She recalled the creation of Gerald Arpino's *Birthday Variations,* in which she had her first solo: "When we were working on it, we had a record, which gave me no leeway as far as tempo goes. When we finally got to do it with an orchestra, it was a big change, and I think it helped me a lot."

Much of the dancers' success is vitally dependent on the conductor. Touching upon this, Victoria Pasquale commented: "When you have a really good conductor, he will watch the dancers. Usually if something is happening where the tempo is ridiculously fast, a dancer will try to go along with it as best as possible. But then if there is a step that requires a certain amount of time that the music will not give them at that speed, they'll just have to take their own time to do it, and that means being slightly *off* the music. Then the *dancer* will be noticed; it is never the conductor who 'looks bad.' "

A VISIT WITH ROBERT IRVING

One company that prides itself on both dancers who look good and music that is tasteful is New York City Ballet, where for many years the orchestra has been led by music director Robert Irving and his colleague Hugo Fiorato.

The author spoke with Mr. Irving one day in the conductors' lounge at New York State Theater, and asked him what it felt like to come into the pit to start an evening's performance.[2] He laughed, and said: "Oh, I've done it for so long I don't think I can say. Well, you know, you feel like what you feel like that evening. Of course, if you are playing a difficult score which the orchestra doesn't know well, that's the only cause for anxiety, really."

"But the standard of orchestral musicians in New York is about the highest anywhere in the world, I think, and you're not going to get let down by insecurity in that department," emphasized the music director. "So there's no reason to be nervous—good God! Some things of course, one especially likes, and others one isn't quite so interested in anymore. But you do *everything* for all it's worth, I hope!"

Theater-goers are often curious about the differences between conducting for ballet and conducting for opera. In a speech to members of the New York City Ballet Guild about this one evening, Mr. Irving summarized his experience: "You have the physical element in ballet. Sometimes, unluckily, you have to distort the music a bit. You have to know what's involved, then produce that. To have a sense of involvement, you have to sort of half visualize the steps *before* you start the music. The need to distort usually comes if you haven't been together with the people who invented the steps."[3]

"And if one day you're feeling low . . . or another feeling good and want to gallop like a race horse," continued the conductor, "that you don't do with the ballet; you've got to really produce. So I think it helps to have a sense of movement. It's no good waiting for the feet to hit the ground. You've got to pay attention. You can make a little leeway and little differences—though it doesn't happen often in *this* company. In companies where you do something like *Giselle,* the music is designed for steps and is capable of being bent more. But at New York City Ballet, all the dancers are well-schooled, and nobody's allowed onstage who can't do the choreography."

Asked to single out some of his favorite scores, Mr. Irving remarked: "I've always had a great liking for French music. I think Balanchine did too. That was one of the bonds between us, really. Chabrier and Ravel and Debussy. And of course, I've always since school days been very interested in Stravinsky. But the whole horizon of Balanchine's long association and interest with Stravinsky—Well!" exclaimed the conductor, "I don't think any other orchestra in the world has ever equalled the number of works we did at the Stravinsky festival."

For that remarkable series in 1972, twenty-two works by Stravinsky were presented by the New York City Ballet in one week. Mr. Irving recalled the preparations for this marathon event: "We had an extra week off performances, beforehand, so we had only that time to prepare. Everyone in the orchestra was very interested in it, I must say. It was a tremendous 'up' for them."

Also among his favorite scores are *Daphnis and Chloe, La Valse,* and *Le Tombeau de Couperin.* Then he singled out Jerome Robbins' version of *Antique Epigraphs,* to Debussy's music. "I also enjoy going back to the full-length classic ballets sometimes," Mr. Irving said. "I have had the opportunity to return to *Sleeping Beauty* in London . . . and good old *Swan Lake!*" he exclaimed. "But I don't know that I would really wish to conduct *Giselle* particularly."

One couldn't even begin to count the number of performances of *The Nutcracker* that Robert Irving must have conducted, yet he could still say: "I love it. I think it's the best score by Tchaikovsky, and I'm always very proud, because we're really the only people who do it in the correct manner."

Turning to his collaborations with Jerome Robbins, Mr. Irving was particularly pleased with the recent reworking of Stravinsky's *Dumbarton Oaks.* "Brisk, brisk, brisk! And that's good," commented the maestro. "It works well like that."

Tempo, tempo, tempo. That is the element one hears about most on all sides—from choreographers, dancers, musicians, conductors; it seems to be everybody's main concern in ballet, at least in terms of the music. Indeed, on occasions it seems that tempo is all the conductor has to be concerned with. For instance, while discussing Robbins' ballet *Glass Pieces,* to music by Philip Glass, Mr. Irving remarked: "There's next to no collaboration with the stage, providing you know what the tempo is supposed to be, and in this one, there's almost no reason even to look at the stage!''

When he does have to look at the stage, in other works, Mr. Irving pays particular attention to the general rhythmical flow, the pace. ''The thing is to set it,'' he suggested, ''not to watch their feet and then think you're playing with their feet. That's a fatal thing to do.''

When the conductor was asked if he had a preference for working in classical ballet or contemporary, he replied: ''I think it's nice to do both. It keeps the circulation going! It's very good to come back to the classics of ballet. I love and respect them. On the other hand, it's very nice to step across the road and do a lot of modern pieces.''

It may well be that Robert Irving has introduced audiences to more modern music than most symphony conductors in this country ever attempt. At New York City Ballet, twentieth-century sounds are dished out as a way of life. And since Peter Martins organized the American Music Festival in 1988, there has been an even greater encouragement for dancers and audiences to be aware of the concert music that American composers are producing in our own time.

Apparently patrons don't complain about all the new music—at least not to the conductor, though he acknowledged that ''they have quite a lot to put up with!'' He also noted: ''I hardly ever get what you might call complaints or surprised comments. Sometimes I think it's surprising myself. A lot of the regular audience, I think, takes rather a pride in just being *subjected* to it,'' he laughed, ''subjected to a lot of complicated unfriendly music.''

In speaking with Robert Irving, one senses—naturally—a great loss when the conductor touches upon his twenty-five-year professional association with George Balanchine. For example, the maestro emphasized Balanchine's unusual musicality: ''Because he could play the piano, he liked to make a choice himself of something that he felt he wanted to do, and then he would ask one's opinion—which he might or might not accept. That was usually the way it happened. I very seldom suggested any music to him, because he was always ranging over the field of music, looking for things.''

During a regular season, things get very busy in the pit, and the pressures of both time and economics have dictated that for much of their repertoire, the dancers at New York City Ballet may never have the opportunity to rehearse with the orchestra at all. When they dance the season's older pieces, the actual performance is often the first time they hear the live music. ''It's gone on that way for a long time,'' Mr. Irving explained. ''There's no complication in the orchestra for works like *Serenade* or *Symphony in C*, and the dancers can listen to a tape for the texture.'' So even most stage rehearsals for the dancers are done with a pianist, who can provide the proper tempos.

Aside from conducting rehearsals and performances, Robert Irving has also collaborated for several television productions, notably *Live from Lincoln Center* and *Dance in America*. For the latter series, the sound track was done separately in New York, and the dancers then went to Nashville for the filming, giving their performance there to pretaped sounds. "It's a good booster," said Mr. Irving of the telecasts.

Another booster are the recordings which he has done with the company's orchestra, featuring the music of some of the best-loved of Balanchine's works. Reviewing one such recording, Edward Willenger wrote in *Ballet International:*

The playing of NYCB's musicians, one should mention, is exemplary throughout A Balanchine Album, with none of the flubs and occasional coarseness that seem inevitably part of the theatrical routine. However, it is, again, to Irving and his orchestra that one will turn to recapture the power of Balanchine's early masterpieces.

Just as the words of a Schubert Lied have become Schubert's words, whoever the poet may have been, so the music of a Balanchine ballet has become Balanchine's composition, not because he appropriated it, but because he seems to have magically re-experienced the creative act, to have relived the decisions, the choices and eliminations that the composer has lived through in bringing it into being. . . . In the light of Balanchine's musical achievements, it is a pleasure to welcome the release of a recording that evokes four Balanchine ballets as vividly as a recording can do. . . . One hopes that A Balanchine Album will mark a new beginning . . . in the recording history of Balanchine's music and musicians.[4]

Mr. Irving himself said in his speech to the Ballet Guild members: "It was marvelous, working with Balanchine. You really couldn't touch him for a musician, because of his superior knowledge of music and the play of music and the construction of music. What a succession of joys! The relationship was, you might say, a relaxed professionalism, which is hard to achieve. I shall never forget it. I'm afraid he's irreplaceable," lamented the conductor.

Then snapping out of his sadness, the British-born conductor cheerily added: "But never mind; we have wonderful dancers around here now. I don't yearn towards London at all. I've been there guesting, but I belong here!" he declared, to warm applause.

When asked how he felt about the audiences interrupting performances with applause, the conductor conceded: "That is a fact of life you get used to. I never get too cast down by a *lack* of applause. I get buoyed up—naturally—by a very responsive audience. Some audiences are going to be rather intrusive, and dancers rather like that. Balanchine used to take steps in certain places to ask the audience not to applaud between the numbers—I think the Mozart *Divertimento* is one, where there is a large series of variations, and the music is of very high quality. I think we've more or less dropped that and let things run their course. It's been so long that it doesn't upset me very much," Robert Irving added philosophically.

DENIS DE COTEAU: COMMITMENT IN SAN FRANCISCO

The San Francisco Ballet gives its home seasons in the city's War Memorial Opera House, where everything is on a grand scale. Even the pit is enormous—

all in the open, and very deep. The musicians do not have to sit under the stage. Consequently, the sound that reaches the audience is quite bright, which encourages the inclusion of the orchestra in the consciousness of those who attend.

The attention and devotion of the ballet's patrons is impressed immediately upon the visitor who steps into the new multimillion dollar home of the ballet company and its school. Inside the doors of these luxurious yet sensible headquarters are the names of the donors—listed, appropriately, in gold. Among the things they financed are pianos in every studio, and spacious offices, including one for the conductor.

That's where the author met Denis de Coteau just after he had led a matinee performance.[5] In his break before the evening program, he described an unusual situation: "The company has made a commitment to the orchestra—an orchestra that is fully resident in the sense that, like any of the major symphony orchestras, you have tenure, and hiring through auditions. We also have a medical plan, a dental plan, an insurance plan for instruments, and so on. It's a rare commitment to a ballet orchestra, that became part of the company's salary structure and comes from the general funding as part of the regular budget considerations."

"In the long run," the conductor pointed out, "the company is making artistic gains when you have an orchestra that is committed to you, and to which you make a commitment. Then you have an orchestra that's going to play well."

The situation in San Francisco was not always this good. Dr. de Coteau recalled that when he first joined in 1970 as assistant conductor, "the orchestra was subject to the whims and fancies of contractors—not the conductor, but the *contractor*. The contractor had—as they all do—many professional friendships that he had built up over the years as a musician himself. So a lot of his friends had retired from other things, and the ballet was just added income for a lot of older musicians."

"I remember days going into the pit to do *Nutcracker* and seeing at least half the string section completely different from the night before," related the conductor with distress. "They were professionals. They could play, so that wasn't the problem. But there were never the same players at almost every show."

Then the maestro told something of a true nightmare: "We went to New York in the seventies. We took our own orchestra from here. Very expensive! But *The New York Times* said, 'This is the finest orchestra we have heard here in the pit since the Bolshoi was here.' Two years later, we went back to New York. Through the advice of various people involved with the company, it was decided to save money, and we used an orchestra that was put together by a contractor in New York." They did not even take any of the solo instrumentalists along.

On opening night, recalled Dr. de Coteau, "there were ten players in the orchestra who had never rehearsed with us. Substitutes! And who were these substitutes? They were sent in by the players who had rehearsed with us, but who had then gotten better-paying jobs. We had different personnel changes every performance, and we were there for a week."

But that wasn't the worst of it, fumed the conductor, still angry years later. "Then we went from New York to Bloomington, Indiana to begin our tour. The orchestra did not travel with us the day that we left, since it was their day off, and the union requirements are that you're not allowed to travel then."

"So the musicians flew out on a Wednesday. They got out to Bloomington in front of the hotel about two o'clock in the afternoon, with an eight o'clock concert that night. I went out to greet the musicians and found that of the thirty-nine players that came from New York, there were eighteen who had never even played a rehearsal or a show with us in New York. They came off that bus—they didn't even have the music because the music was with us—and they went to their hotel rooms, rested, got dressed, went into the pit, and just *butchered* the music," related the conductor, still incredulous.

"The dancers had difficulty dancing," he continued. "Our artistic director, Michael Smuin, was screaming at me during the first number, which my assistant was conducting, and it was going very poorly. I mean, the playing was *awful!* So he kept screaming at me: 'What's going on in the pit? Why isn't he conducting this properly?' And I said, 'Well, he *is* conducting it well. He *knows* about it. But Michael, these are musicians we've never seen. *Eighteen* of them are substitutes.' "

"So when Smuin realized this incredible fact, he was infuriated, because there was no commitment," recalled Dr. de Coteau. "Now, most players do have a commitment to their art, and with such, they would play. But there *are* musicians (they are human beings after all) who, if they can find a better-paying job, will simply go away."

In order to convince the ballet company's board to change all this in 1975, Dr. de Coteau said that all he had to do was make a proposal, and it was immediately approved. "These people are very intelligent human beings," the conductor said of the board. "They appreciate great performances, and they understand that if the lighting is good, the costumes are good, the dancing is good—and if the orchestra plays poorly, then the show is poor. Every facet of a production has to work."

Under the new contracts, allowance was made for sick days, but instrumentalists could no longer arbitrarily send in their own substitutes. Instead, the management has a list of players they feel are responsible artists, so the conductor can now have some control over who is actually playing in his orchestra—at least for the home seasons.

San Francisco Ballet's orchestra does some touring. But when the dancers are sponsored by a symphony orchestra—for instance, in recent years by the

Honolulu Symphony—then the regular musicians have to eat their hearts out at home while the conductor is away. Other cities that provide their own symphonies are Chicago, Cleveland, and Seattle.

In such cases when it's the entire orchestra that is different, Dr. de Coteau has few problems, for as he noted, "with a regular house orchestra, they cannot bring embarrassment to the house by playing poorly." Moreover, the ensemble has already been established by constantly playing together for their own symphonic seasons.

Describing how he felt about his orchestra in recent years, the conductor mentioned, "I would never say we are a 'ballet orchestra.' We are a symphony orchestra which plays special concert performances for which there is dancing. So I don't feel any different about what I do for the ballet than when I guest conduct symphony orchestras. The commitment to the art is the same. The intensity that I feel is the same, because so much of the show rests on my shoulders. I could destroy that show!"

"The orchestra is equally committed now," he emphasized. "As a matter of fact, I think one reason the orchestra is better equipped to play for ballet than any contracted pickup group, is that over a period of time, the musicians have come to know the dancers. They socialize, go to each other's weddings and parties. In fact, we have situations in which a close friend of one of the orchestra members may be dancing a solo that night, and the musician will be sorely tempted not to play his part, because he wants to see his friend dance."

The conductor conceded it would be hard to enforce any rules against peeking at the dancers. On the positive side, he said, "it is true that because of this friendship that has come between the dancers and the orchestra, the musicians have more concern for the dancers. They are co-artists in two different art fields, but they are absolutely tied together by their commitment."

This professional camaraderie is exhibited occasionally in performance, even in some choreography. For instance, in the San Francisco Ballet production of *Papillon* (Eliot Feld's choreography to Offenbach's older ballet music), at one point a delightful giant caterpillar looks down into the pit, and the violist gives him a swipe—as if to say, "Get back into your own territory!"

Artistically, Dr. de Coteau's concerns in the pit center around tempo and the featured dancers. Referring to this particular day, which included a revival of *Filling Station,* he pointed out: "Tonight the young man dancing Mac is about six foot one: big, broad-shouldered, not fat, just well-built. The young man who danced the part of Mac this afternoon was about five-five, slender and very fast. So this afternoon's tempos will not be tonight's tempos. The guy dancing tonight is taller. He's got longer legs and is heavier built, so the tempos for his variation are going to be slightly slower than for the matinee. Not enough to change the musicality of the music-making, but enough to make it possible for him to execute those difficult steps he has to do."

"So my main concern has to be with tempo," the conductor emphasized. "As a matter of fact, before I go into the pit, 90 percent of the time I check to see who's dancing the variations, because in some instances, they *ask* for certain speeds, which I mark in my score."

The musicians, in turn, have to be alert for such variations in speed. "In the pit," warned Dr. de Coteau, "if you vary drastically from what you've been doing, the orchestra *has* to assume that it's related to what's going on up on the stage."

Occasionally, strange things can happen even in the best companies. "For example," related the maestro, "the other day in *Papillon,* there's a place where the harp has a cadenza. When the harpist gets to the bottom of the cadenza, there's a little space, and then a ballerina runs out, and when she snaps into position, we have to play."

"What happened the other night was that they had an electrical short circuit and the backstage speakers went out." The conductor stopped to explain that in San Francisco—as in most big theaters nowadays—there are backstage speakers because the dancers otherwise cannot hear the music coming from the pit.

"So," he continued, "the speakers were not working that particular time and went out while the harpist was playing the cadenza. When he still had about eight more notes to play, the girl ran out and snapped into her pose. I saw her coming and I said 'Oh my God!' and just went with her. The harpist was still playing the cadenza, and the orchestra looked up to see what the hell was going on."

"Looking back on this thing," said the conductor, "I decided that the next time that happened, I wouldn't let it happen! I would let the harpist finish the cadenza, because it confused the orchestra, to start too soon. They didn't play poorly or anything, but it threw them to see me give a downbeat before the harpist's phrase was finished." By coincidence, the same thing did happen again two nights later. Only this time there was only one note left for the harpist. "So I just went with the dancer again," the conductor related.

"Part of this is my fault," said Dr. de Coteau of his relatively minor imperfection, "because I went to ballet school until I was 15 and learned to respond to dancers *too much.* If I had just said, 'Well—tough!' " he laughed.

Denis de Coteau never intended to become a professional dancer. He charmingly confided: "Frankly, I wanted to be a diplomat, a career diplomat in political science. But I was studying music seriously as well. And my parents—particularly my dad—always thought that physical coordination was very important to a young child. So I went to a Mr. Portnoy's School of Ballet in Brooklyn, New York. Nothing like the School of American Ballet or anything, but you know, it was just wonderful!"

"I learned to dance. I learned physical coordination. And I think it's helped me as a conductor, because of the control that I have over my arm," he continued. "You learn in dance that all movements are never finished until they go through the fingertips. The same thing applies in conducting: the movement is not finished until it goes through the end of the baton. In dance, you also learn a sense of tension, release, and arm movements,'' he explained, while giving a delightful demonstration.

''You also learn to take advantage of your height. You have to teach young conductors in the company how to use your height,'' he suggested. ''You know, when you watch a male dancer onstage, he will look *so* tall. If you see him backstage, he seems less so. Then you suddenly realize, it's all in the way you carry yourself. As a student in dance school, I learned to carry myself. I learned how to walk and how to feel this uplift. I love it! I wish every conductor went to dance school.''

Turning again with pride to the subject of his orchestra, Dr. de Coteau mentioned: ''We get great appreciation from board members and other people in the audience. They have a very strong sense of the importance of the music. We *do* get a lot of feedback, and you'll find that people are quite appreciative of this orchestra.''

Paying some well-deserved tribute to the conductor, Janice Ross wrote in the *Oakland Tribune:*

> As the crucial liaison between musicians and dancers, de Coteau takes his job very seriously. . . . Several years ago he was offered an assistantship with one of the country's major orchestras but turned it down in favor of staying with the ballet, a decision others chided him about. ''They said to me, 'Aw, come on! Ballet conductor? That's the lowest thing on the totem pole!' And I agreed, says de Coteau. ''Except that I pointed out that some of the lowest people who came off that pole were Sir George Solti, conductor of the Chicago Symphony; Charles Lynch, former conductor of the Boston; Antal Dorati, and Eugene Ormandy, and those were just a few of the great names who came out of the pit. I consider myself in good company.''
>
> ''When my conducting students ask me what they have to do to be a ballet conductor,'' he smiles, ''I tell them that you have to have a very thick skin, because no matter what you do the tempo is always too fast, or else it's always too slow. Early on you have to develop the ability to take criticism.''
>
> Few conductors are as responsive to their dancers as de Coteau, and it is a sensitivity he demands from any conductor. De Coteau remembers a new conductor who auditioned by conducting a performance of Balanchine's ''Concerto Barocco.'' When he came to the final chord, which he had been instructed to hold, he suddenly cut it off, having decided that it altered the overall balance of Bach's music. ''It was true that it did disturb the balance of the music,'' admits de Coteau, ''but it was *essential* to the choreography that it be held so the dancers could finish out their last position. As it was, he left them hanging on in absolute silence. He wasn't hired.''[6]

MAURICE KAPLOW: KEEPING TIME IN PENNSYLVANIA AND MILWAUKEE

Undoubtedly, much of the upbeat atmosphere in the performances of the Pennsylvania-Milwaukee Ballet is due to the conducting of Maurice Kaplow, who has been with the original Philadelphia company since 1964.

A violist who took special delight in chamber music, he was also a member of the Philadelphia Orchestra. During the course of his conducting studies with Pierre Monteux, the latter had suggested that the greatest thing for conducting experience would be to do ballet, since things happen in ballet that do not occur in other musical circumstances.

A ballet conductor must learn to use rubato (a slight bending of the tempo for purposes of phrasing) and to make the orchestra respond promptly to unplanned events. For example, Mr. Kaplow said that he had to use his hands in slightly different ways to communicate such directions to his musicians. He feels almost as if he must choreograph the orchestra.[7]

Tempo is the one subject that comes up again and again in speaking with ballet orchestra conductors. But Mr. Kaplow manages to maintain his musicality, and is particularly mindful of trying to minimize changes in the well-known classical symphonies. ''If the choreography is good, as with Balanchine, then there is no problem with distorting the music,'' he asserted. He feels a great responsibility to the dancers and mentioned, ''I have always thought that the dance is the greatest experience of classical art.''

Nevertheless, one thing that all musicians seem to bring up when recalling their first rehearsals with dancers is the word ''disaster.'' They discover that playing music for the dance is startlingly different from doing Beethoven symphonies in concert. Mr. Kaplow said he was no exception. But he seems to have developed a winning sensitivity and warmth towards the ballet and its different requirements during his first two decades with the Pennsylvania company. One of the first things he did was to throw himself wholeheartedly into taking ballet classes for a whole year.

At first, he related, many musicians do not foresee problems because dancers rehearse with a pianist routinely. The orchestra learns its new music separately in two or three strictly musical rehearsals. It is in the putting together of these two forces that experience counts.

Mr. Kaplow's familiarity with all the dancers in the original Pennsylvania company led to a very special collaboration, when he composed a forty-five-minute work, *Signatures,* a showcase with choreography by Benjamin Harkarvey. Not only was the choreography tailor-made to highlight each dancer in a very personal way, but the music too was specially created, by a musician who knew each performer and who wrote music to support the specialties of each dancer. The choreographer set only the time: ''This one is two minutes.'' Otherwise on his own, the conductor-composer came up with thirty original dances, including solos, groups, pas de deux, jazz sections, and a grand finale.

Even though the recent reorganization of the dual-city Pennsylvania and Milwaukee Ballet has required Mr. Kaplow to spend more time on administrative work, he nevertheless continues with various composing and arranging projects for the company. For instance, recently he was granted permission by Leonard Bernstein to arrange excerpts from the operetta *Candide* as a ballet for choreography by Richard Tanner. Another project, with Robert Weiss as choreographer, called for Mr. Kaplow to arrange various excerpts from Tchaikovsky's works—from operas, overtures, and incidental music. These were presented as a full-length ballet called *Winter Dreams,* which garnered favorable critical reviews.

And then there is that cantata which Mr. Kaplow keeps mentioning he is working on. It is conceived as a purely musical piece, but, given the varied choices of choreographers nowadays, there seems to be no reason to rule out even a cantata as possible music for the dance.

STANLEY SUSSMAN: JET-SET CONDUCTOR

Another of the nation's dual-city arrangements exists with the Cleveland–San Jose Ballet, of which Stanley Sussman is the music director. In their midwestern home city, the company hires the Ohio Chamber Orchestra; on the west coast, they employ the entire San Jose Symphony.

Speaking with the author in his New York home base, Mr. Sussman emphasized that each of these regular orchestras is not just a ballet orchestra.[8] As concert organizations, they insist on certain things. For instance, he mentioned: "The Ohio group pressures Cleveland Ballet for a certain amount of rehearsal time, because if they don't sound good, or if they don't get good coverage in the press during the ballet season, they are afraid that this will reflect on their organization and work against their own concert season. So we have a situation where the Cleveland Ballet gives more rehearsal time per piece than the Graham Company does, or when I conduct for Nureyev and Friends."

When Stanley Sussman has toured with the Martha Graham Company, a full orchestra has not gone along—with the exception of their 1966 travels. So there has always been a different orchestra, even if the dancers were doing the same repertoire over and over.

Having coped with such situations, Mr. Sussman related: "I have developed a technique of going into rehearsals and rehearsing really very quickly. Waste as little time as possible. I can't approach it as a recital, where I could be very picky and meticulous as much as I want. I must go for the general scope, and be meticulous enough with what I see as the weakest spots before we get into a dress rehearsal. Again, because the music is new—not new in terms of date of composition, but new in terms of most musicians not having played the music in the Graham repertory—if they can get an idea of what the tempos are, then by the time we get into dress rehearsal, we're one step ahead."

Elaborating a bit on what it's like to conduct for Martha Graham's works, this artist said: "It's an intense experience because the music is not generally what we would call 'light music.' It's very serious music, mostly. The lightest piece would be something like *Every Soul Is a Circus,* with Paul Nordoff's score. But that piece had so many sight cues and so many stop-go changes in tempo, that *conducting* it was also an intense experience, even though the music isn't. The *conductor* really has to be on his toes, so to speak, to make sure everything matches.''

''The world knows Martha Graham as a dramatic choreographer, a dramatic theatrical personality, a dramatic creator in terms of movement. So I can't avoid the feelings that I get from the choreography,'' said Mr. Sussman. ''I allow myself to feel the choreography; I allow myself to feel the music, and I conduct the tempos that evolve as a result of finding out what the working tempos are for the dancers. Then I go out and perform as hard as I can! I *have* to keep the orchestra together, so the conducting technique is very meticulous. I'm not free up there. We're not doing free-based stuff. It's very carefully conducted and very carefully played. We're not improvising.''

''One reason why the Graham theater comes off as it does,'' he explained, ''is because the music is used in one way some times and at others more literally. Sometimes the choreography will go 'on' the music without being on the *beat*. You pick up a pulse from the music in your mind, but the pulse of the dancing might be in-between, faster, or slower, to create a dramatic effect.''

''There's a pull between the music and the movement in the choreography of Martha Graham,'' Mr. Sussman went on to observe. ''Whenever a person is portraying an emotion—like Aegisthus in *Clytemnestra*—sometimes his movements are very literal, very linked to the rhythmic structure of the music. At times, during certain seductive scenes between Aegisthus and Clytemnestra, they are not. Yet it is 'with' the music. I think the conductor just has to know the choreography well enough to understand that there were varying places—that it is not a matter of being 'on' or 'off' the music. It's just a matter of what is happening dramatically.''

''If you see on-the-beat dancing in jazz,'' he pointed out, ''you could see if the music is sometimes fast or too slow it might be a problem. It's a little easier to understand why, while time must be spent with something like the Martha Graham vocabulary to get an insight into it.''

In Mr. Sussman's earlier years with the Graham Company, there were new works being commissioned all the time. ''I would work with the composer briefly,'' he related. ''Then I would spend a great deal of time with Miss Graham.''

Tempos were always the main concern. ''I wanted to present the tempos that the *composers* wanted,'' Mr. Sussman emphasized. ''So during the piano rehearsals, and during choreography sessions, I would collaborate with the composers regarding the music, to bring out what they wanted.''

He recalled his work with Carlos Surinach for *The Owl and the Pussy Cat*. ''I loved that,'' smiled the maestro. Again, his primary concern was simply to check the tempos, because the composer's orchestrations were so clear. ''I had conducted Surinach's *Embattled Garden* previously,'' Mr. Sussman noted, ''and there are other works of his that the Graham Company uses. So that by the time we did *The Owl and the Pussy Cat,* we were all familiar with his style. There were no problems.''

Seeing the conductor smile out of a photograph taken with Rudolf Nureyev at Sardi's restaurant, one could momentarily think; oh yes, conducting: lots of glamor, tuxedos, lots of parties, lots of friendships with superstars. But what of the twenty years before that photo was taken? That's part of the total picture.

Stanley Sussman's initial involvement with dance goes back to the time he was a teenager in Brooklyn and belonged to a neighborhood folk dance group that did both European and Middle Eastern forms. As an adult, he studied ballet on and off, just as a hobby, and to help him understand the art form better. However, he doesn't think it's necessary to study dancing to be a musician for dance. ''It helped me in developing a relaxed attitude towards dance, because when people do something themselves, it gives them an easier rapport when they're around those who do it full-time. Studying ballet also helped me understand the length that a person has to go in order to become a good dancer,'' he said.

But what is most important for a conductor of dance music, he thinks, is a general attitude of really liking music and dance. ''I don't think a conductor can see it as a regression in his or her own conducting career,'' he insisted. ''I would say there are those who do it for a living, and if they got a full-time position in something else, with a symphony orchestra or something like that, they wouldn't do the dance work. I don't know about 'hating' it. I've never heard *that* from a conductor for dance—and if they do, they would never admit it. But it *is* a difficult job for a conductor to do, because you have to blend your own conducting techniques to make the orchestra sound good, and make it work with the movement. And that's not an easy task.''

A major impetus for Stanley Sussman's interest in dance collaboration was his service in the Nineteenth Army Band, which required him to play the piano for many USO dances. He loved improvising in ''non-balletic styles,'' as he put it, and he learned to go with the movement on the floor of the dance hall. At the time of his military service, he also enjoyed writing some big band music.

Returning to civilian life in New York, Mr. Sussman was invited, through the recommendation of a friend, to play for studio classes at the Martha Graham School. ''Within a very short period of time,'' he recounted, ''it all blossomed, and I was playing all over Manhattan: at the Neighborhood Playhouse, Barnard, Juilliard, the Graham School . . . and I was developing into a dance musician.''

''There's no fortune in this work, in terms of [the] dollar,'' he acknowledged. ''I was doing it mostly out of excitement, because it was a chance to play structured music without worrying about the material. I didn't play any repertoire whatsoever—just improvised constantly. It was all modern; no ballet at that point.''

"It was also wearing," admitted Mr. Sussman. "About two years into this, I said to myself, 'Now what? It's time for something else.' Then the phone rang at that instant. It was the Martha Graham Dance Company calling to say that in the fall of that year [1966] they were going on a very big transcontinental tour—an eight-week coast-to coast bus and truck tour with full orchestra—and was I interested in going as a second conductor? I said yes!"

"So what happened was for a number of years I would play classes, rehearsals, *and* conduct," Mr. Sussman explained. "At that time, it was extremely exciting, to start with Martha Graham as a conductor working on that scope with full orchestra."

Although with the Graham Company he does not have a cohesive permanent orchestra as he does in Cleveland, Mr. Sussman in recent years has been able to insist that at least in New York the orchestral contractor bring back as many people as possible from past seasons. "Getting a high percentage of return in the orchestra is a serious goal," he emphasized. "It insures a tighter orchestral sound. It gives us a chance to work on the new music that's been added to the repertoire, and it gives the orchestra a chance to review pieces that they've played before, so that they are not looking at ten or twelve pieces for the first time."

JONATHAN MCPHEE: SKILLS OF A CONDUCTOR FOR DANCE

"It *does* take special skills to conduct for dance," agreed Jonathan McPhee.[9] Expanding on the subject, he suggested: "Look at some of these symphony concerts where some of the big ballet stars come in as guests, and watch what happens with the usual symphony conductor." He implied that all does not necessarily go well for the dancers—or the music. Yet one way to learn, he admitted, is just to do it. "Make mistakes and figure out what works. In the end, I think you either have the knack or you don't."

Mr. McPhee himself had already conducted a number of seasons with the Joffrey Ballet and the Martha Graham Company, in addition to guest-conducting with the New York City Ballet and continuing his performing on the oboe. With this perspective, he particularly deplored the strange consensus among many of his musician colleagues who might say, as a general statement about anybody, "Oh, he's conducting for ballet because he can't do anything else." Such observers conveniently overlook the fact that a number of prominent symphonic conductors have chosen to do ballet work for many years—such as Pierre Monteux, Antal Dorati, and Ernst Ansermet, for example.

Noting the lack of special training or courses available for dance conductors, Mr. McPhee expressed the opinion that a conductor for dance should be trained first and foremost as a good symphonic conductor.

"I'm a perfectionist," he continued. "I like to do everything very well, and I'm one of these people who prepares, whether or not something will happen." In line with that outlook, he took advantage of the time when he lived with his family in London. "I had a little system," he recalled. "I would see two operas a month, and four ballets. I figured if I ever had an opportunity to conduct ballet, I should know what's going on and what the problems are."

Similarly, when he was teaching in upstate New York later on, Mr. McPhee availed himself of the opportunity to take dance classes with Edna Simmons. "I'll be forever in her debt," he said graciously of that teacher.

"The point is," the musician went on to explain, "I got to understand body timing. An awful lot of it is physics. For example, if you're a baseball player and you're standing at bat, and the baseball comes at you, you've got a split second to judge, to know where to swing—and when, and how."

"It's the same idea in dance," he said. "There's that athletic quality. When a dancer goes for something, there's a preparation that lets you know how fast, how far, and *when* they are going to get there. The preparation is important. Martha Graham calls it the breath. When you breathe together and are preparing together, it all lines up."

When he was fresh out of Juilliard, Jonathan McPhee's first position in the dance world was as conductor for a European tour with the Martha Graham Company. After several years with the company, he developed a method of learning the extensive repertoire. First he studies the musical scores by himself. Then, if a video of past performances is available, he looks at that. "It's one of the greatest aids of today," he observed, "because that way you learn the choreography. To conduct ballet really well, you *have* to know the choreography. You have to know *why* the choreography went to that music."

"I'm acutely aware of the choreographer's views on music and style," he emphasized. "That has to weigh in the interpretation. The approach is partly psychological. You have to look at the characters in terms of what their impact is. You find your musical approach also through the choreography itself and the individual dancers' interpretations—which affects the timing of the music."

"The next step is to look at the bare bones and technical problems. Where do they need more room? What is the top level of speed you can go at before it becomes a problem and the dancers can't do the steps? So you have the physical aspects, and you also ask, 'What am I trying to say as a musician?' "

"With the Graham dances," said Mr. McPhee, "there is a meshing, but it took me a long time to find it. Instead of going 'this step–this step–this step' as in classical ballet, you might line up every three bars. You have to know it well enough and work it out well enough in your head to be able to know where the music and the movement are supposed to go along. Once you know the style, you don't have to know exactly what happens bar by bar. Then you're looking at it through the right set of glasses, so to speak. I always give myself musically acceptable adjustment places, just to be sure."

It was as an oboist that Jonathan McPhee was first noticed by New York City Ballet's conductor Robert Irving. So before he was given the opportunity to guest conduct for the ballet, he had already worked in the pit as a substitute player.

As Mr. McPhee's career progressed, he went on to become the conductor for the Joffrey Ballet. In that company's Los Angeles location, there is a fairly stable musical group, noted the conductor. "There's a contracted orchestra out there, so at least you can build on that. About 70 percent of the players are the same from season to season. In the other cities we visit, we use the symphony orchestras—which are good. At Kennedy Center, it's the Opera House orchestra; in San Francisco, it's the San Francisco Symphony. We also use the San Diego Symphony, the Rochester Philharmonic, and the Grand Rapids Symphony—which was a wonderful surprise, because it's a young orchestra, but very good."

"All of this gives me a chance to work with several high-level orchestras," noted Mr. McPhee. "But one thing about playing with an orchestra that is *used* to playing in the pits," he emphasized, "is that even if it's a free-lance group, they know from night to night there are going to be fluctuations in tempos. Pauses may be longer—or suddenly not there at all. In contrast, a symphony is used to basically preparing for a concert where everything will be constant. So very often, until they get used to it, there's a little bit of push-pull that happens. For me to do something, and for them to follow, there's a little lag. Then they get used to the idea."

"Once you build up a relationship of trust with the dancers," observed the conductor, "you can understand what the problems are. The thing I always go for is this: if you took away the dance, the musical performance should still stand up. It should be a valid musical interpretation."

"But just as there's no one 'right' recording of Beethoven's Fifth," he suggested, "you can perform something like *Serenade* in a number of different ways. When you know that choreography and understand what Balanchine was listening to when he choreographed it, then you can develop a musical interpretation that supplies what the dancers need, and is yet musically valid."

"For example Balanchine's tempos are not the traditional 'musician's tempos' taken for Tchaikovsky's *Serenade for Strings.* Talk to any musicians, and they'll say it's too slow in various places. I really had trouble coming to terms with the fact that it was different," confided the conductor. "I cornered Balanchine one day briefly and said 'I'm having trouble with this. I don't understand . . .' and he said, 'I know what you're going to say.' (He obviously had heard it before.) 'Rather than accepting the view, the tempo that you know, go back and listen to the inner tempo of the folk idiom. If you listen to it, there is a certain folk quality to it, to the themes. Just look at it with fresh eyes,' " the choreographer advised him.

"So I did," related Jonathan McPhee, "and it gave me a new perspective. Right now I can click into the tempos. They work!

"So Balanchine found other qualities in the music that were not usually brought out. It's not so much the instrumental balance as much as it is the quality of the music's folk roots: singing simply, not going for the power and the technique; looking at the simplicity of it. I think that's it, basically."

GLEN CORTESE: CONDUCTING FOR ERICK HAWKINS

While many others in the field of modern concert dance complain they can't afford live music, Erick Hawkins has always had live musicians play for his dance performances. He has accomplished this mainly by molding his musical repertoire to fit a financially manageable chamber ensemble of seven musicians, and by asking his collaborating composers to write specifically for this combination.

For recent tours and concert seasons, Mr. Hawkins has had an able and enthusiastic conductor at the helm in the person of Glen Cortese. A faculty member at the Manhattan School of Music, with a doctorate in composition from the same institution, Mr. Cortese is one of that rare breed of conductors whose mastery of contemporary scores verges on brilliance. And he delights in his experience with dance.[10]

"Working with Erick is very special because of his theory of dance," he said. "A lot of the ideas he tries to communicate are extremely closely related to the music. He's very shrewd about what's going on in the music."

"Conducting is a day-to-day kind of business," he went on. "You really don't know what's going to happen next. I really do enjoy dance. It is one of my favorite things as a conductor. It's the biggest challenge—even more so than opera—because your reflexes have to be so sharp that you can follow a dancer, even when a movement is made without preparation. With a singer, you can watch. You have words, you have breath, as a preparation. But with dance, there's frequently no preparation at all. So it's timing, rehearsal, and watching—really being on top of what's going on."

At rehearsals, Mr. Cortese does note down precise metronome markings, just to give himself a bearing. "You have to gear yourself flexibly from that," he warned. "I use a metronome as a tool. But you have to be very careful from there, because you never know what the dancers are going to want. It's a pretty precarious part of the business."

The conductor confessed that when he is working in the pit, he cannot always watch everything. What then, does he pay most attention to onstage? "It depends," he said. "Cues can come from any part of the body—sometimes the feet or the hands, sometimes just the turn of a head. It can be just about anything. Usually I write the cue in the score to help me know what I'm looking for. Sometimes it's a line of text if the dance has a story to it. For instance, we do one piece called *The Joshua Tree,* and it's about greed and outlaws who steal some money, and their demise. They have a dialogue onstage, and sometimes the words are cued. Other times, it's the movement itself.''

Describing his pleasure in making an initial tour with the Erick Hawkins Dance Company, Glen Cortese noted: ''We have seven players and a conductor, and there are eight dancers. We all travelled by bus and truck. The tech people went separately to take the costumes and scenery and all. I have trouble keeping count now of how many concerts we actually did—somewhere between thirty and fifty, but it was a lot. In the first two weeks, including lecture demos, I think we had a total of either nine or ten performances. We did a run at Kennedy Center earlier in that year to open their Dance America series. Then we did a run here in New York City for a full week—seven nights and one matinee, straight.''

''On our tour itself,'' he continued, ''we went [to] a lot of interesting places, starting at the University of the South in Sewanee, Tennessee. The next place was Hayes, Kansas. Then we were in San Antonio and Edinburgh, Texas, down there at the border. Next was Louisiana . . . and so on. It was a Southeast and Midwest trip, generally in college theaters.''

When other modern dance troupes tour the college circuits nowadays, they almost invariably perform to tape recordings. ''That's what makes Erick so special compared to other choreographers,'' Mr. Cortese noted. ''He *never* does a performance without live music. He believes it adds an element of intensity and excitement—something you just can't get when people are sitting there listening to a tape. I agree with him. I think it's a very special kind of union of two art forms. If that's lost, the overall performance really does lose a lot of its luster, even if the choreography is fantastic.''

On that first tour, Mr. Cortese especially appreciated the opportunity to talk with the dancers. ''That was really kind of nice,'' he recalled, ''because everything I had done with them up until then entailed running in and out of performances. I didn't really get to know them. You go down the day before; you do the rehearsal; you go and do the job; and then you come home and you don't see them until the next time. But on the tour, you got to talk with people and to know them over the course of several weeks. After it was over, I think all of us felt a lot closer, and the working situation is very comfortable. If there is a problem, there's much less tension now. We can work it out because we know each other better.''

What kinds of questions do the dancers take up with him? ''Tempo!'' he replied, like so many other conductors. ''Tempo! Because whenever you get a new conductor, the dancers are used to whatever the *last* person was doing a certain way. Sometimes what happens is that if you're with a company a long time, a conductor can start to adjust a little *too* much to the dance and not do justice to the music, which is also terribly important.

''Erick has choreographed the dance to the music in an original way, and I think if that gets altered too much to accommodate each individual dancer, you start to do injustice to the music. I'm not inflexible. But I'm only going to bend to a certain point, because I'm very concerned with what goes on in the score too. I am a *musician* first. It's important for me to really honestly play what's on the page. Also, it keeps you on your toes a little bit more!''

Glen Cortese seems perfectly suited to the repertoire of the Hawkins company. ''I've always been interested in modern music,'' he said. ''Because of that, I've seen a lot of modern dance. Sometimes I'll go to *hear* a certain piece, and it happens to be choreographed. Multimedia ideas are a very twentieth-century thing, where people will use more than one art form to get their ideas across. I've seen a lot of these, some pretty avant-garde, and some pretty standard.''

Asked if he found differences between concert audiences and those who attend dance programs, Mr. Cortese replied: ''Yes. If it's billed as a dance event, mostly just people who are interested in dance are going to come. But sometimes not. If you have a special piece of music, and musicians and others who want to hear the *music,* they will come to the dance performance mainly to hear the piece.''

Audiences at colleges frequently include people who are particularly open to trying new things. When the Hawkins Company tours, Glen Cortese sometimes has a chance to talk to the students and to hear what they thought of it all. ''It's surprising,'' he remarked. ''New Yorkers get kind of snobby sometimes and think other audiences are not educated for the arts. That may be true to a certain extent, but outside of New York, they are also much less prejudiced about the arts. I found that on tour, people were much more open to new things than they are here! What's happened in this city is that you get specialized audiences: people who go to new music concerts, people who go to new dance events, and people who go to traditional music concerts. Of course you get some people who go to all of them, but it's become just as much specialized as the city itself. You know, we have specialized jobs here, specialized ethnic sections of the city . . . and specialized concert audiences. It really just goes along with everything else that happens in a big city.''

''On tour,'' he observed, ''I found that people were much more open to hearing new pieces and were not 'turned off' by something they didn't know. They didn't have preconceived notions about 'what music should sound like.' ''

Contrasting the often more practical world of theatrical music-making with the kind of music that all too frequently comes out of academic environments, Glen Cortese remarked: ''I like performing and composing, and personally I feel that a lot of the university composers that I've dealt with are writing 'university type' music. Maybe it's stupid to say 'intellectual music,' because all music is intellectual—*but it's not geared too much to reaching an audience.* A lot of them tend to have the attitude that the *process* is more important than the result. I think the result is a lot more important than the process!'' declared the conductor.

Turning once again to his little chamber ensemble at the Hawkins Company, Mr. Cortese noted that his instrumentalists were fully professional—even virtuosic—but on the young side. Often they were people just recently out of school.

"Money is a prohibitive factor," conceded the conductor. "I couldn't go out and hire free-lancers who have been on the scene for twenty years. I formed the group with people that I had worked with, or otherwise knew that they played well. They either had some exposure to contemporary music, or a special liking for it. I chose people that I knew could handle the job. When you don't have a lot of rehearsal time, you can't deal with people who aren't prepared. Unfortunately, some professional musicians that have been around a long time get lazy and don't care as they should."

Pondering what he himself cared about, Mr. Cortese confided: "It's funny. You do the things you're 'supposed' to do to get ahead in a career, but I really don't think about it so much anymore. You know, you apply for the next job and do whatever the daily events require. But I really do try and enjoy every minute of whatever I'm doing at the time, and don't think of 'Well, what is this going to lead to?' because you miss out on so much, if you do that. You really do miss the thing *itself* if you are always thinking 'Well, what can this project do for me next?' I have found that living this way, and getting the most out of each individual thing, has made me a lot happier person. So I'll just keep doing it and see what happens."

Somehow, Glen Cortese's philosophical outlook seems particularly appropriate for a conductor who works with the fleeting art of the dance.

DONALD MAHLER: BALLET MASTER AT THE METROPOLITAN OPERA

In the world of ballet and modern dance, it is generally the musicians and conductors who are cast in supportive roles. At the opera, this balance is reversed.

Donald Mahler described what it was like to be ballet master at the Metropolitan Opera, where the dancers contribute to the variety and visual pleasures of the musical works—but where they can also serve to deepen the plot or effectively evoke a specific time and place.[11] The dance master also had some things to say about relationships between conductors and choreographers in a medium that focuses essentially on the music rather than the movement.

The starting point of Mr. Mahler's career as a choreographer came when a singer at the Metropolitan Opera injured herself and could not do any kind of movement in her role as *Salome* (by Saint-Saëns); it was decided to enlist the aid of the ballet for some sections.

"I was asked to create a dance at the last minute—like in one-and-a-half days," recalled the artist. "This is really unusual, and it's a ten-minute-long piece with mammoth orchestra. At first, my instinct was to say no. But then I have this other instinct which is to *never* say no. So I decided, and just did it.

"In the music, you hear references to things that have happened earlier in the opera—things that have been said, feelings that have been felt, and dramatic situations that took place. So my feeling was that as she's dancing, she reminisces in her mind. I knew what the themes refer to, because I know the opera very well. She may have sung at one point to John the Baptist, 'Oh what a beautiful body you have,' and then that theme comes back in this dance. So with some kind of acting and pantomime and movement, I kept this feeling, as though she would get lost in her thoughts and then come back to her dance."

"It was a wonderful experience!" exclaimed the pleased choreographer. "I never really expected that I was going to have such a thrill out of it."

Donald Mahler went on to choreograph a total of seven ballets for the Met operas, and to present the ballet company in separate performances. (There were, at that time, twenty-three dancers who would get independent bookings as the Metropolitan Opera Ballet Company in addition to their appearances on the opera stage.)

Giving a further sampling of what it is like to choreograph for an opera ballet company, Mr. Mahler described *Francesca da Rimini:* "There's a scene where there are four demi-solo singers who sing about spring. The director wanted them to move around, but I suggested that it was very difficult to get singers to move at all—much less when they're singing. So we agreed to use the ballet girls, and I did a kind of Botticelli thing with garlands for one part of it, and there was another interesting part, with doves."

Though he spoke with pleasure of his experiences with opera ballets, Donald Mahler seemed to feel rather despondent about what he perceives as "competition" between some conductors and musicians on the one hand, and choreographers and dancers on the other. His impression is that musicians in general often seem to have the attitude that they have to teach the dancers about music. The way that they do this—or the fact that they felt a need to do it at all—can make for some antagonism.

"Basically," Mr. Mahler acknowledged, "for the most part, you're at the mercy of the conductors. They are not really going to give you anything special. The ballet is the lowest rung on the totem pole at the opera." The choreographer did make some exceptions. "Occasionally, I would be able to go to a conductor—for some of them were very nice—and ask for a little slower. Basically, it was usually for a little slower. Usually the conductors like to breeze through."

Commenting about his work on some of the older operas, such as *Vespri Siciliani,* Mr. Mahler said: "You know, there's a kind of school of thought nowadays amongst a lot of the directors at the opera that the ballet should be seen 'very little.' The music is playing, and they don't want you to look like dancers."

However, he pointed out, many operas also have genuine dance forms in them. For instance, in the middle of a celebration, the characters will do a tarantella or some other folk dance. And some of the operas have set artistic pieces like the "Dance of the Hours" in *La Gioconda,* which is actually meant to portray an entertainment for the characters in the opera.

"For *Forza del Destino,*" said the choreographer, "I managed to make more of a dance. Before I got to it, the director had eliminated the dancing almost completely, and I had to sneak it in. I tried to make a dance that looked *natural.* I didn't put in any artificial elements like tour en l'air and entrechats or grands jetés. I tried to do steps that were character-oriented and looked as if they could be done by the people in the scene. You have to find a balance."

Donald Mahler was asked if the Met conductors generally seemed aware of the dancers—if they looked up, and so forth. "Oh yes," he replied. "Jimmy Levine would often come into the rehearsal to see what was going on and some of the others would do that too. It wasn't so bad, but you really couldn't ask for *major* things. They tend to feel that the music is more important than the dance. They don't want to do what they call 'sacrifice' the music. You may have to strike a compromise, that's all."

However, the choreographer offered a few comments that reflected some uncomfortable feelings which other dancers seem to share: "Musicians always feel that their place is more important—even the ones that play for ballet performances. They don't think ballet dancers are musical. They don't think that what choreographers do or ask for in the music is 'musical.' "

"Though I love music more than anything else, I have a very low opinion of that aspect of musicians," Mr. Mahler said. "They're at times some of the worst people to work with," he remarked in exasperation. Relenting a little bit, he added: "Not always—not at *all* always. But sometimes . . . !"

Asked to pick the most important thing that he wished musicians understood about the dance, Mr. Mahler was quick to respond: "That the feeling for the proper tempos is not just a musical thing; it's a *physical* thing with dancers. There are not many people who understand that."

"I'll tell you what it is, actually," he continued, giving an example from his own experience. "I am a very poor pianist. But I play piano, and I used to sometimes, just for fun, accompany a lady who was in our ballet orchestra, someone who played the cello.

"She said that I was an absolutely wonderful accompanist. She wasn't referring to the fact that I could technically play the notes. But I was able to really accompany her—to sense when she wanted to go faster or slower, and to *be with her.* It's the same as a pianist who plays for a singer. It's an accompaniment."

"And that's what a good ballet conductor should do," Donald Mahler concluded. "He should have the feeling that he is *with* the dancers—not subservient. It has nothing to do with who is top dog!"

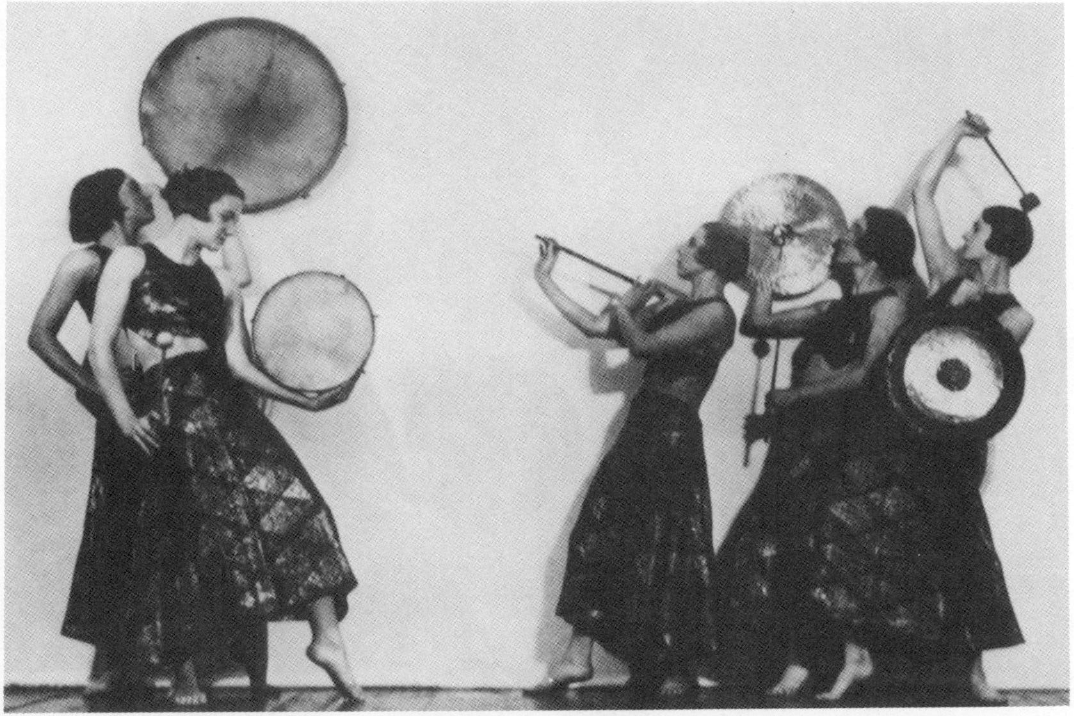

Disciples of Mary Wigman in a Percussion Chorus—including Hanya Holm, at center with flute. Photo by Charlotte Rudolph, Dresden, 1923. Courtesy of the Dance Collection, The New York Public Library at Lincoln Center, Astor, Lenox and Tilden Foundations.

Jean Erdman with two of her collaborators: John Cage (l.) and Lou Harrison (r.). Photo © Robert Holder

Dance Theatre of Harlem production of *Fall River Legend.* Choreography by Agnes de Mille; musical score by Morton Gould. Photo © Jack Vartoogian.

The composer Otto Leuning at work. Photo © Chou Wen-Chung.

Life on Broadway: Mary Martin Lands on Arranger Trude Rittmann. Drawing © Roy Doty.

A Disagreement About Tempo. Drawing © Roy Doty.

Sneaking a Peek. Drawing © Roy Doty.

Tania Leon conducting a rehearsal of one of her own compositions. Photo © Marbeth.

A Musician Dances: Flutist Elizabeth Brown performing *Jolivet Incantations.* Choreography by Jesse Duranceau. Photo © Otto M. Berk.

Alvin Ailey Company, with onstage drummer, in celebration of Katherine Dunham's choreography. Photo © Jack Vartoogian.

Natalia Makarova in her own production of *La Bayadère* with American Ballet Theatre. Photo © Jack Vartoogian.

Mikhail Baryshnikov performing Balanchine's *Theme and Variations* with ABT. Photo © Jack Vartoogian.

A Hawkins Dancer: Laura Pettibone in *Black Lake*, with music by Lucia Dlugoszewski. Photo © 1988 Jonathan Atkin.

Final Tableau of Jerome Robbins' *Ives, Songs.* The New York City Ballet. Photo © Steven Caras.

Conclusion of Eliot Feld's ballet *The Unanswered Question* performed by New York City Ballet in their American Music Festival. Photo © Steven Caras.

SILENT ARTISTS SPEAK

9

Dancers' Tales

Often in ballet classes, teachers shush talkative young students by explaining that Terpsichore, the Greek Muse of dance, was mute. "You don't talk while you're dancing!" they admonish.

Indeed, dancers are usually in the limelight for their visual artistry; yet a number of dancers who were interviewed expressed strong opinions about the musical aspects of their endeavors as well.

TWO HAWKINS PERFORMERS

Long before he danced professionally with Erick Hawkins, James Reedy played percussion at the Chicago Dance Center—a place he called "the essence, the highlight, of what was going on in modern dance in that city."[1]

"They gave me an hourglass drum and asked me if I could accompany a class, because there was an accompanist that did not come. I did it, and the woman who was teaching the class said 'You're terrific. Why don't you accompany my class from now on?' So I did, but I got so involved with the dancing, that I started studying dance myself," said Mr. Reedy.

Then followed many years of learning Balinese styles, ballet, and jazz dance—all on top of finishing law school. However, explained Mr. Reedy, he had been in athletics all his life and had some conditioning which helped his dancing. But this performer really did get involved with dance initially by drumming for it. "Yes!" he confirmed. "In fact, after I accompanied that first class, I joined an Afro-dance class, where I learned how to dance and drum on the congas at the same time. That was my main thrill. I wanted to be a percussionist."

All this explains Jim Reedy's lively studio entrances—by way of the drum sets—before rehearsals with the Hawkins company. Nowadays he can communicate excitement not only with his drumming hands, but also with his entire being. Mr. Reedy nodded. ''That's why I love the dance so much. It builds that sense of cosmos up to such a pitched degree.''

This performer has had experiences that are still very rare: he knows what it is to sit and play music for other people to dance to, and he knows what it is to dance to live music that others are playing for him.

What happens inside? What's different when you are the one who is dancing? ''It's more captivating,'' suggested Mr. Reedy. ''My attention has to be in the moment, especially when I'm with people like the Hawkins company, that are really very good dancers. When I first got here, I had to learn how to be in the moment—constantly, without even getting excited or enthusiastic: to have my complete attention on what the dynamic was, what the rhythm was, and the form that was going on at any given point.''

With so many new works to learn—all of them to initially unfamiliar music—how did he know where he was supposed to be in a dance? ''It's body language—I should say body *memory,*'' explained the performer. ''I can walk in without thinking about a dance, and my *body* will remember the dance before my mind does. So when the music is playing, it's almost like an automatic reflex for the dancer to move to the choreography.''

''When I'm 'clean' in dance—when I feel that I'm totally present in mind, body, spirit, if you will—I can see myself doing the next movement right before I go into it,'' he continued. ''I can 'see' myself extending energy into the image of what I'm doing. I can go through a dance with bodily memory alone, but in terms of the precision and intensity, that always comes back. The image is there too. I'm usually 'into' the image of where the movement is going, of where the phrase is going next.''

''Let me put it this way,'' Mr. Reedy continued. ''One of my exercises is to be able to visualize the dance: just to sit down and visualize it, mentally. Usually when I'm visualizing, it's done rhythmically; it's done dynamically, formally, spatially, sensationally. I can actually remember sensations of moving through patterns.''

When asked what the relation of all this is to the sounds that come out of the instruments, James Reedy explained that he studies the scores. ''Sure! We all do. When Erick choreographs, we are all aware of the score.''

''Erick generally likes to come in first without us knowing the score—just to feel the movement for a piece. Then he'll watch us do that. So he'll work like that for awhile,'' explained the dancer. ''For one piece that he choreographed with us, he came up with over three hundred separate movements. Then he started to weave them together as you might weave a rug, and we had a dance.

''He knows the score so well, that he says things to us like 'Well, I think that this movement, or this series of movements, is going to go here in the music.' And he'll go home in the afternoon and listen to the score, and then come in and choreograph. So a lot of times, he's already got rhythms in his body that he wants to play with. That's what he does: he *plays* with them.''

"He has sometimes composed the dance before the music. Then Lucy Dlugoszewski would take the meter structure. She would watch the movement very closely, and then she would go back and compose. Wonderful pieces. If you ever get to see *Cantilever* or *Overfloating* or *Lords of Persia*—masterpieces!" urged the dancer appreciatively.

Another such collaboration was *Here and Now with Watchers*. "It's an excellent score, an excellent dance," Mr. Reedy commented. "That was really one of the highlights, because of his philosophical dance, because Erick was just interested in 'pure being,' nothing else. And he designed a dance that really *does* communicate 'pure being.' "

Another Hawkins-Dlugoszewski piece, revived in 1987, was *Black Lake*. While the musicians were busy with the myriad of instruments needed to evoke the sounds of this score, onstage Laura Pettibone floated by in the role of the evening star.

Like James Reedy, she too was at first more oriented to making music than to dancing. But while growing up in a town just outside of Chicago, she was fortunate because her public schools offered both music and dance. Of particular impact upon her was a program that used Orff instruments to teach movement. Miss Pettibone retained some vivid impressions of this, and commented that the Orff approach seemed like a "great way to introduce children to music-making. You are not overly concerned with the quality of tone or the pitch using these lovely instruments."[2]

By third grade, she was proficient enough to be part of a group that was sent around to different schools to perform. She remembers "showing her stuff" while playing finger cymbals. "I was so nervous, I could barely see," confessed this now-seasoned professional performer.

Years after that childhood debut, the thing that most drew Laura Pettibone to Erick Hawkins was his musical approach to dance. She herself had studied composition in high school, and in college she played flute and harpsichord quite seriously. Simultaneously, she managed to find some "quasi-dancers" who would get together with her to design their own dance classes and arrange their own shows.

Her musical composition studies got a boost during a term under the supervision of David Ward-Steinman in California. Importantly for Miss Pettibone, this included lessons in editing tape as well as manuscripts. Her mentor recognized the young student's interest in dance and introduced her to a teacher in San Diego. From there, she went directly to Erick Hawkins in New York.

"I loved it," she said simply. "It was the first thing I did that combined all my interests. And Erick has a wonderful sense of design and a sense of music." She also found that the people associated with Hawkins were stimulating. They were people with different interests beyond focusing on how to point their toes, observed the young artist.

A bonus at the Hawkins school was the series of workshops taught by the composer Lucia Dlugoszewski. "She has a wonderful sense of structure and design, and an amazing eye," Miss Pettibone noted. Lucia Dlugoszewski taught the dancers to break down the elements of dance, with studies that would focus just on the rhythm, or just on dynamic, or just on space, or just on structure. For music, she would have each person play for the others in turn. At the end of the workshop, the dancers would give little performances, which Mr. Hawkins would of course attend. "We would stay up all night, finishing our music scores," recalled Laura Pettibone vividly.

Asked about what it is like to be onstage dancing to music by Lucia Dlugoszewski, this performer immediately thought of the piece *Angels of the Inmost Heaven:* "I love dancing to her music. It has a wonderful rhythmicality in it, but it also deals with texture. Unlike much music that is linear, hers is somehow three-dimensional. Your image of her music doesn't go in a straight line. It's more as if she surrounds you with a wonderful cloud of sound. Her sense of timing is different, too. But she is very good about putting in cues for the dancers. They are very obvious, and you can listen for them easily."

It is not uncommon for modern dancers to try creating their own choreography. When Laura Pettibone presents her own concerts, she also designs the scenic sets and makes the costumes, in addition to composing the music and dancing in the performances. She enjoys working with a variety of instrumentations not normally found on dance programs. For instance, one solo she danced was accompanied by a double bass player alone.

One such program took place at the Pineapple studios in lower Manhattan. The audience—a young crowd that did not mind sitting on cushions on the floor—seemed exceptionally encouraging towards such experiments. As James Reedy observed, "it's like family." Typical of the enthusiastic explorations of these musician-dancers, Mr. Reedy was waiting for Miss Pettibone to compose a piece for him to choreograph.

Such interchanges are rare in the ballet world.

HOLLY REEVE: DANCING FOR DE MILLE, BROADWAY, AND "FAME"

One of the dancers who toured with Agnes de Mille's Heritage Dance Theater was Holly Reeve—"a very gifted girl," according to the choreographer herself.

A native of Altoon, Pennsylvania, this young artist was just completing her studies at the new North Carolina School of the Arts when Miss de Mille began her theater company there. The dancer toured with the troupe during its entire existence, and five years later, she worked with Agnes de Mille in a revival of *Brigadoon* on Broadway. Still later, she assisted Miss de Mille in the creation of *The Informer,* a work premiered in 1988 by American Ballet Theatre.

In addition, Miss Reeve has performed in a wide variety of styles—ranging from a season with Kathryn Posin's modern dance group to several years of purely classical ballet with the Ohio Ballet. She was one of the principal dancers—

the one in long hair and a leopard's skin—in the movie *Fame,* and she performed in American Ballet Comedy.

This versatile performer was asked if she thinks any kind of music can be danced to. "Yes, I do," she replied. "But it does depend on the choreography."[3] Elaborating on the subject, she suggested that certain types of music are more conducive to the dance than others. Since she married a jazz musician, she acknowledged she had become a bit partial to that genre. "But," she added, "I think that one can also dance to nonmusic. You can dance to silence. You can dance 'over' music. It can be a background. It can be just a different level or layer. When I move, I think I usually move *with* the music. But I've also worked with music where you dance to counts rather than to the music itself—especially with some electronic pieces. But I *do* think any type of music can be danced to."

While working with Agnes de Mille, the dancer learned her roles first with counts. Later, she said, "you can throw away the counts when you know the piece. If you're not really familiar with the music or the dance, then you might continue to count . . . or you may go back to that if you feel a little nervous one night. But if you've performed it enough and know the music really well, you can dispense with the counts altogether."

Although she has never performed the type of avant-garde works in which dancers don't know how the music and the movement are going to mesh until they are onstage, Miss Reeve has reacted to this type of performance as an audience member. "When I see that kind of piece," she said, "I usually think: 'Well, the dancers and the musicians are probably having a great time, but what am *I* doing here as a viewer?' They're doing it for themselves, so to speak."

"Actually," she corrected herself, "I *have* done that sort of thing, but in workshops where we did a lot of improvisation and working with the *moment.* It was a lot of fun at the time—but it's something that you do in private, not in front of an audience."

Holly Reeve was pleased to share her memories of performing to live music, which in her case ranged from the sound of country fiddlers all the way to full symphony orchestras. "It adds so much! First, there's the technical aspect of being able to adjust the speed. But I think there is something more. I think *life* comes from the live music, and dancers can feed on that. It makes a big difference, even in class."

On Broadway, what goes on in the dancer's head? Miss Reeve explained: "The choreography is worked out with counts, and you *think* the counts until you become comfortable with the part. You also start out with the character." Musically, the preparations are all with a rehearsal pianist. And how does it feel the first moment that one hears, instead, a live orchestra in the pit? "Very exciting!" said the dancer.

It is the musicians' sounds—not their persons—that the dancers associate with. For example, Miss Reeve would never have occasion to speak with the bassoon player. "No!" she exclaimed, almost in horror at the impropriety of such an idea. Dancers talk with choreographers; choreographers talk to conductors; and conductors talk to bassoon players.

Holly Reeve mentioned that she could see into the pit. Was it a distraction? "No, not usually," she said. "But you shouldn't have your mind on it. If you're performing a character, you're supposed to be thinking of your character. So theoretically, you don't even see the orchestra."

Working as an arts administrator at the YM-YWHA of Mid-Westchester while she awaited the birth of her first child, the dancer had a taste of what it is like to be the one in charge of musicians, for a change.

She laughed heartily when asked what the particular problems were in this endeavor. "Egos," she replied. "It's hard to find musicians who can do dance work . . . really! There aren't very many of them. We get recommendations from other studios, and we have a file of accompanists for class, but usually it's just by word of mouth. It takes real talent and ability, and it's something that has to be worked on over a period of time."

Holly Reeve herself is musically very literate, having played violin and piano while she was growing up. Since she can speak from practical knowledge of both arts, what does she feel is important for musicians to know concerning dance work? "That usually dancers in a classroom will need a really strong beat," she emphasized. "That may be boring to play, but it is necessary. For interpretative music, I imagine a player might want to draw one part of the music out, and so forth. But for working in the classroom, there needs to be a real strong regular beat."

Yet when it comes to performance, she noted that there are various changes in tempo possible—ritardandos and accelerandos, and so on. These shadings become built into the muscle-memory of dancers as they work with the same musicians, she pointed out.

For example, the dancer recalled one pianist who performed with the Ohio Ballet. Since he had also played for classes, the dancers came to be familiar with his style. "I remember that being very special," Holly Reeve said. "I remember he did some Schubert *Waltzes* and he played the piano onstage. It was beautiful dancing to that because if he saw you were holding the balance for a little bit extra longer, he would hold the music too, and then wait until you were ready to start into the next phrase. That can be really special. With a live pianist, you take a breath, and you breathe together and go into the next phrase."

"I just said one thing for class and exactly the opposite for performance," she realized. "For class, you want a specific, measured movement. But that's worse for performance. When you've done something enough times, the special qualities do come out when you breathe together, and you can be more expressive."

IAN HORVATH: EXPERIENCING MUSIC WHILE ONSTAGE

"Go right back to the pianist in class," suggested Ian Horvath in an interview.[4] The advice came from someone who has been a principal dancer with American Ballet Theatre, a cofounder of the Cleveland Ballet, a choreographer, and more recently, an associate director of the Limón Company.

"When you're taking class and you have rhythmic changes and you have that human one-on-one relationship with the music, you develop a different kind of dancer than you do in class where the dancer hears a record or a tape," he pointed out. "There is just no comparison! It is just absolutely *essential* that there be live music in all dance performances as far as I'm concerned—unless the music is such that you can't do it live, such as an electronic score or something like Twyla Tharp's *Sinatra Suite*. You obviously can't have Frank Sinatra on every performance, so you have to do with recorded music."

Thinking further about taped recordings, he suggested: "One of the things that one has to take into consideration from the artistic director's view, is what you're putting onstage in terms of feasting the eye has to be matched for the ear, so that if you're producing something like a big nineteenth-century Fokine piece—*Swan Lake* or *Nutcracker,* for instance, and you use taped music, it's *hideous*. It just doesn't work. It loses all of its magic, because you're not supporting the visual impact with the audio at all."

Speaking only of the artistic considerations, Mr. Horvath emphasized: "There's no way to support such dance without live music. There's an ambiance about taped music that's just—wrong, when everything else is live. There's an electric quality about taped music that needs film or video to be consistent with it, because it's *all* electric, and you accept it. But when the dance is live and you've got real dimension as far as 'visuals' are concerned, then you have that flatness that comes from reproduced music. You don't have the same dimension that you have from live music. It doesn't work. There's no *way* for it to work!"

However, what happens when the dancer has no choice and must perform to tape? What sprang to Ernie Horvath's mind were some of the things that went wrong. "The tape would get stuck. The machine would break." And he couldn't refrain from telling one of his favorite stories. Once he was dancing Arpino's *Viva Vivaldi* with the Joffrey Ballet. The piece starts with a procession which stops, center stage, and the woman does a huge penché arabesque. When she comes up, that is the cue for the music to start.

One particular evening, one of Horvath's friendly partners, Trinnette Singleton, went down, came up . . . and still there was silence. She took a pose in fifth position to wait, and Horvath whispered, "Trinnette, let's just bourée off!"—which they did. The curtain came down, and that was the total ballet for the evening: a big crossover. Once backstage, the partners discovered that the tape had broken totally in many places. Such dangers are the reason that it is now common practice to run two simultaneous tape recorders. They can be synchronized and controlled by computers.

Thinking back on his career with American Ballet Theatre and later with the Cleveland Ballet, Mr. Horvath reflected upon his awareness of the music when it was there on time: "The consciousness onstage during a performance is basically one of survival, unless you're used to the situation—which doesn't really happen that often in dance. Unfortunately, if you get to do one piece six times in a year, that's a lot, because of rotating repertory, multiple casting, and all kinds of things. So it takes maybe five years to be really comfortable with a particular piece, where you feel that if anything happens, you're on top of it and it's not going to ruin the performance.

"Initial performances, if you've been rehearsed well, for me have gone by almost without consciousness. Sometimes they have even been transcendental kinds of experiences where I'm not conscious of anything. The body takes over and just goes into automatic pilot. You do it, and you're just experiencing things that are completely different from the rehearsal situation."

"You're dealing with so many things that you have no control over," Mr. Horvath went on to explain. "A lighting cue is a little bit off, and suddenly you're blinded. It wasn't supposed to be there when you have to do a pirouette, and so you're concentrating on that. Suddenly there is a distraction in the wings, and you're trying *not* to deal with that. Suddenly, there's an audience out there, and you're not sure you can really make contact. You're not sure. You start to think, 'Gee, is this a fourth-wall ballet, or a ballet that is supposed to be projected and played to an audience?'

"A lot of times, those things are not taken into consideration in the rehearsal, because sometimes the choreographer doesn't know until the piece is performed, what it is! So you are all of a sudden experimenting: you start to smile; you start to play with the ballet; and you start to tease the audience. You say, 'No, that doesn't seem right.' So you pause. . . ."

"The performance is actually a continuation of the rehearsal," Mr. Horvath suggested. "It's just a situation where you can't stop. You have to make do with whatever happens."

"Dance is never there forever," he emphasized. "It's totally ephemeral. It's only there at the moment that it's happening. I've had highlights, as a performer, of particular pieces like Dennis Nahat's *Brahms Quintet*. It was a wonderful role for me. I remember a performance in Chicago with the Fine Arts Quartet playing. It was magic! Everything that happened up from the technical level was in place, and we were verging on *art*. We were making it right there, and I was dancing with someone that I loved to dance with, Naomi Sorkin. We were well-matched and loved the piece, and that has a lot to do with it."

"Dancers tend to be very judgmental about pieces," continued Mr. Horvath, "and it's very difficult to do a piece you don't really like." Did he ever have to dance to a piece like that? "My God!" he exclaimed, "The majority of my career. Not dance to *music* that you don't like, but to do a *piece* that you don't like. Quite often, the situation is that you love the music, and you think the choreographer has butchered the music or has not understood the music and has not realized any of the parameters of the piece, and *you* have to make up the difference. You don't have any structure to rely on, so it just becomes a real burden."

"In many instances," he noted, "it's very difficult for even a discerning and sophisticated audience to see the difference between interpretative quality and structure, because there is no score in front of you. So there are lots of ballets that have been 'saved' as it were, because they have been brilliantly performed, and it isn't until later that they start to see the holes in the structure, because other casts come in. The dancers in the original cast with a piece are almost as much responsible for the creative choreographic structure as the choreographer is, depending on how the choreographer works."

Giving some examples, Mr. Horvath noted: "Balanchine's choreography was structural, totally. You do the steps, and the ballet will work. Period. You don't have to bring anything to it as an interpreter other than the ability to be musical, basically, and have enough technique to do the movements.

"But Tudor, in addition to the moves, has all these things happening: motivation, character development, and all kinds of things. You need to know *who* you are all the time and *why* you are doing the movements. Consequently, Tudor's is an extremely difficult repertory to preserve and is very difficult to pull off."

How does a former principal dancer like Ian Horvath feel when he sees others performing the ballet roles that he used to do, to the same music? "It depends on the dancers and on the ballets," he observed. Speaking about a recent all-Tudor evening he had seen at ABT, he remarked: "They danced it better than any of us could ever have done, because the technical level of dancers today is so superior to what it was. It just grows each year, almost."

But what of his own experience of the music, when he is sitting in the audience, watching and not dancing? Of this, he said: "You're experiencing the music the way Tudor wants you to, or the way any choreographer is asking you to interpret the music. There's a give and take between the two of you as to how ultimately you will experience it. But that 'mindset' is what you're trying for: 'Here's a point of view about the music' is what you're trying for, and the more technically proficient a dancer is, the more he or she is able to achieve that."

Ian Horvath left ABT in 1974, having already started his own ballet school in Cleveland. Speaking of the founding of the Cleveland Ballet, he noted: "It was assumed right from the beginning that there would be a live orchestra from the first day of our performing as a fully professional company. And there was—a full orchestra of forty-four people!"

"One of the reasons we felt that was very important," explained the former codirector, "was because we were in the home of the famous Cleveland Orchestra. The sophistication of musical tastes in Cleveland was substantial, and much of our audience would be shared by the orchestra.''

The Cleveland Ballet's first conductor was Dwight Altman, who soon shared the podium with Stanley Sussman. ''The key is the music director,'' said Mr. Horvath. ''That music director has to have the sensibility and the flexibility to go with the dancers. The dancers have to understand that theirs is not an inflexible art either. It is not only the music director and the composer that are making the decisions. Unless the choreographer has made very bravura demands on the dancer in a specific passage, the dancer must be victimized, as it were, by the music director, and not the other way around. If there is a particularly difficult technical passage, certainly there has to be give and take. But it really is in the music director's hands.''

''I look upon the music director as an associate artistic director,'' said Mr. Horvath. ''I wouldn't make a decision about the music without consulting the music director in terms of commissioning new pieces, and musically, in terms of, 'Well, can we play it?' or 'What are the acoustical problems going to be like?' So you become a kind of liaison with the elements.''

''Music and dance are synergistic and *one,*'' underscored this artist. ''Now a lot of people would disagree with me,'' he admitted. ''Those people who come from a Merce Cunningham sensibility would say that the music and dance are equal but *independent;* they operate in their own dimensions, and they don't necessarily have anything to do with one another.''

''I respect that opinion on paper; I *hate* it as an audience member,'' declared Ian Horvath. ''I don't understand it at all. It's a great *idea,* but it just doesn't work for *me.*''

LARRY CLARK: EXTENDING THE CUNNINGHAM THEATER CONCEPTS

Choreographer Larry Clark could be considered part of a third generation in the lineage of Merce Cunningham's experiments with music and movement. Formerly he danced with Viola Farber, who in turn had been one of Cunningham's lead dancers.

Seeking to expand the kinds of activities engaged in by concert dancers onstage, Larry Clark collected about him a dedicated group of dancers who had had training in both ballet and modern dance—dancers who were were willing to enter into the possibilities of both singing while they were moving and acting in artistic ways (as contrasted with ''show'' styles).

To his experimentation, Clark brought a solid schooling in traditional musical forms. ''My whole background has been with the Louis Horst tradition,'' he explained.[5] ''I went to Ohio State, and their composition courses required all the students to go through a pre-classic series. You had to choreograph pieces to the gavotte, the gigue, the pavanne, the sarabande, and so on.''

Such strict adherence to older forms seemed like a direct contradiction of the methods employed sometimes by Merce Cunningham and composer John Cage, especially when music and movement are put together randomly during a performance. Larry Clark distinguished between training and new invention: "Here, we're talking about basic building blocks, and learning about movement, and exploration, and understanding music and dance. Merce and John Cage are *not* into the pre-classics and the history of music. They are making an obvious choice."[6]

"I worked with Viola Farber for ten years," Mr. Clark went on to relate. "She was very, very musical. But you know, Merce's *choreography* is also very musical. I mean it is intricately counted, and it is all set."

This presented a puzzle. When it comes to a finished performance, if the relationship to the music is not set beforehand, then the totality certainly is not controlled by the creators. "Sometimes it's very provocative," agreed Mr. Clark. "Sometimes John Cage's idea of doing music to a beautiful piece of movement work is to come out and turn on a radio to any station you happen to turn on. At the time I may like it, but it's not something I want to do all my life!"

"However," continued the dancer, "I am certainly very open to the idea, and it certainly does provoke interesting reactions, between what's predictable and what's unpredictable. You have two predictable units: a set piece of music that is going to be played, and a set dance. Then you put them together, and they never before have come into contact. There *are* some wonderful things that can happen."

"I have performed with Viola, where we were onstage and didn't have the music until the opening night," he recalled. "The movement piece had a whole different feel. I would have a story in mind that I basically made up for myself, that made sense to me. It was a really heavy piece. Then all of a sudden, this music came on, and that just completely changed the dance the night that we opened."

Concerning the specific music for some of those dances, Larry Clark mentioned doing Beethoven's *Moonlight Sonata,* for which Farber herself played the part on the piano. Then there were tapes, which Larry Clark acknowledged were certainly the most economical way to provide music. "If I had the option, I like both, to tell you the truth," he said. "There are some phenomenal things you can do electronically that you can't do live. I love live music, but. . . ."

"I like everything!" he burst out enthusiastically. "I like marbles thrown against a slate floor, for example. You couldn't do that live onstage, of course, because it would be dangerous. But I've had the idea of doing this *behind* the stage and miking the sounds. That's in one of my pieces to come," he grinned.

A musical omnivore, Mr. Clark added: "I like nonmusical sounds as well as sounds one *expects* to hear from instruments. I love homemade instruments too."

Indeed, one of the musicians who worked with Mr. Clark when he was teaching at Princeton University is Skip La Plante—who was once written up on the front page of that bastion of the establishment, *The Wall Street Journal.* "He was a young kid when I was at Princeton," reminisced the choreographer. "He would come in—tall, lanky, long hair, sixties-looking kid, never wore shoes, most of the time half his pants were missing, no shirt. . . . He would play pots and pans and guitar and bass and a little bit of piano. He was amazing, though, and he had some good ideas about creating new sounds." Subsequently, that musician went on to start his own concert group performing on homemade instruments.

Concerning his own current theatrical innovations, Mr. Clark explained that he had two active companies. After holding auditions for the second one, he and his collaborative composer, Joseph Reiser, arranged intensive two-day workshops every week for a complete year, at which specialists would come into teach acting, singing, drama, and music.

"We felt that the orientation of modern dance is going more theatrical now," explained the director, while carefully distinguishing that what he is after is an amalgamation of the arts that is quite different from popular Broadway-style productions. Part of the thrust of his search is a greatly altered role for music as incorporated into his dance works, such as his hour-long work based on Edgar Lee Masters' *Spoon River Anthology,* with a score by Joseph Reiser.

HELEN STARR: SHINING IN KENTUCKY

"It is a great art: to conduct for ballet, to play for ballet. There is no doubt of that in my mind," commented Helen Starr in an interview with the author.[7]

A former soloist with the Royal Ballet and also a former principal dancer with the London Festival Ballet, Miss Starr brought both experience and enthusiasm to her multiple roles in Louisville, Kentucky. There, she has continued to dance major parts, in addition to serving as associate artistic director of the Louisville Ballet (headed by her husband, Alun Jones). On top of that, she directs the city's Civic Ballet and teaches classes.

Miss Starr has not only restaged great classical ballets; she has also created unusual roles in new works. Among these was the part of the writer Colette in *Paradise Gained,* which was premiered in a recent Louisville season. For this work, choreographer Domy Reiter-Soffer himself arranged a score, using various pieces by Darius Milhaud.

Writing about the new work for *Dance Magazine,* George R. Hubbard observed:

> Top honors belong to Helen Starr. . . . Starr has danced many leading roles with the company since 1975, but Colette is arguably her finest achievement. Her poignant Cinderella and Juliet, her fragile Marguerite Gautier, and her elegant Aurora have to yield place; no other role has coupled her elegant classical technique with her flair for bravura acting in such a convincing manner.[8]

Speaking with the author about the relation between music and dance, Miss Starr remarked: "I believe you need to have a particular affinity and even love for dance to appreciate what music can do for dance. With the classics, where you are using what is known of the 'original' choreography, you are tied musically with whatever they did with it at that time. It is not necessarily what Tchaikovsky intended with *Swan Lake* and *Sleeping Beauty*—we know that; and for some musicians, that becomes unacceptable. But that's no good. You have to have a musician who will understand all aspects of the work."

She felt that the best way for musicians to learn is by taking dance classes. "This is where you can see the difference between a committed dance conductor and a noncommitted conductor," she suggested. "The one understands how the body will phrase with music—if the music is sympathetic to the dance. But there are those who are unable—totally unable—to see that or to feel it."

Drawing from her earlier experiences in London, Miss Starr recalled an attempt to train conductors. "The Arts Council had a brainwave and put up the money for new young conductors to try out. Now the *idea* was wonderful, but the way it was put together was a disaster. They'd stick him in the pit with a score and say, 'Conduct it!' "

"This lasted a whole tour," lamented the ballerina. "Every so often a new conductor arrived, and the first performances were just hair-raising. The ballet mistress came back crying when one man knocked four-and-a-half minutes off *Les Sylphides*. It is only twenty minutes to start with, and without four-and-a-half minutes, it came out like a silent film run too fast."

"Another day, one came and he had been told 'Just watch the dancers.' Disaster!" Miss Starr exclaimed. "I absolutely disagree with that out of hand. He watched me, and in the first variation of the Lilac Fairy, I hit a wonderful balance, and I would normally have used—and caught up with—the music by myself. But he thought, 'Oh. She needs it slower.' So he waited until I came down. I missed the next part totally, and I had to fill out to make it come together. It was the biggest mess."

In her days of touring, Helen Starr always danced to live music—with one exception. "It was a terrifying shock," she claimed. "We were on tour in the Far East, and they recorded a performance and then used that when we moved on. We did a rehearsal to the recording: it was *Swan Lake*. I did the first entrance, and I went up, and then I tried again. Still nothing happened in the music. I said, 'For goodness' sake, whose performance is this?' They said, 'Yours!' " laughed the ballerina.

"This was Jack Carter's version," she went on to explain. "He does it the way Tchaikovsky wrote the first entrance: thunder, and she goes to the floor directly, and from there, you get up, and the recovery is slow. He maintained that the feet were painful. The feet were only on at night, and a swan only uses its feet to swim. So he was trying to put all this on, and it gave a wonderful feeling to the entrance at the beginning. But I obviously that night of the recording took a lot of time between the landing and the getting up from the floor,'' related the ballerina with amusement.

A totally different kind of musical experience for the dancer was the role of Hecuba in Alun Jones' work *Trojan Women,* which was set to a score commissioned from Karel Husa by the Louisville Ballet. Miss Starr recalled the collaboration: ''Husa said it was the hardest piece he ever had to write. But what he put into it! As a teenager, he had been witness to one of the 'demonstrations' in Czechoslovakia where the Nazis literally erased a village. The men were lined up. The women and children watched while the men were shot, then all the women and children were taken away. They watched the entire village be obliterated.''

''He was there. He knew all this—and then this music!'' said the dancer quietly. ''It wipes you out. But he was just incredible. We loved him so much. He came in to conduct. We were so excited, and it was the most wonderful score.''

Regardless of the tone of a work, Helen Starr emphasized, ''music is *my* motivation for dance. When I look back, it always has been. As a small child, I heard music. My father had a string band and was also a church organist. In addition, both he and my mother played the piano. So there was always music in the house—as there is in our house now!''

LISA DE RIBÈRE: ON POINTE

Much attention has been paid to the musical taste of George Balanchine. But what did it feel like to be onstage dancing to the music he chose? In search of answers to that question, the author interviewed Lisa de Ribère during one of her weeks at the Carlisle Project, a center for the training of choreographers, in Pennsylvania.[9] She had just emerged from a session of choreographing her newest ballet in the red barn studios of Marcia Dale Weary.

Years ago, the artist was herself a promising student in that same barn. She also studied with Barbara Weisberger at the Pennsylvania School of Ballet, and subsequently at the School of American Ballet.

Accepted into New York City Ballet at the age of 16, Miss de Ribère remained in the corps there but was given a number of unusual roles—some considered demi-solos, others actually full solos. Later, she became a full-fledged soloist with American Ballet Theatre. In recent years, she has been developing as a very promising choreographer. Already she has created more than three dozen ballets, including works for the Stars of American Ballet Theatre at the Aspen Festival, for Baryshnikov and Company, the Pittsburgh Ballet Theater, the Florence Opera Ballet, and others.

To watch her spin out her beautifully crafted and poignantly touching pas de deux to Arensky's *Variations on a Theme of Tchaikovsky* was to enjoy a sample of her creative work.[10] But for an hour or so, Miss de Ribère recalled what it had felt like to be the one dancing onstage.

Concerto Barocco, set to Bach's *Concerto for Two Violins,* was one of her favorite Balanchine works to perform. "The thing about *Barocco,*" she said, "is that the corps is on the stage from beginning to end. It's a tough ballet! So by the time you get into the third movement, it builds and builds, and you could get so you just wanted to walk *offstage*. But for some reason, it also gets you so excited, that by the end you're doing as much as you can. There's something about the music that makes it so. Of course, the choreography has something to do with it as well," she smiled.

"But I think we *all* felt as if we were in heaven when we danced to that," added Miss de Ribère nostalgically. "In fact, people who were with the company for years and were due to be replaced in that ballet because they were becoming soloists, would say 'Please don't take me out of *Barocco*.' "

When she herself achieved the rank of soloist at ABT, Miss de Ribère found that the unknown elements concerning the music would make each night's performance different. She noted that at ABT, "a lot of ballet conductors were very good about coming back and saying, 'OK. What tempo do you want?' "

At New York City Ballet, however, it was her impression that Mr. Balanchine would say to music director Robert Irving, "I want this and this and this. . . ." Even so, it seemed to her that the conductors would sometimes go out and do exactly what they pleased. Then, observed the former dancer, Balanchine would be likely to get angry. "Not often, but once in a while. Usually Hugo Fiorato and Robert Irving really did not like to be told by the dancers what they wanted, so in City Ballet, we got used to following whatever the orchestra did—*no matter what*. That was something Balanchine liked. He liked the dancers to have the ability to adjust. So when I went to Ballet Theatre, I was used to doing whatever tempos were set by the orchestra. Whether it sped up or slowed down, you just rose to the occasion."

For example, Lisa de Ribère remembered one dress rehearsal for ABT's *La Bayadère*. John Lanchbery was conducting, and Miss de Ribère was doing the first variation in the "Shades" scene. "We got to the end," she said, "and I started with piqué and the relevé-arabesque, moving across the stage, and the funny thing that happened was I was following him, but he was looking up at me and following me. I was sort of doing it a little faster. He started speeding up to get caught up with me, and we were going on like this until at the end it was so fast that I thought 'My God! I can't believe it.' "

"Usually, when we like the tempo—and sometimes even when we don't—we go up and thank the conductor. We make a point of it, because it's really helpful to have a good relationship with the conductor. So I went up to Lanchbery and said, 'You know, the tempo was fine, except I felt it was a little too fast at the end.' He looked at me and said, 'I thought so too. I was trying to keep up with you!' "

In contrast, said Miss de Ribère, she has also experienced cases where the conductor would not look up, but just kept on conducting with his head down. This was not in the big ballet companies, but rather during special concert tours. "It was scary," said the performer, "because you wouldn't know what was going to happen next. Those were usually conductors who were not used to conducting for dance. They weren't used to looking up at a stage."

It was surprising to hear that a dancer could keep an eye on the conductor while performing—but it seemed to be a source of reassurance during a performance. "Oh yes," confirmed Miss de Ribère. "You can look, and you can notice. Usually you just listen, but if something doesn't sound right—you *look!*"

"Ballet Theatre went to Miami, and we were doing *Bourrée Fantasque,* which is a Balanchine work," continued Miss de Ribère. Luckily, she has forgotten who was conducting, but here is what happened: "We got to the end, and there was this pause, just before the finale. Half of the orchestra played its part, and half played four counts *behind.* Onstage, nobody knew who to follow. Now, I have heard conductors actually yell in the orchestra pit. There have been lots of funny experiences. But I'm sure that night it also looked like a mess onstage, because the music is usually the glue that holds us together.

"Normally, the first thing you're conscious of is the tempo. Of course, you're also conscious of the actual piece of music itself, and of how the steps are supposed to be within the music. Then you become conscious of the texture, and whether or not the music sounds dead. There are times when the music just sounds so boring, and other times when it's so alive."

But of course, the music is only one of the things a dancer has to be concerned with. Another important element is the counting of the beats for the choreographed steps. "Balanchine *insisted* that we count," emphasized Miss de Ribère. "And if we didn't count, he'd get mad at us. So you just memorized the counts, and once he told you what they were, it made so much sense."

This dancer felt that she personally absorbed the music both through the counts and by listening over and over again in rehearsals. She never looked at the scores or the piano music. What she had to know would all be in the movement that Balanchine had devised to go with the music. But even during a performance, would she be counting in her head? "Yup!" came the unequivocal answer.

"You're doing a million things at the same time when you're dancing," Miss de Ribère explained. "If you have an injury, you're thinking about how to adjust your weight to cause the least problem. You're thinking about the music. You're thinking about the steps. You're thinking about how you're relating to other dancers on the stage. You're thinking about your spacing—a million things! Sometimes you get into trouble: you get hooked on somebody else, and you have to think instantly how to get out of it—or if you fall, how to get up and get right back into it."

"In fact, when you're counting, a mistake in the music is really going to be more evident," the dancer pointed out. "For instance, once when I was doing the 'Rubies' section of *Jewels,* suddenly the instruments that were playing the melody just disappeared—didn't play. The rhythm was still there, but I didn't know what to do. I kind of stopped for a second, because it was as if *my* point of reference had disappeared for a few seconds, and it really threw me. But that was a good lesson for me, because then I learned how you don't just listen for the melody and for what you're familiar with; you listen for the *rhythm*. If the rhythm is still there, you can just keep going."

Working as a choreographer herself, Lisa de Ribère found that it was no longer enough to absorb the music just by listening. She felt a need to know more about the structure of the works that she intended to set. To help with that process, she became the very first choreographer-in-residence at the Carlisle Project. She mentioned that working there with composer-teacher Juli Nunlist had been particularly helpful.

After undergoing such training, did Miss de Ribère have any suggestions for musicians about what is important to know concerning a dancer's needs? "This brings up a whole thing between musicians and dancers," she sighed. "There is often an abrasiveness between musicians and dancers, which comes out at contract time," she added ruefully. "But this can be an uncomfortable feeling."

"Musicians feel that dancers are very young, and maybe immature," she continued, voicing opinions heard from many others. "Generally, musicians in the pit *are* older, and I think it may bother them to see us (and we *are* very young) reaching positions of soloist or whatever."

"I don't really feel comfortable with musicians in general," she confided. "I always get the feeling that they're looking at us as though we're stupid kids." That sounded harsh, for many musicians express a great deal of awe for the dancers and their art. "Yes," she acknowledged, but then turned to economic disparities: "The musicians feel that they should be making more money because they often have families to support. They are married or whatever, whereas most of us aren't."

The dancer was asked whether that should be a relevant basis for payment—any more than it is in sports, for instance, where the stars are also often quite young. Miss de Ribère responded: "The people who are going to get more money are the ones who scream the loudest, and I think dancers tend to be not very vocal about their rights. It's sort of the nature of classical ballet, that dancers stay quiet and take what's given to them: take correction, and do what you're told. It's a very different kind of mentality from that of musicians."

Yet one wonders how this is any different from the situation of instrumentalists who sit in the pit and take corrections from the conductor. That is their whole life, too, it seems. One crucial difference in the professional world may be that the musicians have over the decades built up a stronger union.

Commenting on how she feels since switching to the position of being the one in command, Miss de Ribère confided: "I think that may be one of the reasons why I'm a choreographer! I didn't like being in that submissive position that you're pretty much forced into as a dancer. Not that I want to be the boss and be *oppressing* dancers; quite the opposite,'' she hastened to add. ''But I definitely prefer the position I'm in now to the position I *was* in. A lot of dancers feel powerless about their lives. I *know* they did.''

As for the musical aspects of Lisa de Ribère's artistry, throughout her entire career, colleagues and audience members alike always considered her extremely musical. What did she think that meant? ''I heard various things,'' she replied, ''like the way I *feel* the music to the way I moved to the music to the way I'm always 'on' the music—that I'm never late or jumping the gun.''

''Being musical seems to mean a lot of different things to different people,'' she reflected. ''I will tell you about a secondhand compliment that I received. Someone told me that a musician in the pit at ABT said that I was the most musical dancer he had ever seen. That to me was the ultimate compliment! Whatever feelings, negative or positive, that I've had about musicians, that was special.''

Noting her own favorite performers, Lisa de Ribère remarked: ''Violette Verdy and Suzanne Farrell and Mikhail Baryshnikov are some of the most musical dancers *I've* ever watched. I don't know if I should say who wasn't! But what amazes me is how few really truly musical dancers there are.''

When one sees a Baryshnikov or Verdy or Farrell, a viewer cannot, of course, know what is going on in those dancers' heads. ''But you can see by what they're doing,'' suggested Miss de Ribère. ''For Violette, it was like second nature. I may be wrong, but I think it's something that you're either born with or you're not. People can learn to dance *with* the music. They can teach themselves. But they never will be quite like a Violette or a Suzanne or a Misha. It's just something really special. You can't buy it!''

10

What Is Musicality in a Dancer?

Like many other musicians, conductor Robert Irving unhesitatingly names Violette Verdy as one of the most musical dancers he ever worked with. One day the author questioned him further about this: ''Mr. Irving, is such musicality an *inborn* thing?''

''Oh no!'' he laughed. ''Very much *out-born!''* Asked to elaborate, he suggested: ''Well, they can hear the music while they're dancing. And they *do* hear it and listen to it. They understand it. That's not very complicated. And yet—'' he paused to consider. ''Some of the people haven't got the basic auditory apparatus to distinguish the sounds, to analyze them. I mean, there *is* an immense variety in the musicality of human beings, isn't there!''

VIOLETTE VERDY

A chance to hear Violette Verdy's thoughts concerning musicality came one morning with her gracious invitation to observe her teach the company class for New York City Ballet.

Long considered one of the most delightful of Balanchine's ballerinas, Violette Verdy went on to become artistic director of the Paris Opera Ballet, and later the Boston Ballet. Most recently, she has rejoined New York City Ballet as a master teaching associate. In addition, she devotes considerable time and effort to setting both Balanchine's choreography and her own works on other companies in the United States and abroad. Her *Set of Seven,* to piano music by Mary Jeanne van Appledorn, was among the works featured in the American Music Festival presented by New York City Ballet.

When this dance artist finally sat down to rest for a few minutes, she was asked: ''What is musicality in a dancer?'' Miss Verdy responded: ''That's difficult to answer simply. It's such a question! But I feel that *I* danced because of my love for music. I feel that even some of my physical technique and the courage it takes to have it, came from my musical conviction. I think that music has been the conviction for my dancing, even from the start. I think that's what has made me dance.''[1]

''*Musicianship,*'' she continued, ''is a combination of the most extraordinary rhythmical exactness, and yet freedom. In other words, you leave it, and you know when to come back. In the sense with the melody, there is a freedom with rubato, also going off and returning to the beat.''

''So it is things like this . . . also, being able to 'tune' yourself to the instruments that you reverberate. If it is to a piano, it is sometimes more staccato; if it is to a violin, it's sometimes more legato. If you dance to a full orchestra, there's a power; if you dance to voice, there's a fluidity and a delicacy that you have to treat.''

''If the music is already in existence in a recording, or if you have a chance to listen to the orchestra, you already begin to get the picture of what you are in for—what you will have to express, and how you will have to 'tune' yourself up, either as an orchestra, or as a single instrument. When you dance to a solo instrument, it's different from when you dance to a full orchestra. Also if you dance alone or with others, there's a given collective effort or personal effort involved that's very different,'' advised the ballerina.

''You know, the French are very analytical,'' she pointed out. ''When I was going to school, we were always asked to do a lot of analysis and a lot of composition in writing. When I learned music, it was the same thing. Then I learned it was the same everywhere: perspicacity and judgment are very important. You need to have perspicacity and analysis. You need to analyze elements to know what you are in for. With that clearly in mind, you proceed to place yourself within that context of what is expected.''

''Balanchine knew that I would analyze and not be passive, and that I had been developed in Europe by coaches and teachers so that I knew how to analyze and how to work on a role. You really work on every single element, so that you make a presentation of *all* the elements,'' Miss Verdy emphasized.

As part of her preparation, she did study scores a little bit; she can read music. But mostly, it seems, she just had a very good ear and could learn simply by listening. Speaking of her own development, Miss Verdy noted that before she started dance lessons, she studied violin when she was six. Later she also took a little bit of piano.

''I would love to be a musician,'' she remarked. ''I realize now that I *could* have been a conductor! In many ways, I act as a conductor would. Now that I've directed ballet companies, I realize that the way that I work with dancers is very much like the work that a conductor would do with an orchestra.''

Guessing about her own inborn musical abilities, Violette Verdy recalled: ''Very often, without meaning to do it, I have remembered a piece of music, and people have told me that I was exactly on pitch. So apparently I have a sense of pitch also. But some singers have it, and some singers don't have it. Some musicians don't exactly have it—but that doesn't stop them from being good musicians,'' she noted, implying that perhaps dancers with varying musical aptitudes can also work to develop whatever it is they have naturally.

For younger students, she suggested that it could be very beneficial to study some musical instrument, and particularly to have some knowledge about the structure of classical music, if they intend to pursue ballet.

''I have done a lot of things on Baroque and classical music,'' said Miss Verdy, speaking now as a choreographer. ''There's a sense of *form*. I cannot work with 'formlessness.' I would immediately recreate form in 'formlessness.' I would *have* to recreate form, because ballet *is* form.''

At New York City Ballet, the choreography has been very largely based on classical musical form. But if an artist wanted to project a particular story or particular character in addition, that is something different to think about.

''Oh yes,'' agreed Miss Verdy. ''But I think that either you choose to do a ballet character and then you have to look for the music that reflects that—or you let the music give you the plot and the character, and you go along with what the music sort of *tells* you to do. Two ways of doing that: you can illustrate an idea you have, or you can choose a piece of music and see if you can extract a plot out of it somehow.''

In her own performing career, the ballerina noted, ''Balanchine gave me roles with *style,* and he knew he could let me analyze, study, and finish a role without having to tell me what to do. So he would not even bother to finish little things in between. He would just let me do it.''

Are there different ways of being musical, as a ballet dancer? ''Of course,'' said Miss Verdy. ''But it depends what choreographer you are working with. Some of them are very exacting in their demands, and some of them are much more free and let you respond.'' This means, in her view, deciding ''how to use the music, how to phrase *yourself.* Often you cannot go 'word-word-word-word,' but you want to make a phrase. Again, it's another approach: even in class, if you do separate little jumps, or if you want to make a phrase out of those separate little jumps.''

Good dancing is both technical and musical, emphasized the ballerina. ''It's both; otherwise, it's gymnastics—athletics.''

The quality of musicality is sometimes difficult to pinpoint, but it is definitely one of the criteria of a good dancer from around the world. This consideration came up again as Violette Verdy commented on the New York International Ballet Competition, for which she had served as both a judge and a teacher during several gatherings of young dancers from around the world. Speaking about how one judges the contestants' musicality, Miss Verdy acknowledged, ''It's so difficult. There *is* something about the quality. It is so indefinable—and yet you know it's there.''

Then she pointed out that, especially in New York, audiences generally do sense these musical, artistic differences in performances. In the competition itself, Miss Verdy noted: "The audience knew perfectly well. The dancers that got cheered were really doing something right: either technically they were fiery, or spiritual . . . though they *all* did some beautiful things." (All the contestants danced the same pieces to the same recordings.)

"Artistically, of course, we love performers that give us fiery, passionate, warm performances—it's always wonderful, so divine," mused the ballerina. "But then, an even more rare—extraordinarily rare—quality that, for instance the Chinese gave us, is the sense of the sacred, a sense of the sublime."

In the case of the two dancers singled out—Xin Lili and Yang Xinhua—according to Miss Verdy, the musicality of their pas de deux from *Swan Lake* went far beyond merely being with the music. "It's *artistic* musicality: how they take the music and how they give it back to you. Nothing could be more musical than what they did, because it was completely translated into a spiritual essence of the music—completely. They were so immersed in the music, that they were just in the heart of the expression of the music. They were more than on the beat; they were in the *heart!*"

LARRY CLARK

For modern dancer Larry Clark, the experience of hearing totally different music emerging either from the pit or from electronic speakers during an actual performance was at times a normal part of his career. But in his teaching of younger students—most recently at the State University of New York, Purchase—he has some demanding definitions of musicality.

"There's a certain way of feeling the movement in the music," he suggested after a class one day.[2] "You know, a lot of dancers dance 'behind' the music, not really on top of it. They don't know what it means to dance *around* a note. If, for example, you are doing archery, there's a bull's eye. You either hit the center of the bull's eye or shades of the bull's eye, or you miss it. That's the way very often a lot of dancers move—even people with musical training."

He was asked if working with a jazz beat could become pretty insistent. "Like somebody hitting you over the head," said Mr. Clark. "But when I worked with Viola Farber for years, we danced full-length pieces *without* any music. Do you know how boring that can be unless you're really, really musical—*physically?* It's one thing to be musical mentally; it's another thing to be musical physically, with the dynamics and all the shadings. This is one thing, I think, that one never stops learning."

The artist clicked his fingers. "If there is a beat going, how do you hit that beat dynamically? The whole dynamic involvement of hitting *around* the beat is also very important in movement."

"A lot of things with Viola were in silence," he explained. "But she was so musical, we learned to count and be so articulate in the divisions of a beat, both in movement and in the music. We learned how to be very musical with our bodies. We learned how the body stays alive and doesn't just rely on the music as a support system. So I think we had more of an *internal* musicality. Then, when there *was* music, it was wonderful."

"You see," the dancer went on to observe, "Viola often does stuff like Merce Cunningham, where the music is totally unrelated to the movement. There might be abstract music going on, or David Tudor's dinosaur sounds. . . ."

"Normally, dancers adjust right away to the music and the musician," Larry Clark continued. "For example, if I have set movement with set phrases for my students, they can do an improvisation on those phrases by taking the movement out of sequence. For this I might have them improvising to a really strong jazz beat. The more inexperienced dancer often will not be able to control the *quality* of the movement. It will immediately take on the feeling of the jazz music."

"Then if you play something like a pavanne or an Americana piece, this forces the students—with a set phrase of movement—to go through various quality changes, being influenced by different music. I give them set material and say 'You can use no other movement than this. Improvise to the music.' I might give them some sections from *Cosi fan Tutti* or *Tosca,* then something by Benny Goodman or Chopin. So we get all kinds of quality changes. The beat and the pulse could be much different, but since the dancers are improvising on *movement* phrases, they can make variations as long as the improvisation is still on that material. The tempo is not set; the rhythm is not set."

"That's a great way for students to learn. I also might do a phrase of movement and have the dancers improvise to just chords—strong chords—on the piano. Then we might change it to something more light, like a little gigue, taking the same movement and trying to make it work real fast. It's very difficult. Also, free improvisation is wonderful: no movement given; the dancers just parallel the music."

LOU HARRISON

"Musicality in a dancer is *sensitivity* to music, in the first place," observed the composer Lou Harrison. "It's a sensitivity to music through *kinetic* resources. There are dancers who are sensitive to music: that is, they feel it emotionally, but that is not in some sense connected to their own kinetic resources. That is to say, it doesn't come out *immediately.* There can be a little gap there; the synapses don't quite connect." In contrast, he suggested, "a *really* musical dancer has an *immediate* response, and it comes out kinetically with the music."

"I've known several like that who have an especial sensitivity," the composer added. "It shows itself kinetically the minute you see the body in action. Jean Erdman is among them. I was also thinking of a woman I worked with here on the West Coast, Lorele Kranzler. She's a born music lover. It's in her body too. There is that *combination*. Carol Beales had it. I think Erick Hawkins has it too,'' he noted.

Having heard that, it seemed appropriate to elicit Mr. Hawkins' own views on the matter.

ERICK HAWKINS

''The basis of musicality, of course, is feeling the evenness of the pulse,'' Erick Hawkins told the author. ''Once you can feel and experience the evenness of a pulse, then you can make that into patterns, and that's what we call rhythm.''

''But there is something in the actual organism. The psyche, and the soma, the body, are healthy when they're rhythmical,'' he added philosophically.

''The main image of creation in India is the *dance* of Shiva,'' Mr. Hawkins said. ''Shiva is the King of the Dance. The very *image* that the world is created, maintained, and destroyed comes from the rhythmical play of the in and out. It's a metaphysical idea, of course, but the very fact that they embody it in somebody supposedly dancing is absolutely. . . .'' The choreographer left his thought unfinished.

''We have no comparable image in Western culture,'' Mr. Hawkins continued. ''The main notion of how to show what the divine is, in our Western culture, is by a man who of all the Western artists is one of the most sensitive physically, William Blake. He has a watercolor of God with calipers, measuring. And that measuring, you see, is the theoretical component of how you know. It's not the *directly perceived* way of knowing, the way that the rhythm of the dance is.''

''So those are two polar ways of knowing,'' he mused. ''That's why Jacques Barzun was right in talking about the treason of the artist when he tries to be 'sciency.' Science is right in its place, but just because science is so highly developed with us and has gone so far and has done so much and yielded so much in the Western ways (the ways non-Western people didn't discover), it doesn't mean that's the whole thing. That's why you need the *complementary* ways.''

HANYA HOLM

The choreographer Hanya Holm also stressed a nonmechanical way of knowing. What did she think makes a particularly musical dancer? ''Talent!'' she laughed. ''When you have no talent for it—forget it. You can't manufacture it. You have to have that feeling for music.''

''You can be aware of the basics of things—sure,'' she acknowledged. ''But you cannot mechanically multiply it. It doesn't work.'' She related her experience of watching the pianist Vladimir Horowitz on television. ''I watched Horowitz, and sometimes when the chords come, it's not methodical; it's *dy-*

namic. You see, there are such fine differences: off the beat and on the beat at the same time. You *are* in rhythm; you *are* in meter . . . and yet, your beat is not mechanical, like a clock tick tick tick. It may be a little bit faster, a little bit broader—but not so that it becomes irregular.''

Hanya Holm, unlike some dancers nowadays, never worked out her choreography with a metronome or an electronic drum machine. ''No no!'' she exclaimed, ''I couldn't do it. It takes all the life out. And yet,'' she added, ''it's *on the beat*. In the musical theater, that's very important: to be on the beat, and *off* the beat at the same time. You are not *mechanically* on the beat; yet you *are* on the beat.''

In her days of teaching in Colorado and elsewhere, Miss Holm often had her dance students take up percussion instruments and make their own music. ''To play percussion for dance, it's not easy,'' she suggested. ''It's not just hitting. They have to have rhythm. It is not so farfetched,'' she laughed. ''Dance is rhythm; music is rhythm. Melody has timing, pulses, and tempi, and so forth, and that is all so closely related.''

Sometimes a few of her students would make the music for the others to dance, ''because sometimes they couldn't find music,'' she explained, ''so they made it up themselves, by percussion. It was a matter of using it with discretion—not just banging along. Eventually they understood. An instrument is a different animal, I would say. It's almost living! It's not a dead piece and you hit it.''

Miss Holm went on to give a personal demonstration of *timing,* which both dancers and musicians have to understand together. ''You see, when you have a 4/4 going along,'' she said, clapping lightly, ''it is no tapeworm, but there is in it a caesura; there is a rhythm. It is continuous, but not monotonous. It has *dynamic* in it, and *that* makes a difference.''

''It is a little bit like breath control,'' she suggested, demonstrating how one can hold the air in slightly, let it out in small portions, or all at once, in a forceful way. ''So it's the same, and yet not the same. When there is breath control, there is a hidden rhythm to it, but it's not pronounced; it's not sharp. It's like breathing: there's a lot of rhythm to it, but it is not absolutely regular. It's irregular, and not monotonous. But in the repetition, it has *dynamic*. It doesn't jump the rhythm, and it doesn't jump the pulse. The pulse *flows*.

''So when you breathe, regularly, in and out, it is subconsciously; it's rhythmical, but *not stiff*. It has its own pace, but it doesn't go suddenly in snorts; it keeps going, but it has dynamic. In other words, it's a life. And that is a difference that people make when they *learn* it; it becomes mechanical. They cannot have regularity and keep it alive. It keeps going . . . and that is for some people impossible. You are on the beat—and yet you are not. Otherwise, it becomes hard and mechanical—and dead.''

''So there you are,'' Hanya Holm concluded. ''That is a thing you have to work hard for musicians to understand too. So when I listened to Horowitz, he had that inner dynamic. He plays regularly, but it is never monotonous. It has that wonderful quality of 'breath control.' That's why he is so alive—not mechanical!''

PAUL TAYLOR

''I'm the most musically uneducated person you can imagine,'' announced the choreographer Paul Taylor, knowing full well that his visitor regarded his ear for music as quite phenomenal. ''In a way,'' he added, ''it's been good not reading music or being terribly familiar with its history and everything, because it does force me to listen very hard, and I think that can be a benefit.''

He recalled his own performing days, and explained how he knew where he was supposed to be in relation to the music. ''You know the music, just by listening, and when you learn a piece, you learn counts—but not necessarily the way a musician would count. Both to teach dances and to learn them, they're *always* done by counts—*millions* of counts,'' he groaned.

Even for something like Donald York's macabre and atmospheric score for *Last Look?* ''Even *Last Look,''* he confirmed. ''Eventually, you don't have to count, because the rhythm gets in your body if you do it over and over. And there are some dances that you just have to listen to the music, and it's perfectly obvious where you are.''

The counts are precise, the choreographer emphasized. ''Absolutely. In terms of movement, not the music necessarily. But they jibe. There's a relationship that is very accurate, and you do the same thing every time. The counts are for the dancers' convenience. It's according to what makes sense on the movement. Movement phrases don't necessarily have to match music phrases. You can do a movement that takes maybe five counts and do it while three are going on in the music. They don't have to match.''

''Most people don't realize that dancers are actually doing something that's practically scientific, and not improvised,'' the choreographer pointed out. ''Although there are interpretative things that go on in a performance, the accuracy of the dance itself is a constant. Dances don't change.''

But there's no single way that the music and the movement have to relate, Mr. Taylor emphasized. ''It's all relative to what's to be accomplished. There are many people who think musicality is Mickey Mousing the music. Mickey Mousing is—if I had a dictionary I'd give you the proper meaning,'' laughed the choreographer. ''It's like in a Mickey Mouse cartoon where they add a soundtrack of sounds that go with the action. Mickey Mouse goes *bong* over Donald Duck's head, and the music goes *bong*.''

''In a dance, often people think that the dance should go *bong* every time the music goes *bong*. They think we should follow: if the music goes up, the dancers go up; if the music goes down, the dancers go down; if the music goes fast, we go fast . . . or slow, you know: just follow and do what the music does. This is *not* musicality!'' Mr. Taylor declared. ''This is Mickey Mousing.

It's a tool. It's part of the palette, one of the ways to deal with music. But it's only one means to an end.''

''Therefore,'' concluded the choreographer, ''it would seem, in my opinion, that musicality can *include* Mickey Mousing, but it is more a matter of creating a dialogue between the music and the dance. The matter of contrast—going against the music—can come in very effectively, and has all kinds of meanings (if you want to call it that) to an audience: going fast when the music is going slow, and vice versa; not following the musical phrasing, but running across the musical phrase and making your own phrase end amidst the music's. There are ways to play one thing against the other—play music against movement. And this to me is a much more interesting thing. And it assumes the audience is much more sportsman!'' said Paul Taylor with a smile.

Then the choreographer considered what people in an audience might be receiving as they attend a performance. ''True, we don't know what everybody is aware of,'' he commented. ''Personally, my visual sense is much stronger than my ear, and what I'm seeing predominates. But that's just a matter of perception. We hear and see what we *want* to hear and see.''

''But the combination of music and movement to me has been one of the most interesting parts of my job, along with the discoveries that I've found for myself—though many other people may already know them. As I started as a young choreographer and learned through doing it, one of the joys in the work was to discover all the different possibilities that there are in the combination of music and movement. It's fun!''

AGNES DE MILLE

When the choreographer Agnes de Mille was asked what she wished young dancers would know more about in regard to music, she fired back: ''Oh! They don't know music! They know their dancing, but they know nothing of music, as a rule. Every choreographer I know—including Jerome Robbins—can read a score, pick out the music, go to the piano and play it, and say, 'No, I don't want that; give me more of *that.*' If you can't cut your own music, you can't say 'Go back to *there;* try *there.*' Today, they're aliens at the keyboard.''

While Agnes de Mille was growing up, she studied piano many years and reached a level of accomplishment that enabled her to master some Chopin pieces. ''I got through most of the *Scherzi* and the *Etudes,*'' she told her impressed visitor. ''I did lots,'' she went on. ''But I have a very small hand. I could barely do an octave, so I was confined. But I was very fast,'' said the choreographer smiling gently. ''I had gossamer fingers. Not much power, but—''

It gave her pleasure to remember her own music-making. What other composers did she enjoy? ''Bach. Scarlatti. Schubert.'' What about twentieth-century composers? ''Debussy? Well, that's sort of wispy,'' ventured the choreographer. ''But in the end, I guess I laid down a pretty solid foundation. I remember starting on the Magdalena book of Bach and *adoring* it. I first started the piano at about five.''

She initially had a teacher who was trained by legendary artists. But what had he set his pupil to learning? ''He wouldn't let me play anything very much,'' mourned Miss de Mille. ''Oh, 'Brownies in the Rain,' you know . . . 'The Dewdrop,' '' she sniffed in scorn.

Her visitor laughed and said: ''Not the sort of thing you'd want to dance to.'' ''Not the sort of thing I'd ever want to *hear,* either!'' declared Agnes de Mille, raising doubts about the musicality of some music teachers.

DENIS DE COTEAU

In San Francisco, conductor Denis de Coteau has at times taught courses in music for dancers. To this effort he brings not only his practical experience with the San Francisco Ballet, but also his theoretical studies that culminated in a doctorate degree from Stanford University.

What is the main thing he likes to get students to think about concerning musicality? ''What I *hope* to get them to understand is that they have to listen to the music,'' he replied quite simply. ''The problem is that many times dancers count. Their choreography is all to counts. So they count and they count and they count—and they don't listen to the music because they are so busy counting. The music 'says' to do something; the choreographer feels it; the choreographer lays it in there . . . then the dancers do the step, but they do the step to the *count* and not to the music. So while it matches the music in terms of counts, it doesn't always match the music in terms of *intensity.*''

''So what I hope to teach dancers is that—yes, you have your counts to learn your steps, but you must also listen to the music, because the music gives you the quality and the intensity level.''

The conductor singled out the talent of Evelyn Cisneros. ''She is so musical when she dances. She's got the counts, but it's something special that she does. It's *more* than just dancing to counts. And that's what we have to teach dancers to do. Listen to the music.''

ALAN BARKER

When asked his views on musicality in dancers, conductor Alan Barker replied: ''It's an understanding of the structure of the music, of the basic lifeblood, the rhythm, the flow, the impulse, the pulse of the music . . . learning how the choreography should fit with that . . . and more. Some of the dancers know that music has a flow and is going in a certain direction, but they're not going to be bound rigidly by that. They can vacillate slightly to either side, but they find a guide-place where they must meet.''

''I think this may be one of the reasons I like working with Cynthia Gregory so much,'' he remarked. ''Working with her is like working with an extremely fine jazz singer. She knows exactly where the music is, and she knows exactly how much time she has if she wants to diverge slightly from the flow of the music, because she knows when she must get right back onto the note again."

The conductor also spoke of Mikhail Baryshnikov: "He's an extraordinary man. He is totally unfazed by whatever music comes out of the pit, even if it is something totally different from what he has requested in rehearsal. It could be twice as fast or twice as slow, and he never gives an indication of 'suffering' because he has the extraordinary ability to make music work, no matter what it is."

"I'm not sure he analyzes it either," ventured Mr. Barker. "But I just love it. I watch him while I conduct. Other times I've watched him dance to music that is too fast; I've watched him dance to music which is too slow, and he still makes it look like it's exactly right. That is a most unique gift . . . a most unique quality. But then, he's a most unique performer!"

"It seems that one of the things he does is that when he gets onto a stage, he devotes himself solely to dancing and performing. By this I mean that he seems to cease to analyze the individual step, as he would in the studio or the classroom, because the time for that has passed, and his only preoccupation at the moment that he's onstage, seems to be to dance and perform. Many dancers will get onto a stage, and they will think, 'I have to do an arabesque on the count of five . . .' and so, their dancing is a series of disconnected poses or attitudes or steps, but it's not really dancing; it's a classroom exercise. The person who is most far removed from the classroom while he is on the stage is Baryshnikov."

LYNN STANFORD: A CLOSE VIEW OF BARYSHNIKOV, MAKAROVA, AND OTHER DANCERS

"Touring with Misha is first class!" said pianist Lynn Stanford. "He takes me around with him—sort of the way Elizabeth Taylor takes around her hairdresser," he added, explaining what it is like to work with superstar Mikhail Baryshnikov.[3]

Unlike most musicians affiliated with major ballet companies, Mr. Stanford rarely plays for repertoire rehearsals or for stage performances. Instead, he has made a professional specialty of providing music for ballet technique classes. This is a valuable service for the dancers, and a constant creative challenge for the musician.

Fortunate enough to have been introduced to this art through the coaching of ballerina Dame Margot Fonteyn, Lynn Stanford has developed his skill as a cheerful and effective improviser of appropriate, encouraging music that aids the dancers in their daily workouts. For twelve years, he played for classes at New York City Ballet and its affiliated training institution, the School of American Ballet.

After Balanchine's death, the pianist entered a new phase of his career. For about five months of the year, he has continued playing for the professional-level classes at David Howard's private studio in New York City, and has filled a number of composition requests. For instance, he wrote the incidental music for two of Arthur Miller's recent plays that were produced on Broadway.

The rest of this musician's calendar has been filled largely by touring dates with Mikhail Baryshnikov, both in the United States and abroad. Much of this travel has consisted of one-night stands with the little troupe called Baryshnikov and Company. For performances, the group has taken along what Mr. Stanford characterizes as a small ''gypsy'' band consisting of violin, keyboard, synthesizer, bass and drums—a substitute for a live orchestra that apparently left something to be desired.

But that wasn't his department, explained Mr. Stanford. Normally, he does not perform in public. He has, however, from time to time appeared with the group for such pieces as *The Class,* which was choreographed by Peter Fonseca at Mr. Baryshnikov's request.

When asked to describe what he did in his own piece, the pianist replied with a smile: ''A lot of carrying on. As you know, I play with a 'free-spirited' style. Note-for-note, it wasn't exactly the same for each performance. But of course, the *structure* remained the same, and the steps were the same.''

The piece received a favorable review from critic Jennifer Dunning, who saw a performance in Springfield, Massachusetts:

> ''The Class,'' a new work by Peter Fonseca, had an ingenious and lively score composed, arranged, and played on stage by Lynn Stanford, a noted ballet class accompanist. . . . The ballet incorporates elements of a class, from barre warmup to center combinations, in a suite of fleeting dances that gives everyone a chance to shine. ''The Class'' is not another ''Etudes,'' however, but sleek, fast-paced entertainment that would be as much at home in a television variety show as on the Ballet Theatre stage, where one hopes it may someday be used as the inspired opening number it is.[4]

Offstage, Lynn Stanford's musical responsibilities lie in the real studio each morning. Regardless of which city they are in, regardless of whether the project of the day is a live performance before adoring crowds or a filming of a movie or television show, every day begins with Mikhail Baryshnikov doing his private workout alone with Lynn Stanford at a piano—with no printed music on the rack.

''He's trying to stay in shape,'' explained the pianist concerning his work with Baryshnikov. ''It's very difficult to do that if you are by yourself. So at least if I'm there, it gives a sort of formalized structure.''

What Lynn Stanford provides is personalized music, created on the spot and instantly tailored to fit each movement exercise as it evolves before his eyes. When he finishes his private session with Mr. Baryshnikov, the pianist in effect turns the hourglass upside down and begins all over again, playing a separate class for the other dancers.

On tour, Mr. Stanford's other responsibilities have encompassed diverse nonmusical functions that can best be described as assisting on location. Sometimes this has included such fun as playing a walk-on part for the crowd and party scenes in the recent movie *Dancers* starring Mikhail Baryshnikov and other artists from American Ballet Theatre. When the author commented that this must be an interesting way to see the world, the musician injected a note of realism: ''Well, I'm seeing the hotels and theaters—a *lot* of those!''

Another thing that Mr. Stanford has seen a lot of is the dancing of Mikhail Baryshnikov—not only in the studio, but also in performances, which the musician often watches from the wings of the stage. Yet when asked what Mr. Baryshnikov does to give the viewer an impression of being so musical, the pianist was hesitant to express in words what the magic ingredient might be. ''I can't articulate it,'' he acknowledged. ''I can't say that I think I can tell you what it is.''

But contrasting his experiences with Baryshnikov and another Russian superstar of ballet, Natalia Makarova, the pianist remarked: ''Natasha is very musical! I'll tell you a thing I find about the two of them, about their musicality: it's that their phrasing—whether it's onstage or in the classroom—relates *thoroughly* to the music. The movement is an extension of the music. It's not necessarily 'on' the music; it's not necessarily a visualization of the music. It's *through* and *in* and *over* and *around* and *about* the music!''

''Now the curious thing about Misha,'' the pianist went on to note, ''is that he's very quick, impatient and all that. He's always running slightly ahead of the music. You can't watch Misha when you are playing for him and try to be 'with' him, because he's always slightly anticipating everything. But he is very *consistent*. So you just have to play and have your experience tell you that you are playing the right tempo, and leave it up to him to do with it what he wants.

''Now Natasha Makarova, on the other hand, is kind of laid back and languid, retiring and sylphlike. So Natasha is always—curiously—slightly behind the music. Just *slightly*. The music sounds, and she moves, but it is in such a consistent way that it all works, because it is always all *about* the music. It's never 'in spite of' the music. It's always totally and absolutely related to the music.''

''So my point,'' Mr. Stanford continued, ''is that if you see them taking class—one at this end of the barre and the other one at that end of the barre—and you're watching them work, because one is slightly ahead of the music and one is slightly behind, they can be as much as a beat apart. So you just go ahead and give them the musical framework to work in. That's what I'm doing: I'm providing the impetus.''

''Now of course,'' he went on to say, ''this wouldn't work necessarily if they were standing side by side in a corps de ballet. But obviously, it does work for *them*. And they dance beautifully *together*—I think, magnificently!''

Miss Makarova, for her part, paid Lynn Stanford a compliment. On her videotape ''In a Class of Her Own,'' she is heard saying: ''He has spice in his music, that gives me joy to dance.''[5]

Speaking about his collaboration for this and other videotapes, Lynn Stanford himself communicated a sense of dissatisfaction. What happens when an improvised piece of music, one created to suit a specific moment and functional purpose, gets transformed into a permanent record? "What may feel good or right in the studio is not necessarily going to look or sound right on camera or on tape," remarked the pianist.

"I don't know that one is ever really head-over-heels about anything that one does," said Mr. Stanford. "I listen to everything with such a critical ear—don't we all? Oh, I think it would be wonderful to hear something and say, 'Gosh, I'm thrilled,' or have some sort of really self-satisfied comprehension. But that hasn't happened to me yet." Until it does, Lynn Stanford—like other pianists in ballet studios across the world—continues his close and immediate musical collaborations with dancers.

When asked if he had any general ideas concerning what makes some dancers give an impression of being more musical than others, he suggested, "One thing is a proper understanding of what the relation between music and dance is. I can't necessarily tell you what's 'proper,' but I can tell you what I think is improper! One thing I feel very definitely about is that the music is not another element that is 'added on,' like lights and costumes or make-up. The whole reason that we dance, and what dancing is about, is an impetus to respond to the sound."

Continuing his train of thought, Mr. Stanford suggested: "You hear the music, and you want to dance. I feel this is a very instinctive, natural, basic reaction. People in Africa do it. People here do it when they go into a disco and hear the music and want to dance. You hear a beautiful Strauss waltz and feel like waltzing. You go to the theater and you hear something on Broadway, and you walk out of the theater with a lighter step! I feel that the instinct to respond to music with movement is a very natural one. I feel that it carries on regardless of how formalized the structure is or how classical we get. I feel that the impetus is still the same, and I think that's what shows on the best dancers that I work with. Visually, what seems to be happening, is that they seem to be responding to the music."

"It's hard to say what musicality is," he acknowledged. "I do want to say just a couple of things that it's *not*—like relating to music as just another element. There is unfortunately a saying that is quite fond among conductors, that the only relationship between music and dance is *rosin*. This is because with a lot of dancers, it has not been instilled in them that they have to *respect* the music."

"Something I learned from Balanchine," the pianist observed, "is that it has to start in the classroom. The dancers have to be made to dance *on* the music rather than indulged by having musicians follow them. Misha agrees with me entirely. And Misha very seldom says anything to me about 'It's too fast' or 'Too slow,' or anything like that. *He* goes with the music."

A DANCE CRITIC CONSIDERS AURAL ELEMENTS

Elizabeth Lee brought an unusual combination of experiences to her work as a dance critic for the *Durham Morning Herald.* She had studied piano and music history, but went on to become a college teacher of English, and also took up modern dance very seriously. She performed with the Carolina Dancers, then went on to choreograph and present her own works. Furthermore, as a panel member for North Carolina's Council for the Arts, she became familiar with a wide variety of companies, productions, and concerns.

In recalling her impressions while reviewing more than 500 programs in Durham, including many at the American Dance Festival (ADF), Dr. Lee made the dismaying observation that nearly all the professional dance performances were to taped music. That fact was further commented upon by ADF director Charles Reinhart, who pointed out that live music is often at least potentially the single most expensive item in the budget of small modern dance companies.[6]

Concerning the music used by local dance companies in Durham, Dr. Lee again said that it was usually taped—except she recalled the Carolina Dancers doing one piece where the performers created their own sounds. "Stomping and clapping, and talking, and then giggling. I liked that," commented the dancer-critic. "You giggle in rhythm; you giggle in time; you giggle together. There are all kinds of ways of giggling. You can giggle in canon, for example."

This simple live sound device seemed to her a pleasant change from taped music—even though the recorded choices of the local choreographers had been quite eclectic, spanning music of Charles Ives, Irish folk tunes by the Chieftains, jazz works, Brahms, and Bob Dylan, for example.

Such variety—and such dependence on tape—probably exists in many community and student dance performances throughout the country. How does this piped-out aural element strike the professional audience member—which is what a critic is, after all?

"I'm very visual," Elizabeth Lee remarked. "That's something I discovered by doing choreography myself, even though I love music and have an ear for it. But if you give me both inputs at the same time, I'll go right for the visual. I'll turn the audio off if I have to turn something off."

"I have a feeling," she explained, "that when the music is live, then my experience is much more intense. It's not always true, either, that I turn the music off," she added half-apologetically. "I think that intellectually I don't attend to the music, when I'm thinking about reviewing, because I'm not going to have to *discuss* the music!"

Why not, when the music is such an important ingredient of a theatrical work? "Well," she relented, "maybe it's different if it's taped. Maybe I feel as if nobody's there. As a matter of fact, once I reviewed a dance concert where the musicians were onstage, and I spent half the review talking about them, not so much because of the music, as because of their movements! And when I am at orchestra concerts where you can see the musicians, I get very interested in their movements. Since I *see* them producing the sounds, I can also apprehend the sound a lot better.''

The practical aspects of journalism became clear as the author followed Elizabeth Lee around on her American Dance Festival assignment one evening. Having positioned her car carefully for a fast getaway from the theater, the critic zoomed to the newspaper office and typed her story on a word processor, which was hooked up to the editor's desk so he in effect could read over her shoulder. Just before midnight, he finally asked her to ''cut a couple of inches.'' That particular night, the critic had precisely twelve inches of space allotted to her story, and less than an hour to review the Limón Company's performance of three major works.

After finishing her review, the critic mentioned that she would be more likely to devote some of that precious space to the music if the score had been specially commissioned. ''But even a commissioned score that's not performed live probably doesn't *seem* commissioned,'' she mused. ''I *would* talk about the music in Laura Dean's works,'' she went on to say. ''But to me, in Dean's works, everything goes *past* the perceptual apparatus, so you're getting rhythm as if it's generated in *you,* from what they do.''

''Maybe partly because it's live,'' she reflected. ''But I find that Dean's works are very integrated. She does her own composing and works directly with the musicians—so you *are* talking about where the artistic consciousness is.''

SOME MEMORABLE QUOTES ON MUSICALITY

''The worst thing to do is to work with a dancer who only cares about the steps,'' suggested choreographer Jennifer Muller to a group of aspiring students gathered at the Alvin Ailey School. ''You gotta know musical styles!'' she advised.[7]

Some further advice for students can be found in Alexandra Danilova's autobiography *Choura.* Based on her long experience both as a ballerina and as a teacher at the School of American Ballet, Mme. Danilova suggested:

> Many teachers believe that musicality is rare and God-given, beyond their power to shape, but I disagree. I think that for any dancer it is a necessity, and I know that it can be cultivated because I cultivate it in my students. I teach them to associate music with movement, to listen hard, so that they learn to sense immediately the places where the choreography fits the score. . . . I demand that all my pupils, even little children, be right on the beat.
>
> Good dancers are made every day, by good teachers; but great dancers are born. A great dancer has something extra—I think it's personality. She isn't just a dummy who waves her hands in time to the music; her movements have meaning.[8]

In her autobiography, the ballerina Natalia Makarova touched upon some of the deeper layers of relationship between music and dance:

Classical ballet is, in this sense, closer to music than anything else. In music, sound is arranged harmoniously, and what it asserts can be only partially rendered in words. In the classical ballet, it is the body, subject to the harmony of the steps it is executing, which speaks. And it speaks to the heart in as direct a language as does music. Of course, the body's range of meaning is more limited—it cannot completely overcome its concreteness—and it can only make music concrete, translating its abstract language into plastic form. I believe that the body can overcome its corporeality through the magic of inspiration and can be transfigured into a musical phrase. But how to accomplish this? It cannot be taught, and however much I have tried to find the magical formula, I have been unable to. It is possible that I am encroaching now on the very secret of art and inspiration, and that it has not been given to anyone to decipher it.[9]

TOWARD THE FUTURE

11

Building Theaters, Patronage, and Artistry

In contrast to the fleeting presence of dance itself, lavish new theaters are typical of a nationwide trend in the United States.

Not only have major dance companies become affiliated with particular buildings and cultural centers; the organizations of performing groups themselves have also become increasingly complex and structured. Particularly when new or live music for ballet and modern dance is involved, large financial investments are often required for each new production. And in recent years, artistic decisions—including those involving the musical elements—are increasingly influenced by boards of directors whose members may be more oriented toward business, social, or political interests than they are toward the art of dance.

Some of the dangers in these developments were addressed by several speakers before a national gathering of Dance USA (a service organization for professional companies). Former Ford Foundation executive W. McNeil Lowry, for one, warned that "management has become the right hand not of artistic directors, but of boards of directors. Creative leaders must take control of their institutions." Similarly, in his keynote speech, choreographer Alwin Nikolais voiced concern that performing companies are becoming removed from the creative initiatives that sparked them in the first place.[1]

Another development that has brought both benefits and challenges is the increased involvement in the arts on the part of both government and private corporations. On the one hand, their support and funding is most welcome. But on the other hand, there are some accompanying dangers to be wary of. For instance, Agnes de Mille warned students at the Graham School about some of the pitfalls of bureaucracy. Though she herself had been one of the original panelists of the National Endowment for the Arts, she nevertheless pointed out that to divide up public funds according to certain considerations, such as electoral districts, might make "good politics, but not always good art."[2]

Somehow, while we juggle all the concomitant aspects of the performing arts—buildings, funding, social galas, the attraction of performances in connection with political and community prestige, the health and educational values, and so on—we must not lose sight of the arts themselves. The best creations, after all, begin somewhere in the imagination of individuals. The end products also exist within individuals—namely, in the awareness and feelings of audience members as each person experiences a work in the theater.

In the long run, our present "golden age" of dance in America will continue only if the works presented have meaning and pleasure for audiences beyond mere saturation in watching a variety of physical movement patterns.

The musical choices that choreographers make, the way that they use music, and the way that dancers relate to the music, can often spell the difference between disaster and artistry. And of course, the way that musicians fulfill their collaborative functions for dance performance can make a difference too, for better or for worse.

BEN STEVENSON: BALLET FOR HOUSTON, CHINA, AND CHILDREN

Speaking to the author some months before the opening of Houston's elegant new theater for opera and ballet, artistic director Ben Stevenson was both proud of his ballet company's orchestra and uneasy about the financing of it, since patrons' contributions were very much contingent on the ups and downs of oil prices.[3]

"We try to keep a good standard in Houston," said Mr. Stevenson, "because that is where we have to *glow!* The company regularly has a small orchestra of twenty-four musicians for tours, but at home, they may employ as many as seventy musicians for large works. It is a big expense, but I think our backers feel it is very important."

Along with the building of the physical theater, the director was also pleased with the company's home-grown conductor, Glenn Langdon. "He was a pianist in our school," Mr. Stevenson explained. "Then he became affiliated with the company. I am very excited about him. It is very difficult to find a young conductor that is used to dance. But Langdon is disciplined. He is very interested in developing the orchestra, and he is very loyal to the musicians. Thanks to him we have this group now, because he has built it up."

Grooming a conductor and the musicians is one part of the artistic director's job. So is nurturing musicality in each generation of young dancers. Ben Stevenson made it a point to mention that in the Houston Ballet's affiliated academy, there are both lectures about music and choreographers' workshops in the summers. He explained that "the teachers talk about music and how it should be used—how not to suddenly use great [Gustav] Mahler for your first piece.

We try and listen to what they want to do first. If they say 'We want to do Beethoven's Fifth or something like that which is so ridiculously enormous, we suggest something not so difficult for dance. We try and guide them.''

Mr. Stevenson is also very much involved in the cross-cultural practice of ballet. Formerly a principal dancer with the Royal Ballet in London, he now spends many weeks each year at the Beijing Central Ballet Academy. Back home in Houston, he choreographed a new work to a commissioned score by the Chinese composer Mao Yuan. ''It sounds Chinese,'' observed the choreographer, ''but it is written for Western instruments. It is very sweet, very nice, very charming.''[4]

When asked what he does on both sides of the globe to train dancers in musicality, Mr. Stevenson replied: ''I think it is partly in the steps you give and the way you use music within the steps. If a *teacher* is unmusical—and I think that sometimes happens—then students learn how to do the steps, but they can't do them to the music. So sometimes their phrasing is off.''

''Some people just dance to a beat,'' he observed. ''But I think you have to listen to the music. I think it starts at the barre, learning how to phrase and how to be continuously moving until the end of a phrase. If you've got something in four counts, then make it last four counts, and don't do it in two and then be standing there for two.''

As part of the early training for dancers, Ben Stevenson is much in favor of classes in creative movement. ''Four- or five-year-olds really learn to experience themselves in these classes,'' he said enthusiastically. ''Someone plays some music and they go march-march-march, or they are giants, or they do little fairies running around. All the while, they get to listen to live music and appreciate it. We see that with the people who come through this, that when they reach their first year of ballet, they are much more expressive than the people who don't. They have more appreciation and are more used to listening.''

Ben Stevenson keeps his own listening very up-to-date and has collaborated with a number of composers. Among these is Robert Prince, who did the score for Mr. Stevenson's *Space City*. Then there was a young composer from the Houston Ballet Academy, Glen Tarachow, who was only 18 when he composed a score for the director. ''He also danced,'' noted Mr. Stevenson, adding, ''he is very talented, and he wrote a very good piece.''

Another collaboration was with John Dankworth, the well-known English jazz composer, for *Lady in Waiting*. This was a major two-hour ballet in two acts, and it also involved the composer's wife, the popular jazz singer Cleo Laine.

Looking towards the future, Ben Stevenson seems a master at transforming the best of classical traditions in ways that are immediately meaningful for younger generations. As he taught emerging artists at the Southeastern Regional Ballet Festival in Miami, it was obvious that the young dancers found him very inspiring. It is no wonder that his colleagues wrote in the festival's program notes:

Ben Stevenson has transformed Houston Ballet into one of the major dance companies in America with a reputation throughout the world. . . . Internationally known as one of ballet's great master teachers, Mr. Stevenson has overseen enormous growth in the Houston Ballet Academy, which has become the essence and the future of the company. His conviction that the development of a major company stems from the success of a well-established professional school has produced one of the finest dance training centers in the United States.

THE ATTITUDE OF CONSERVATORY MUSICIANS

Music is part of the dancers' training in Houston and at other good dance schools. Unfortunately, the complement of this statement does not hold true, for most music instruction in this country does not place major emphasis on dance as a closely related art.[5]

Ideally, all music students would have direct experience of dance; serious musicians, especially composers, would receive training in collaboration for the dance. In addition, courses about the history and aesthetics of dance would be helpful, as well as specialized analytical study of musical scores and forms intended specifically for dance purposes. If such offerings exist at all in any institution of higher learning in the United States, they are not widely known.

The Juilliard School is unusual in that it houses professional divisions for both music and dance. Upon speaking to a number of the students who were studying modern dance intensively there, it was impressive to hear one of them mention that "at Juilliard, you take L & M—Literature and Materials of Music—until you die!"

Wondering if the musicians were also required to take "L & M of Dance," the author spoke to William Schuman, who had been president of Juilliard before becoming the first president of Lincoln Center. "I started the dance department at Juilliard," he said. "There had been no dance at Juilliard, and I brought in Martha Hill to head the department, and all those teachers, all those wonderful dancers."

Yet when asked whether there was much collaboration between the musicians and the dancers, Mr. Schuman answered: "I wouldn't say there was collaboration. I always hoped that there would be. But there wasn't an awful lot. Of course the musicians were around to play for the dancers, and *some* musicians were interested. But professionals usually go their separate ways, even within the branches of music. You won't find string players talking to singers. It just doesn't work that way."

Such divisions of association and activity exist at other schools that emphasize the arts, though perhaps not to such an extent as at the Juilliard School. But unfortunately, collaboration between the music and dance departments is not automatic anywhere.

For example, at the State University of New York at Purchase, which was established to provide professional training in the performing arts within a liberal arts program, there is an elegant center with four theaters equalling some of the best facilities in New York City. Yet for some years, the dance students and the music students seemed to go their separate ways. The musicians performed without dancers, and the dancers performed with tapes. So it was a particular pleasure for local audiences to see one of the exceptions to that rule, when the Purchase Dance Corps performed *Coppélia* with a student orchestra conducted by faculty member David Milnes.

Discussing the event with dance teacher Larry Clark, the author observed that it must have been an advantage to have a free student orchestra. "No!" he replied. "We pay. You bet we do! There's nothing you get for free. The whole school is set up to interact, hopefully, on a freebie basis, but it has never worked that way."

Another deterrent to frequent collaboration is the pressure of time. "The music department has their own format," Mr. Clark noted. "They are naturally concerned about their own schedule. You know, it took almost a whole semester to do *Coppélia*—so it probably knocked some students out of purely musical performances they might have liked to schedule."

Turning to the ballet itself, Mr. Clark said he heard some instrumentalists say: "This is boring music. It's not pretty music."

"I heard that from a *lot* of musicians," emphasized the dance teacher. "However, once they played it with the conductor, I think they got a lot out of it, and they *learned* a lot."

"You know," the artist asked pointedly, "what are they going to do when they graduate? If they are lucky, they'll be in an opera pit or a ballet pit in New York City making a ton of money—*if* they are lucky."

"I don't know why those kids had the attitude they did," pondered Mr. Clark, "whether it's because of their teachers, or because of their own expectations. I would think they would be very enthusiastic about playing for dancers—ballet *or* modern. But the orchestra was marvelous," he continued. "The conductor helped. You could hear the growth at every rehearsal. So when they finally performed, it did not sound like what you would anticipate as a college orchestra."

In regard to the dance students, Mr. Clark noted a similar learning experience. "A lot of things seemed unfamiliar to them when we went from tape to live orchestra. It didn't even sound like the same piece to some dancers. Something magical can be confusing at the same time. Also, when there are human people playing with heart and soul in the pit, it really affects the dancers energy-wise. I think the live music elevated the dancers' performing ability quite a bit."

Finally, when some of the instrumentalists were asked if they had received any extra academic credit for playing in *Coppélia,* one violist replied: "No—but we certainly don't fail orchestra!"

12

Obtaining New Music for Choreography

MEET THE COMPOSER

One of the most ambitious recent projects aimed at the creation of new music for ballet and modern dance is the Composer/Choreographer Project initiated by Meet the Composer, supported by the Ford Foundation and The Pew Charitable Trusts.

Over the years, Meet the Composer has been helpful to smaller dance groups as well. The organization is under the leadership of John Duffy, a composer who has collaborated with such fine dance artists as Pearl Lang. Speaking in his office, Mr. Duffy was justifiably proud of his organization's function as a catalyst for new works.[1]

Asked whether contemporary music is anathema to most audience members, Mr. Duffy offered reassurance that audiences by and large seem to love hearing—and seeing—fresh works. Moreover, he observed, there seems to be a softening of former harshness in musical style, as well as a kind of spiritual awakening among composers. Whereas some twenty years ago, it seemed as if there was a widespread "ivory tower" attitude on the part of some of our best-trained composers, nowadays they are eager to meet with their audiences—and in fact are writing warmer, more accessible music.

As part of its careful preparations for the Composer/Choreographer Project, Meet the Composer enlisted dance artist Ian Horvath as consultant. He visited thirty leading companies around the United States and wrote a detailed report, which turned out to be a fine overview of professional dance in America today. In it, he noted:

Dance's innate collaborative nature and its audiences' and artists' insatiable appetites for new works gave rise to the idea of a new program that could substantially benefit each discipline while allowing individual artists the opportunity to create together.[2]

He went on to emphasize:

The single most important need in dance today is the development of a body of work large enough to sustain the repertory demands of our major institutions. Compared to that of our sister disciplines, our standard repertory is miniscule.[3]

Then, focusing on the relative lack of music composed specifically for the dance in this country, Mr. Horvath suggested:

The continuing divergence of concert and popular music, the inaccessibility of much serious music during the second half of the century, and Balanchine's sanctioning of musical masterworks as dance accompaniment have all contributed to the fact that very little new concert music is being commissioned for dance.[4]

Despite the sustained and dedicated public relations efforts of organizations such as Meet the Composer, ASCAP, Broadcast Music, Inc. (BMI), the American Composers' Alliance (ACA), the American Music Center, Composers' Forum, the International Society for Contemporary Music, Composers Recordings, Inc., and many others in the field of contemporary concert music, the word about our country's vast supply of well-crafted new music and competent composers apparently has not reached all performing dance groups. In his report, Ian Horvath touched upon this lack of familiarity:

In institutionalized music today, including most of this country's orchestral and chamber ensembles, new musical literature is relatively unknown. Even the music field is grossly undereducated and uninformed regarding new music. Dance, needless to say, shares this unfortunate plight.[5]

Turning to the performance aspects, the report suggested:

Performing with live music is a "way of life" for only the very large dance institutions. Smaller organizations . . . simply do not have the financial wherewithal to engage musicians. . . . There is a great need and desire in the field to perform with live music. All companies participating in this study found their performances immeasurably enhanced by live music. All need and want to perform more frequently and consistently with live music.[6]

Elaborating verbally on his findings, Mr. Horvath spoke about some of the problems involved in embarking on new collaborations. He suggested: "The difficulty that so many choreographers have, especially choreographers that come from the ballet vocabulary, is that they are totally motivated by the music, totally inspired by the music. They want to hear the completed score before they start to do a step, or before they start to make figures and motifs and movement phrases and things like that.''

''That's not possible with a commissioned score,'' he observed. ''And yet, some choreographers have rather sophisticated knowledge, from a compositional point of view, about music. They can read and understand orchestration, but they just feel as if they are going to miss something important unless they can hear the piece totally. That is one of the great problems. I understand that, for it's an incredible fear to go into a piece and have only the piano reduction. You're talking about the orchestration; you're seeing it—but you're not really hearing it.''

''But it has worked for me several times,'' said Mr. Horvath of his own collaborations with composers. ''The key here,'' he explained, ''is that whenever I have commissioned a piece, I did so because I had a specific concept that I couldn't realize with existing music. This also makes a collaboration more meaningful as far as the composer's input is concerned.''

A FIRST STEP

Precisely because of some of the points raised by Mr. Horvath, many choreographers feel most comfortable embarking on new works to contemporary music that has already been composed. But even then, if they present their performances with live musicians, there can be considerable artistic risk—as well as satisfaction.

For example, a young dancer named Todd Hall performed in the Washington, D. C. premiere of Robert Steele's *Other Selves,* and couldn't say enough enthusiastic things about the whole experience. Mr. Steele later described his feelings during the project.[7]

Inspired originally by a sculpture exhibition called ''A Woman's Journey,'' the choreographer selected existing music by Victoria Bond for his new dance. Although the score itself had been used for choreography previously by Lynn Taylor-Corbett, *Other Selves* had the added interest of considering the musicians performing, in terms of lighting, placement and so forth. The choreographer remarked that it particularly pleased him afterwards when the composer came to him and said that he had expressed in movement what she had meant to say in her music.

Of the score itself, Mr. Steele observed: ''It's very eclectic; it's very contemporary. Some musicians might consider it trite—people who are 'learned' in the field of music. To me, it was *not* trite. To me it was very challenging—very! It's atonal, very dissonant, and very hard to count. I had to feel my way through. I had to feel where I thought there was a phrase.''

''So what happened,'' continued the choreographer, ''is that I stuck to my guns and felt what I felt, and did what I did, and the dancers were doing what I gave them to do. They really interpreted it the way I wanted it.''

"I said to them before we went on, 'Just go out and do it like a gig, with a great deal of conviction. Really believe in yourselves doing it. And no matter what happens—you know, we may get applause, we may even get booed—but do what you do and finish it with a great sense of conviction and responsibility, because *we are making our comment.* It may not be enjoyed by everybody, but we're making our comment.' "

"Afterwards, much to my glee, the audience was extremely favorable," said Mr. Steele. "The musicians themselves came to me and told me how much they enjoyed working with me in that position, doing what I was doing, and what artistry and sensitivity I had for their music and for their playing. All around, it was just a respecting of each others' work!"

RON CUNNINGHAM: EVOKING MUSIC THAT REFLECTS THE AMERICAN PAST

When the Boston Ballet performed Ron Cunningham's staging of *Cinderella* in the People's Republic of China, the performance was televised to an estimated thirty million viewers—possibly the largest ballet audience in history.

Back in the United States, this choreographer has made other artistic breakthroughs—ones which, though not as heralded by international publicity, nevertheless required a different kind of risk-taking, as well as some self-financing.

For example, he related to the author his first experiences in collaborating with William Sleater, who at the time was untried in composing for the ballet stage.[8]

Describing his collaborator's unusual background, Mr. Cunningham noted: "Sleater makes his living as a writer of everything from children's fiction novels to psychology textbooks. He's a kind of interesting guy. He studied at Harvard as a pianist. He had come to the Boston Ballet to write a kind of ballet–murder mystery type thing, and he offered his services as a pianist so that he could be around the company to observe. He went on tour with us, and ended up being there for many years—and he never wrote that book!"

However, author-musician Sleater did compose three musical works for the choreographer. "The first was *Saturday Morning,*" Mr. Cunningham went on. "It was an idea I *had* to do, about cartoon characters, a satire on Wonder Woman and Captain America, the sort of stereotype role models that we have.

"Billy wrote the music for me. I believe there were six instruments, and we recorded it in a studio with musicians from the New England Conservatory of Music. The performance was actually with tape. But it was an experimental piece. There was no budget for it whatsoever. Billy did it for free; I did it for free. They were real good musicians, but they were students."

The collaborators' second project together, *Incident at Black Briar,* was quite successful, and turned out to be one of the choreographer's most "portable" ballets, with performances at over fifteen locations within a few seasons.

Based on D. H. Lawrence's story *The Fox*, the ballet had a slightly altered plot. It portrayed an intense relationship between a mother and her daughter, and a man who comes between the two. "You know that kind of symbiotic relationship that many women have with their daughters?" asked the choreographer. Concerning his own version, he explained, "it's a very powerful kind of psychological dramatic piece, done in a sort of quasi-Victorian setting."

Instead of simply using some older European classical music, as many other choreographers might do, Ron Cunningham took a route that is perhaps more difficult: he attempted to to elicit a score from the composer that would closely reflect the setting, emotion, intention, drama, and kinetic requirements of his particular dance. Mr. Cunningham even searched his own experiences of American life to suggest particular instrumentation to the composer.

Ron Cunningham described the way the two collaborators decided together on what they wanted to do: "On an intuitive level, Bill and I would get together and go out and have an Italian dinner and make these grand plans and write all over napkins. Usually, in our collaborations, Bill likes to be able to have an outline of the *quality* of what it is we want to do.

"So in the case of the D. H. Lawrence theme, I would start out talking about the story: what elements we wanted, and what we wanted it to say—talking about what I, as a choreographer, was trying to get at . . . what was important, and what was my reason for wanting to choreograph this mess! Out of that, we asked, how can we distill our characterization down to a minimal, just the essence of it, so you won't have a long complicated thing?"

"Billy and I have real good communication," continued the choreographer. "He would throw out some observations on why various things were important to me. This would make me think psychologically about these things. Then we tried to make a *structure*. I felt it was important to assign instrumentation for the characters, and Billy thought it was a good idea as well."

"The instrumentation for that ballet," he explained, "was piano, percussion, dulcimer, cello, oboe, and accordion. The cello was for the older woman; the oboe for the younger; and the man was associated with the accordion. When Bill suggested the accordion, I said, 'You gotta be kidding.' But he fought for that, and he was right. It really gives a very sleazy sound and is just right."

Focusing on the unusual use of the dulcimer, Mr. Cunningham explained: "I grew up in Chicago, but my family is from Tennessee. I remember when I was a small child, going up into the hills of the country—kind of isolated, backwoods communities. They have a lot of dulcimers there, of course, and the dulcimer has always reminded me of something very remote, very private, very secretive and secluded . . . far away.

"I understand that the dulcimer was an Elizabethan instrument. When the English immigrated to the United States and moved to the various communities, those instruments like the dulcimer, which they brought with them, sort of stayed locked up there with them. So I have always thought of the dulcimer as a very delicate, private, secret kind of instrument that has very special qualities, and also is rooted in the past history.''

''Similarly,'' Mr. Cunningham pointed out, ''I saw the drama of these people in the story as very private, with the shutters closed, and the door also. Whatever happened, was happening inside their house, very confined and very uptight. And so for that reason, the dulcimer became one of the instruments for the dance.''

It was a particular pleasure to find an American choreographer taking the initiative and searching for distinctly American music to accompany his dance.

13

A Festival of Ballets to American Music

To celebrate its 40th anniversary, New York City Ballet presented an ambitious two-week Festival of American Music. The events of the Festival, while unique, also served as a good barometer of the current atmosphere for music and dance collaborations in the United States.

Musically, there was a spectrum of styles ranging from the romantic lushness of Samuel Barber to the urban suaveness of George Gershwin and Duke Ellington. There were craggy serialist scores and mesmerizing minimalist ones. There was a variety of instrumental groupings, ranging from the delicacy of solo art songs with piano to the robust enthusiasm of Ray Charles and his jazz band onstage for the grand finale.[1]

The festival was originally conceived by New York City Ballet's co–ballet master, Peter Martins. Prior to the events, Mr. Martins told *Dance Magazine:*

> I spent more than two years researching American music before any active work on the festival was begun. I called publishers, talked to musicians, asked everywhere, and then listened and listened and listened. Obviously, the festival is not going to be comprehensive. . . . But I hope that [it] will help contribute to an awareness of American music, because I think that American music is underplayed in America—undervalued. It's the old story. Europeans are fascinated by Americans, and Americans love everything that's foreign, especially in the ballet world. Neither side can afford to be close-minded that way. American music should be honored and celebrated.[2]

For theater-goers who tried to see everything, the festival soon became mind-boggling. But with all the emphasis on the music—including the attractive orchestral overtures which were played while a commissioned art poster was projected on the screen—it was intriguing to listen to the reactions of audience members.

"What? There's no dancing in this one? Just music? It's a gyp!" one man was heard to comment. A lively-looking young woman of 30 or so, when asked what she thought of Jean-Pierre Bonnefoux's setting of Charles Wuorinen's cello concerto, responded: "Oh, I loved the music, and I loved the dancing." Had she ever heard any of Wuorinen's music before? "No." Well, would she like to go home and put some of his recordings on for her own listening pleasure? "Probably not," she answered, with a telling wrinkle of the nose.

Even music critic Bernard Holland of *The New York Times* admitted that "it was all a little bewildering to the innocent." He went on to observe:

> One had the troubling feeling that sound, while progenitor and sustenance for stage movement, is conceived—and ultimately received—as a second-class operative in the politics of dance, an essential prop but one whose clarity and shape is readily sacrificed when the stage so demands. In the concert hall, sound rules; in the opera house, it pretends not to but usually does. The ballet seems quite different. In its home, music is the indispensible family servant who nevertheless lives over the garage.[3]

Touching upon two of the new works which had been commissioned from two prestigious Pulitzer Prize–winning composers, the critic suggested that "Mr. Wuorinen's music struggled awkwardly with the stage, while Ellen Taaffe Zwilich's 'Tanzspiel' seemed to render it numb and drab."

Judging by the strong reactions expressed both in print and by word of mouth, it seems fair to say that one of the positive effects of the festival was simply that it got people thinking about new possibilities in collaboration.

For instance, judging by the amount of applause and even cheering after the premiere of the Wuorinen-Bonnefoux piece, *Five,* it seems accurate to report that quite a few of the audience members reacted favorably, in contrast to the negative impressions of *The New York Times* critic. And yet, there were many people present, including the author, who upon only one viewing experienced very uneasy feelings about this collaborative work.

However, the orchestra musicians seemed pleased with the Wuorinen composition. They found it well-crafted, and the cello solo as performed by Fred Sherry seemed to many little short of dazzling in its virtuosity. Furthermore, some knowledgeable musicians in the audience suggested that perhaps the choreography was not up to the music.

Everybody seemed to have a different viewpoint on the performance, and a different emotional reaction. In light of these diverse opinions, one wondered how the commissioned composers were feeling about the festival. Charles Wuorinen, for one, was asked about his participation—which had included not only composing the new piece, but also conducting performances of it.[4]

Apparently undaunted by any adverse press coverage, Mr. Wuorinen had nothing but good things to say about his entire experience with the American Music Festival. "I was very pleased with the way everything went," he said. "My only regret was that because of the combination of the ballet rehearsal schedule and my own, it was impossible for me to see a piano rehearsal or have a chance to see the choreography without being busy in the pit myself.''

Although Mr. Wuorinen had not previously collaborated for the dance (except for a youthful attempt some thirty years before), his music had been used by a number of choreographers. One of these was Jean-Pierre Bonnefoux, who had once mentioned to the author that Charles Wuorinen was his favorite contemporary composer.

The esteem was mutual, it seems: ''This is a company of distinction,'' Mr. Wuorinen commented, while noting that he had attended many performances by the New York City Ballet. The commission was arranged almost a full year before the premiere performance. Mr. Wuorinen considered it a major piece, and his collaboration was very focused: he talked with the choreographer, found out what he wanted, and then sat down and composed—totally apart from the dancers themselves.

For the performances, his role as conductor was a familiar one, for Mr. Wuorinen had worked in theater pits before, with other dance groups. In preparing the orchestral performance itself, Mr. Wuorinen estimated that he had about four or five hours of rehearsal. ''Never enough,'' he commented, while acknowledging that such an amount of time is about all one can expect nowadays even for concert performances with major symphony orchestras.

Just a few weeks after the festival, Charles Wuorinen had already been approached about the possibility of writing another piece for a ballet. So one outcome of Peter Martins' experiment may in fact be tangible encouragement to composers in various styles to enter into creative collaborations with the dance world.

It works the other way, too: festivals may make dance artists more aware of the wide range of expressive concert music that is being written today by American composers. No need to be constantly returning to the European past for inspiration and musical accompaniment; there are new, contemporary sounds out there waiting, and there are many competent American composers who will gladly craft new pieces made to order for dancers.

Yet no matter how eagerly musicians approach their projects for dance, it might help if they have had their initiation into theatrical work under less pressured circumstances—perhaps with smaller companies in smaller theaters, or with longer preparation time. It seemed as if some of the creative collaborators for the New York festival—both the composers and the choreographers—apparently did not bring enough of this kind of experience to their projects to achieve entirely masterful new productions in their Lincoln Center premieres.

From the audience's viewpoint, it must be admitted that in such a professional setting, most theater-goers do expect, if not masterpieces, then at least a high quality of expert craftsmanship. If this skill was not always present at the Festival of American Music, then perhaps it is not surprising, considering the lack of training in collaboration that characterizes the education of both musicians and dancers in this country.

Pondering all this, one recalls Virgil Thomson's comment: ''Oh, you can't *make* situations; they grow.'' Growing takes time and attention. To expect instant masterpieces from all first-time collaborators is perhaps unrealistic.

MORTON GOULD LOOKS TO THE FUTURE

Since he had participated in the American Music Festival not only as a composer, but also as a conductor and a piano soloist, Morton Gould's impressions were of particular interest—especially since he spoke from the vantage point of past collaborations with exceptional choreographers such as Jerome Robbins, Agnes de Mille, and George Balanchine.

While discussing the whole series of festival performances, Mr. Gould was asked for suggestions about various ways that other ballet companies might elicit good scores in the future. He observed: ''One of the things I think that Peter Martins was trying to do was to involve some of the younger composers of our time and get them into this orbit.''

When it was noted that composing for New York City Ballet was a pretty high-level initiation into the art of collaboration, Mr. Gould agreed. But even this composer, who is also the president of ASCAP, did not know of any training ground where the thousands of composers in the United States might learn the craft of writing for dance. ''However,'' he added, ''what Peter Martins has done has opened up a lot of possibilities. In a way, that festival happened as a workshop, and the fact that not all of it might work is beside the point. That's part of the nature of the beast.''

''One of the things that one has to do is have contests and commissions,'' Mr. Gould suggested. ''That means you have to get money for it. You have to get support: national arts endowments, state arts councils, corporate support. There again, a great deal of aesthetics has to do with finance.''

Returning to the question of how composers are to be trained artistically for collaboration, Mr. Gould could only say: ''I don't know the answer to that. The answer might be in a *climate* where you have a number of ongoing opera houses and theaters that are also using ballet, and where young composers can try their wings in a smaller community and in a smaller setting.''

Morton Gould's word ''ongoing'' was pleasant to consider. ''Yes,'' he agreed, ''but now you're talking Utopia!''

THE REACTION FROM THE PIT

Though many of the instrumentalists in the New York City Ballet Orchestra learned what was happening onstage only through hearsay, they nevertheless seemed to agree that what the dancers were doing was still the most important thing—even in a festival devoted to American music. But principal horn player Paul Ingraham probably spoke for many of his colleagues when he said: ''I think it's always kind of fun to do a new idea. It certainly gave us a shot in the arm, to have the challenge of some new music to work on.''[5]

Concerning the choice of pieces, the orchestra members gave divided and mixed reviews. Reflecting on this, Mr. Ingraham said: ''I think when people in the dance start choosing music, sometimes their background and choice of music is somewhat limited.''

In fact, speaking to members of the New York City Ballet Guild, Danish-born Peter Martins explained: ''I began to be very curious as to 'where was American music today.' I felt it was a very important part that I was lacking in my knowledge, so I wanted to investigate it.''[6]

Associate principal flutist Paul Dunkel, for one, was most appreciative of this approach. ''I think people don't realize what an effort the festival was, and what a courageous thing Martins did,'' he said.[7] ''I think it was one of the best events, regardless of the results, that has happened in New York that I can remember! The New York Philharmonic has not done anything like this, nor the Metropolitan Opera, nor the City Opera. And I think that this was more of a real 'festival' than, say, the Stravinsky or Ravel or Tchaikovsky festivals. When you do one composer, on a certain level it's easier, because you don't have the research. But when you're doing lots of composers, that's really something!''

Nevertheless, there were a number of negative comments from some of the musicians regarding one score or another: ''I hated it passionately. . . . It was hideous . . . garbage.'' It seems that the minimalist scores were especially unpopular with the players.

So the moral is: even the most courageous, and expensive, experiments do not always meet with universal success and approval. Perhaps what it also suggests is that we all need more experiments, so we can find out what works well and what does not.

MUSICAL ASPECTS OF THE PERFORMANCES

The ballet orchestra itself came under unusual scrutiny during the festival. Bernard Holland, music critic of *The New York Times,* was especially harsh:

> The two inseparable points of discomfort (for a music critic, at least) were, first, music's diminished role in these proceedings and, second, the easy acceptance of shoddy musical performance. . . . Mediocre musical performances—ones that would have been scarcely acceptable elsewhere—seemed to trouble no one.[8]

Amazingly, some members of the New York City Ballet Orchestra did not refute this criticism. For instance, when flutist Paul Dunkel was asked if he agreed with the review, he replied: ''I did. Totally. I find that for a variety of reasons, nothing is ever rehearsed properly down there. They are in the habit now of saying, 'Well, we only have time to run through this once; we'll do it as best we can.' We cared about it, but not enough to make it first-rate. You know, the orchestra tries. But it should have been done much better—and it could have been."

From his place under the stage, the flutist's viewpoint was this: "When you're playing, you try to play as though it's a concert, so you really don't care about the dancers. You know they are there, but you don't have the involvement, obviously. It's really almost as if they weren't there. It's the conductor's responsibility to make sure that the tempos are within a ballpark so they can dance."

But speaking of the entire scope of the festival, Mr. Dunkel was full of admiration. "I think it was really rather impressive. You can't possibly hit *all* styles. Some of it I didn't like, but—what the hell! We weren't unanimous in the orchestra about what we liked, but that doesn't matter. You have to give Martins credit for taking a shot. I find people—especially the dance critics—are being a little picky now. He gambled! And very few people will gamble."

What seemed uppermost in the mind of horn player Paul Ingraham was the importance of having conductors who were familiar with the various contemporary styles. He was particularly enthusiastic about Charles Wuorinen's guest conducting, since obviously the composer knew his own piece and how he wanted it performed. "But," Mr. Ingraham cautioned, "You have to balance that with the dance company's wishes to have somebody who they think knows how to work with the stage."

Reflecting on these sometimes contradictory needs, Mr. Ingraham recalled another recent experience at New York City Ballet—one that exemplified some of the ongoing problems which all collaborators have to deal with, whether they are instrumentalists, conductors, composers, choreographers, or dancers.

"We had a young man from the Netherlands who did some conducting. But he really was not interested in being a 'ballet' conductor. He was there simply to try to get a good musical performance—which he did. And the people on the stage got a little bit upset, because he didn't pay as much attention to them. But *we* were glad to have him!"

"With Balanchine," reflected the horn player, "the dancers were basically trained to be able to dance with the music as it was coming from the pit. Not that the conductors were never watching or never in tune with them. But he recognized that if you put the orchestra in a straitjacket, you don't get a good musical performance."

"Now, since he's gone, we have a great deal more rehearsal with the stage; a great deal of stopping on the part of various dancers and complaining that the tempo is too fast, too slow, or faster than before, or slower than before. And you know," Mr. Ingraham confided, "it gets very tedious. So it seems like we might be sliding back a bit to the old days of the ballerina deciding that the music has to go a certain way, and the conductor saying, 'OK; I'll try and do that.' "

So he considered that a backsliding? "I certainly do," exclaimed the musician, "because dancers basically, as a group, do not have the training in music, and do not understand how a piece is to be played. They get a recording of a piece to do their work with, and they think that's the tempo. When they hear it live, they think it's different—even though in many cases, if you put a metronome on, you'll find it's the same. They *hear* it differently."

Many members of the ballet orchestra not only hear differently, but also play differently—when they are performing with other symphonies that specialize in contemporary music. In contrast, Mr. Ingraham pointed out that in most ballet orchestras—not just in New York City—the conductors are not apt to have the same kinds of experiences as symphonic conductors, precisely because their job is to devote themselves to the service of choreographers and dancers onstage.

For various reasons, therefore, time and effort are not generally spent in the ballet orchestras to take apart and practice even difficult new scores so as to achieve the polished performances that many of the instrumentalists are capable of giving. "So from a musical, orchestral standpoint," Paul Ingraham acknowledged, "I think one goes elsewhere to get that kind of gratification."

And yet, how many years had he been playing with New York City Ballet? "Twenty-eight," replied the horn player. "Time flies when you're having fun," he added with his enigmatic chuckle.

A GROWING INTEREST IN AMERICAN CONCERT MUSIC?

Attempting to sum up the events at New York City Ballet's festival, Anna Kisselgoff wrote in *The New York Times:*

> In the final analysis, the American Music Festival was a giant workshop. . . . Insofar as Mr. Martins' idea was to introduce his audience to new music and new ballets, framed by previous works set to American music, the festival was a success in its workshop spirit. . . . In the end, it was a dancer's festival. They got the most out of it.[9]

Not necessarily. The festival provided many moments of interest and pleasure for large audiences, and it certainly served to raise some curiosity about further use of American music for American choreography, as well as to indicate some changes in public taste.

One indication of changes in the musical tastes of both theater-goers and performers was the number of festival dances choreographed to music by Charles Ives, who during his lifetime had difficulty securing performances of his scores.[10]

Of all the works seen by the author during the course of the festival, none seemed so profoundly moving as Jerome Robbins' *Ives, Songs,* sung simply and hauntingly by David Evitts, with Gordon Boelzner at the piano. Musically, visually, emotionally—in all respects, the work seemed beautiful. Robbins' choice of the songs, and his pacing, drew the audience into a gentle remembrance of young life in the early part of the century. Though clouded by war and loss and the yearning to retrieve past happiness, the work was in turn poignant, funny, fresh, evocative—and it touched the deepest part of one's feelings. For this observer, it was the standout of the entire American Music Festival.

The festival also presented several revivals of older works set to the music of Charles Ives, including George Balanchine's *Ivesiana,* and Peter Martins' *Calcium White Light.* These were most interesting in juxtaposition with brand-new ballets, some of which made use of the same music.

Among these new works were Eliot Feld's ballet *The Unanswered Question* and Paul Taylor's *Danbury Mix,* performed by his own company. Both pieces were well received by audiences and critics alike. Indeed, some observers claimed they even felt that Paul Taylor had stolen New York City Ballet's show, especially with the light, barefoot solo of his company member Kate Johnson in Peter Martins' ballet set to Samuel Barber's *Violin Concerto.*

While watching these new pieces, the author was amused to recall her own youthful efforts to promote American music, by starting The Modern Listeners' Record Club, offering both the Barber *Violin Concerto* and Charles Ives' *Holidays* to prospective listeners.[11] One mail-order customer returned some discs with this letter:

Dear Sir:

Your music is simply horrible. Please do not disturb anymore!

Perhaps some of us need time to get acclimated to radical changes in musical style. At any rate, audience members at New York City Ballet's festival seemed quite open to sampling a variety of twentieth-century styles, even if they didn't necessarily like everything they heard and saw. By and large, the audiences also seemed quite appreciative of both the effort and the performances being given by the orchestra.

One of the author's personal favorites from the festival was Eliot Feld's dreamlike ballet set to *The Unanswered Question* and other pieces by Charles Ives. Indeed, how could a musician be anything other than completely captivated by a piece which features a dancer with his head in the bell of a sousaphone? The work ends with one dancer climbing a rope ladder and reaching with great yearning towards the strange instrument, now suspended in midair, center stage.

Among other things, this ballet seemed to epitomize the ongoing effort by musicians and dancers to achieve a satisfactory merging of their two arts. The process is certainly not without problems, both funny and serious.

Maybe there is no such thing as a perfect alliance that pleases all the creative collaborators, the performers, and the audience. But the process of combining sound with movement is an ongoing challenge—and one which continues to produce many interesting, expressive, and delightful works of art. That artists at New York City Ballet and elsewhere are beginning to delve more into the diversity of American music is surely a healthy sign which bodes well for the future of musical collaboration with theatrical dance in this country.

Appendix

At the time of the author's observation of rehearsals and interviews with instrumentalists, the rosters of the leading orchestras mentioned in the book were as follows.

THE PAUL TAYLOR DANCE COMPANY ORCHESTRA

Donald York, *Conductor*
Jean Ingraham, *Concertmistress*

First Violin: Martha Caplin, Timothy Baker, Ronnie Bauch, Diane Bruce. *Second Violin:* L. P. How, principal; Carol Minor, Leonard Rivlin, Junko Ohtsu. *Viola:* Lois Martin, principal; Maryhelen Ewing, Michael Bloom. *Cello:* Chris Finckel, principal; Lindy Clark. *Bass:* John Feeney. *Flute:* Susan Palma, principal; Laura Conwesser. *Oboe:* Stephen Taylor, principal; Pamela Epple. *Clarinet:* Anand Devendra, principal; Dennis Smylie. *Bassoon:* Michael Finn, principal; Jane Taylor. *French Horn:* Robert Carlisle, principal; Stewart Rose. *Trumpet:* Edward Carroll, principal; Stephen Ametrano. *Trombone:* Jonathan Taylor, principal; David Titcomb, John Rojak. *Contrabass Trombone:* Thompson Hanks, Jr. *Percussion:* Richard Fitz, principal; Norm Freedman, Louis Odo, Benjamin Herman, William Moersch. *Keyboard:* Elizabeth Wright. *Guitar:* Frederic Hand. *Harp:* Susan Jolles.

NEW YORK CITY BALLET ORCHESTRA

Robert Irving, *Music Director and Conductor in Chief*
Hugo Fiorato, *Principal Conductor*
Gordon Boelzner, *Assistant Music Director and Conductor*
Lamar Alsop, *Concertmaster*
Alan Martin, *Associate Concertmaster*

First Violin: Dominic Vaz and Joyce Flissler, associates; Jean Ingraham, Bira Rabushka, Murray Schnee, Helen Shomer, Sabina Skalar, Marilyn Wright. *Second Violin:* Jack Katz, principal; Janet Berman, associate; Nancy Elan, Paul Peabody, Joseph Schor, Joseph Siegelman, Eleanor Waalen. Also Marin Alsop, Sue Ellen Colgan, Sylvia Davis, Joe Rabushka, Martin Stoner, Helen Strilec. *Viola:* Warren Laffredo, principal; Laurence Fader, associate; Herbert Fuchs, Liane Marston, Susan Pray, Carolyn Voigt. Also Barbara Baird. *Cello:* Fred Zlotkin, principal; Eugene Moye, associate; Nellis DeLay, Robert Gardner, Esther Gruhn, Ruth Alsop. Also Daven Jenkins. *Double Bass:* Theodore Flowerman, principal; David Walter, associate; James Brennand, Harold Schachner. Also Barbara Wilson, Jay Blumenthal. *Flute:* Andrew Lolya, principal; Paul Dunkel, associate; Victor Harris, flute and piccolo. Also Marie Owen. *Oboe:* Randall Wolfgang, principal; James Byars, associate; Jane Cochran, oboe and English horn. *Clarinet:* David Weber, principal; Milton Moskowitz, associate. Also Gary Koch. *Bassoon:* Donald MacCourt, principal; Jack Knitzer, associate; Richard Lawson. *French Horn:* Paul Ingraham, principal; H. Robert Carlisle, associate; Michael Martin, horn and librarian; Kathleen Wilber. Also Thomas Beck. *Trumpet:* Ronald Anderson, principal; Robert Haley, associate; Theodore Weis. *Trombone:* John Swallow, principal; Ronald Borror, associate; Robert Biddlecome. *Tuba:* Thompson Hanks, Jr. *Harp:* Cynthia Otis, principal. *Piano:* Jascha Zayde. *Tympani:* Arnold Goldberg, tympani and orchestra manager. *Percussion:* Ronald Gould, principal; Robert Bush, associate.

AMERICAN BALLET THEATRE ORCHESTRA

Alan Barker, *Music Administrator and Principal Conductor*
Paul Connelly, *Principal Conductor*
Jack Everly, *Conductor*
Dennis Cleveland, *Concertmaster*

First Violin: Suzanne Ornstein, Assistant Concertmaster; June de Forest, Sherman Goldscheid, Joanna Jenner, Barbara Randall, Lenard Rivlin, Nina Simon, Dorothy Strahl, Sandra Strenger, Carol Zeavin, Bernard Zeller. *Second Violin:* Ronald Oakland, principal; Martha C. Silverman, assistant principal; Joe Diamante, Anne Gillette, Michael Gillette, Elizabeth Kleinman, Lucy Morganstern, Richard Rood. *Viola:* Janet Lyman-Hill, principal; Ronald Carbone, Maryhelen Ewing, Joan Kalisch, Jake Kella, Olivia Koppell. *Cello:* Daniel Morganstern, principal; Scott Ballantyne, David Calhoun, Eleanor Howells, Maureen Hynes, Ellen Westermann. *Double Bass:* Lou Kosma, principal; Andree Briere, Charles Urbont. *Flute:* Mary Landolfi, principal; Diva Goodfriend-Koven, flute and piccolo; Susan Stewart. *Oboe:* Joel Timm, acting principal; Livio Caroli, oboe and English horn. *Clarinet:* Harold Themmen, principal and librarian; James Douglas, clarinet and bass clarinet. *Bassoon:* Cyrus Segal, principal; Bernadette Zirkuli; Lauren Goldstein, bassoon and contrabassoon. *French Horn:* Frank Donaruma, principal; Virginia Benz, Ronald Sell. *Trumpet:* Jim Stubbs, principal and orchestra personnel manager; Robert Lang, Thomas Lisenbee, Hank Nowak. *Trombone:* Clifford Haynes, principal; Thomas Olcott. *Bass Trombone:* Charles McKnight. *Tuba:* David Braynard, principal. *Harp:* Robert Barlow, principal. *Percussion:* Fred Eckler, principal; David Wilson, Ben Harms. *Tympani:* Lou Barranti. *Piano:* Harold Barr.

SAN FRANCISCO BALLET ORCHESTRA

Denis de Coteau, *Music Director and Conductor*
Roy Malan, *Concertmaster*

First Violin: Janice McIntosh, Tanya Rankov, Terri Sternberg, Greg Mazmanian, Martha Simonds, Lily Li Burton. Also Celia Rosenberger, William Rusconit, Dan Smiley, Lev Rankov. *Second Violin:* Ruggiero Pelosi, Marianne Wagner, Yehudit Lieberman, Patricia Van Winkle, Clifton Foster. Also James Shallenberger, Lisa Pratt, Leonid Igudesman. *Viola:* Ruth Sudmeier, Adrian Stenzen, Leonore Kish, Susan Bates. Also Patrick Kroboth, Natalia Igudesman. *Cello:* David Kadarauch, Nancy Stenzen, Victor Fierro, Gretchen Elliott. Also Dawn Foster-Dodson. *Bass:* Steven D'Amico, Shinji Eshima, Jonathan Lancelle. *Flute:* Barbara Chaffe. Also Susan Wallter. *Oboe:* William Banovetz, Marilyn Coyne, oboe and English horn. Also Deborah Henry. *Clarinet:* Donald O'Brien; James Dukey, clarinet and bass clarinet. *Bassoon:* Jerry Dagg; David Bartolotta, bassoon and librarian. *Horn:* David Sprung, Brian McCarty, Paul McNutt. *Trumpet:* Charles Metzger, Ralph Wagner. *Trombone:* Don Benham, Hall Goff. Also Mitchell Ross. *Bass Trombone:* Kurt Patzner. *Tuba:* Peter Wahrhaftig. *Tympani:* Danny Montoro, tympani and personnel manager. *Percussion:* David Rosenthal. *Harp:* Marcella DeCray. *Keyboard:* Daniel Waite.

MARTHA GRAHAM ORCHESTRA

Stanley Sussman, *Principal Conductor*
Jonathan McPhee, *Associate Conductor*
Israel Chorberg, *Concertmaster*

Violins: Abram Kaptsan, principal; Ruth Buffington, Yaba Goichman, Sheila Kles; Stanley Kurtis, violin and librarian; Sheila Manuel, Marina Markov, Carol Pool, Leonard Rivlin, Louis Simon, Meyer Stolow, Thomas Suarez, Elain Sutin. *Viola:* Morris Sutow, principal; Claire Bergman, Madeleine Frank, Jack Rosenberg. *Cello:* Alla Goldberg, principal; Jerome Carrington, David Heiss, Bruce Rogers. *Bass:* Richard Fredrickson, principal; John Feeney. *Flute:* Susan Palma, principal; Florence Nelson, Susan Stewart. *Oboe:* Marsha Heller, principal; Diane Lesser. *Clarinet:* John Moses, principal and personnel manager; Mitchell Kriegler. *Bassoon:* Lester Cantor, principal; Charles McCracken. *Horn:* Brooks Tillotson, principal; Richard Hagen, Jean Martin, Debra Poole. *Trumpet:* Neil Balm, principal; Grant Keast, Lee Soper. *Trombone:* Ronald Borror, principal; Clifford Haynes, John Rojak. *Tuba:* Stephen Johns. *Tympani:* Leonard Schulman. *Percussion:* Norman Freeman, principal; Michael Aaronbson, Jonathan Haas. *Keyboard:* Elizabeth Wright, principal; Harriet Wingreen. *Harp:* Susan Jolles. *Orchestra Contractor:* Loren Glickman.

Notes

All tape recordings of interviews, as well as transcripts, correspondence, and other documents, are in the possession of the author.

CHAPTER 1

1. The section on Agnes de Mille is based on the author's interview at the choreographer's home on December 2, 1985.

2. Miss de Mille wrote a full account of her collaboration with Morton Gould in *Lizzie Borden: A Dance of Death* (Boston: Atlantic Monthly Press, 1968).

3. Doris Humphrey, *The Art of Making Dances* (New York: Grove Press reprint, 1977; orig. ed., 1959), p. 132.

4. Humphrey, *The Art of Making Dances,* p. 143.

5. The section on Paul Taylor is based on the author's interview with the choreographer on June 25, 1985. Highly recommended is Mr. Taylor's autobiography, *Private Domain* (New York: Alfred A. Knopf, 1987).

6. The section on Hanya Holm is based on the author's interview at the choreographer's home on January 4, 1986.

7. "Holm Dancers Make Debut at Mecca Temple," *New York Program,* January 4, 1938.

8. Walter Sorrell, *Hanya Holm: The Biography of an Artist* (Middletown, Conn.: Wesleyan University Press, 1969), p. 157.

9. For an explanation of the Dalcroze approach, see Emil-Jacques Dalcroze, *Rhythm and Music in Education* (London: Dalcroze Society, 1980).

10. Mary Wigman, *The Language of Dance,* trans. Walter Sorrell (Middletown, Conn.: Wesleyan University Press, 1966), pp. 10–11.

11. Wigman, *The Language of Dance,* pp. 37–38.

12. For a complete list of Balanchine's works, with indications of the music used, consult the Eakins Press Foundation volume, *Choreography by George Balanchine: A*

Catalog of Works (New York: Viking, 1984). The most complete study of the choreographer to date is Bernard Taper, *Balanchine: A Biography* (New York: Times Books, 1984).

13. Stravinsky's memoirs, compiled with Robert Craft, have been extensively published, but of special interest here is his *Autobiography* (New York: W. W. Norton, 1936), which includes comments concerning the composer's general attitude toward ballet.

14. George Balanchine, "The Dance Element in Stravinsky's Music," in Minna Lederman, ed., *Stravinsky in the Theater* (New York: Da Capo Press, 1975), pp. 75–84.

15. In Nancy Goldner, *The Stravinsky Festival of The New York City Ballet* (New York: Eakins Press, 1973), p. 13.

16. Solomon Volkov, *Balanchine's Tchaikovsky: Interviews with George Balanchine* (New York: Simon & Schuster, 1985), p. 139. For a detailed analysis of Tchaikovsky's scores, written by a musician, see Roland John Wiley, *Tchaikovsky's Ballets: Swan Lake, Sleeping Beauty, Nutcracker* (Oxford: Clarendon Press, 1985).

17. Lincoln Kirstein, *Union Jack: The New York City Ballet* (New York: The Eakins Press Foundation, 1977), pp. 55–61.

18. The section on Erick Hawkins is drawn from the author's interview at the choreographer's studio on November 17, 1986, and from personal observations of company class and rehearsal.

19. Ned Rorem, *An Absolute Gift* (New York: Simon & Schuster, 1978), p. 110.

20. *The New York Times,* December 19, 1985.

21. Jamake Highwater, "Erick Hawkins: Unharnessing Animal Energy," *Dance Magazine* (February 1984): 56–58.

22. An essay by Lucia Dlugoszewski appears in the booklet *On the Dance of Erick Hawkins,* available from the Erick Hawkins Foundation for Modern Dance.

23. Lynne Anne Blom and L. Tarin Chaplin, *The Intimate Act of Choreography* (Pittsburgh: University of Pittsburgh Press, 1982), p. 156.

24. Alwin Nikolais was interviewed by the author at his studios on May 20, 1986.

CHAPTER 2

1. Ernestine Stodelle, *The First Frontier: The Story of Louis Horst and the American Dance* (Cheshire, Conn.: privately published, 1964).

2. Louis Horst's two books are *Pre-Classic Dance Forms* (New York: Dance Horizons, third printing, 1979; orig. ed. in *The Dance Observer,* 1937, 1940, and 1968); and with Carroll Russell, *Modern Dance Forms in Relation to the Other Modern Arts* (New York: Dance Horizons, republication 1967; orig. ed., Impulse Publications, 1961). The manuscript collection of Louis Horst is in the Americana Collection of the Music Research Division of The New York Public Library at Lincoln Center.

3. Stodelle, *The First Frontier.*

4. Walter Sorrell, "The Music Man of Modern Dance: Louis Horst," *Dance Magazine* (December 1984): 90.

5. Sorrell, "The Music Man," p. 92.

6. The section on Otto Luening is based on the author's interview of January 23, 1986. *Theatre Piece No. 2* is available on a Composers Recordings Inc. (CRI) disc. Mr. Luening has donated his manuscripts and notes to the music research library at

Lincoln Center. Highly recommended for an overview of music in twentieth-century America is Otto Luening, *The Odyssey of an American Composer* (New York: Charles Scribner's Sons, 1980).

7. Ruth and Norman Lloyd, "Un-Can the Music," *Anthology of Impulse, Annual of Contemporary Dance, 1951-1966*, pp. 75–78.

8. Ernestine Stodelle, *Deep Song: The Dance Story of Martha Graham* (New York: Schirmer Books, 1984), p. 113.

9. The quote is taken from an undated brochure written by Oliver Daniel and published by Broadcast Music, Inc. Future generations will be able to examine Henry Cowell's manuscripts and papers at the Library of Congress. Meanwhile, recommended reading is Cowell's *New Musical Resources* (New York: Alfred A. Knopf, 1930) and *American Composers on American Music* (Stanford, Ca.: Stanford University Press, 1933).

10. Material for the section on William Schuman was drawn from two sources: an address by the composer at the Martha Graham School on November 5, 1986; and the author's telephone interview with Mr. Schuman on November 14, 1986. The composer has donated his papers to the Lincoln Center library. Also of interest is an interview with Mr. Schuman in *Ballet Review* (Fall 1986): 35–36. *Judith* was recorded by the Louisville Symphony.

11. Carlos Surinach was interviewed by the author on April 30, 1986.

12. Virgil Thomson was interviewed in New York City on January 6, 1987. His writings include *Virgil Thomson on Virgil Thomson* (New York: E. P. Dutton, 1985, orig. ed. 1966); *A Virgil Thomson Reader* (New York: E. P. Dutton, 1981); and *Selected Letters of Virgil Thomson*, Tim Page and Vanessa Weeks Page, eds. (New York: Summit Books, 1988). Also useful is Michael Meckna, *Virgil Thomson: A Bio-Bibliography* (Westport, Conn.: Greenwood Press, 1986).

13. Trude Rittmann was interviewed by the author on February 19, 1986, at the composer's home in Waltham, Massachusetts. Trude Rittmann's manuscripts and notes may be studied in the Americana Collection of the Music Research Division of the New York Public Library, at Lincoln Center. See also Marcia Marks, "Like Trying to Explain Color to a Blind Person," *Dance Magazine* (March 1971): 67–69.

14. Agnes de Mille, *And Promenade Home* (New York: Da Capo Press, orig. ed. 1968), pp. 68–69.

CHAPTER 3

1. Richard Cameron-Wolfe was interviewed by the author by telephone, during the summer of 1983.

2. Norma Reynolds Dalby was interviewed in White Plains during the summer of 1983.

3. Jean Erdman was interviewed in New York City on April 14, 1986.

4. The section on Lou Harrison is based on an interview in Aptos, California, on April 6, 1986. Additional insights were provided by the composer's public lectures and gamelan performances during his period as composer-in-residence with the Philadelphia Orchestra at the Saratoga Festival in August 1986. To celebrate the composer's seventieth birthday, Peter Garland edited *A Lou Harrison Reader* (Santa Fe, N.M.: Soundings Press, 1987).

5. Richard Philp, "Revivals," *Dance Magazine* (June 1987): 149.

6. The section on Laura Dean is based on a telephone interview with the author in August 1983. The private showing was on October 15, 1986, at the Dia Art Foundation.

7. "Two Different Whirls," *Village Voice*, February 14, 1977.

8. The material about Steve Reich, where not otherwise indicated, was drawn from a telephone interview with the author on August 15, 1983.

9. The radio interview with Terry Gross was broadcast by WNYC in March 1986.

10. Steve Reich, *Writings About Music* (Halifax: Nova Scotia College of Art and Design; New York: New York University, 1974), pp. 28, 41.

11. Reich, *Writings About Music*, p. 44.

CHAPTER 4

1. Stanley Sussman was interviewed in Manhattan on July 18, 1986.

2. Beth Tyler, "John Herbert McDowell: Composing for Dance," *Ballet Review* (Summer 1985): 27.

3. Tyler, "John Herbert McDowell," p. 26.

4. Tyler, "John Herbert McDowell," p. 26.

5. The section about Donald York is based on the author's interview in the summer of 1983. A recording of York's dance compositions is available from the Musical Heritage Society.

6. Susan Reiter, "Taylor and York to Show a Decade's Collaboration," *Dance Magazine* (April 1987): 6.

7. Tania Leon was interviewed by the author in New York City on April 8, 1988.

8. Lee Norris was interviewed in New York City on July 7, 1986. A picture volume about the National Dance Institute is Jacques d'Amboise, Hope Cook, and Carolyn George, *Teaching the Magic of Dance* (New York: Simon & Schuster, 1983).

9. Morton Gould was interviewed by the author on May 25, 1988. A brief profile is Harvey Phillips, "Morton Gould, Musical Citizen," *The Instrumentalist* (July 1987): 10–16. Mr. Gould's article "Music and the Dance" is still pertinent; see Walter Sorrell, *The Dance Has Many Faces* (New York: World Publishing Co., 1951), pp. 41–48.

CHAPTER 5

1. Michael Rudiakov was interviewed by the author by telephone on December 1, 1986.

2. Gregory Squires was interviewed in the summer of 1983.

3. Edward Birdwell was interviewed on May 23, 1986. A cover article in *The New York Times Magazine* concerning his free-lance work as a horn player has been reprinted as the chapter titled "An American Free-Lancer," in Helen Epstein, *Music Talks: Conversations with Musicians* (New York: McGraw Hill, 1987), pp. 149–161.

4. Interviews with the Pennsylvania Ballet Orchestra musicians and staff took place during July 1983. Maurice Kaplow updated some information by phone in May 1988.

5. Barbara Weisberger was interviewed at the Carlisle Project in June 1986.

6. Judy Sugarman was interviewed by telephone in the spring of 1986.

7. Cynthia Jersey was interviewed in New York City on February 3, 1986.

8. Jennifer Dunning, "Nancy Allison in American Program," *The New York Times*, June 23, 1986.

9. Edward Carroll was interviewed on March 20, 1986.

10. The author observed rehearsals of the Paul Taylor Dance Company in April 1986. Members of the orchestra are listed in the Appendix.

11. The author observed New York City Ballet Orchestra rehearsals in April 1986. Members of the orchestra are listed in the Appendix.

CHAPTER 6

1. Conversations between the author and members of the American Ballet Theatre Orchestra took place during the summer of 1983 and the spring of 1986. Members of the orchestra are listed in the Appendix.

CHAPTER 7

1. The author observed rehearsals of *La Bayadère* in the spring of 1986.

2. The May 1980 issue of *Ballet News* includes an article about Ludwig Minkus, "Maligned Minstrel," by Barrymore Laurence Scherer. In the same issue is "The Tale of La Bayadère," by Gennady Smakov. The articles coincided with PBS's *Live from Lincoln Center* telecast of this ballet, with John Lanchbery conducting his own arrangement.

CHAPTER 8

1. Victoria Pasquale was interviewed by the author, on December 1, 1986.

2. Robert Irving was interviewed by the author at the New York State Theater on June 20, 1986.

3. Robert Irving's address before the Guild of the New York City Ballet was given on June 10, 1986.

4. Edward Willenger, *Ballet International* (April 1987): 46.

5. Conductor Denis de Coteau was interviewed by the author on April 6, 1986. A good survey of the San Francisco Ballet repertoire is Cobbett Steinberg, *San Francisco Ballet: The First Fifty Years* (San Francisco Ballet Association, 1983). Members of the San Francisco Ballet Orchestra are listed in the Appendix.

6. Janice Ross, "Life is the pits and he likes it," *Oakland Tribune*, February 15, 1981.

7. Maurice Kaplow was interviewed in July 1983.

8. Stanley Sussman was interviewed on July 18, 1986.

9. Jonathan McPhee was interviewed on June 12, 1986.

10. Glen Cortese was interviewed on March 18, 1986.

11. Donald Mahler was interviewed at the Carlisle Project in the spring of 1987.

CHAPTER 9

1. James Reedy was interviewed by the author on March 20, 1986 at the Hawkins studios.

2. Laura Pettibone was interviewed by telephone in the spring of 1986.

3. Holly Reeve was interviewed in Scarsdale, N.Y. on November 1, 1985.

4. Ian Horvath was interviewed by the author in New York on September 16, 1986.

5. Larry Clark was interviewed on December 16, 1986, at the State University of New York, College at Purchase.

6. A good introduction to John Cage's aesthetics is his *Silence: Lectures and Writings* (Middletown, Conn.: Wesleyan University Press, 1973).

7. Helen Starr was interviewed by the author during the Southeastern Regional Ballet Association (SERBA) festival in Miami in April–May 1986.

8. George R. Hubbard, "Louisville and Colette: A Life for Love," *Dance Magazine* (March 1988): 74.

9. Lisa de Ribère was interviewed in May 1986.

10. *Variations on a Legend* was premiered by the School of American Ballet at the Juilliard Theater on July 24, 1986.

CHAPTER 10

1. Violette Verdy was interviewed by the author on June 24, 1987, at the choreographer's home. A well-documented account of her performing career is Victoria Huckenpahler, *Ballerina: A Biography of Violette Verdy* (New York: Marcel Dekker, 1978).

2. These remarks, and those of the following several artists, are drawn from interviews cited earlier in the text.

3. Lynn Stanford was interviewed by the author in New York on June 8, 1988. A profile of the pianist by Marian Horosko appeared in *Dance Magazine* (March 1982): 82–83. Mr. Stanford's recordings of music for ballet studio classes are available from Bodarc Productions in Dallas.

4. Jennifer Dunning, "Baryshnikov Offers Diverse Program," *The New York Times*, August 7, 1985.

5. The videotape "In a Class of Her Own" was produced by Video Arts International, Inc.

6. Elizabeth Lee was interviewed by the author during the American Dance Festival at Duke University, June 13, 1987. Charles Reinhart made his remark concerning the costs of musical services for dance in a conversation with the author during the course of the festival.

7. Jennifer Muller made these remarks during a panel presentation on careers in dancing, held for students and the public at the Alvin Ailey American Dance Center in 1987.

8. Alexandra Danilova, *Choura* (New York: Alfred A. Knopf, 1986), p. 208.

9. Natalia Makarova, *A Dance Autobiography* (New York: Alfred A. Knopf, 1979), p. 35. Further discussion of musicality in dancers appears in an article by John Mueller and Don McDonagh, "Making Musical Dance: Robert Irving, Richard Colton, Kate Johnson, Karole Armitage," *Ballet Review* (Winter 1986): 23–44.

CHAPTER 11

1. The remarks by Mr. Lowry and Mr. Nikolais were made during the January 1988 convention of Dance USA in New York City. The impact of the Ford Foundation grants for ballet is chronicled by Elizabeth Kendall in *Dancing* (New York: Ford Foundation,

1983). Mr. Lowry presents a broad perspective in his two books: *The Performing Arts in American Society* (Englewood Cliffs, N.J.: Prentice-Hall, 1978); and *Arts and Public Policy in the United States* (Englewood Cliffs, N.J.: 1985). In 1988, Mr. Lowry accepted the position of president of the San Francisco Ballet.

2. Agnes de Mille's speech was given at the Martha Graham School on February 20, 1986.

3. Ben Stevenson was interviewed by the author in Miami during the SERBA festival in May 1986.

4. Mr. Stevenson's work with the Chinese was the subject of a PBS special, *Pas de Deux: Dance of Two Countries, China and America.*

5. A true-to-life portrait of the way conservatory students view dancers appears in Judith Kogan's *Nothing But the Best: The Struggle for Perfection at the Juilliard School* (New York: Random House, 1987).

CHAPTER 12

1. John Duffy spoke with the author in July 1983. A very helpful handbook, "Commissioning Music," is available from Meet the Composer.

2. Ian Horvath, "Considerations and Recommendations Concerning the Establishment of Meet the Composer's New Dance/New Music Funding Program" (unpublished report, September 1986), p. 1.

3. Horvath, "Considerations and Recommendations," p. 4.

4. Horvath, "Considerations and Recommendations," p. 11.

5. Horvath, "Considerations and Recommendations," p. 13.

6. Horvath, "Considerations and Recommendations," p. 14.

7. Robert Steele and Todd Hall spoke to the author at the Carlisle Project in the spring of 1986.

8. Ron Cunningham was interviewed on April 31, 1986, during the SERBA festival in Miami.

CHAPTER 13

1. New York City Ballet's American Music Festival took place April 26–May 15, 1988, in the New York State Theater at Lincoln Center. Other composers whose music was performed—either as an overture or for a ballet—included: John Adams, Milton Babbitt, Irving Berlin, Leonard Bernstein, William Bolcom, John Cage, Elliott Carter, Tom Constanten, Aaron Copland, David Diamond, Joseph Fennimore, Lukas Foss, Stephen Foster, Peter Gena, Philip Glass, Louis Moreau Gottschalk, Morton Gould, Charles T. Griffes, Charles Ives, Hershy Kay, Edward McDowell, Robert Moran, George Perle, Cole Porter, Steve Reich, Richard Rodgers, Ned Rorem, Christopher Rouse, Paul Schwartz, Roger Sessions, Stephen Sondheim, John Philip Sousa, Leslie Stuck, Ivan Tcherepnin, Virgil Thomson, Michael Torke, Joan Tower, Mary Jeanne van Appledorn, John Williams, Charles Wuorinen, and Ellen Taaffe Zwilich.

2. Otis Stuart, "Made in the U.S.A.," *Dance Magazine* (April 1988): 72–75.

3. Bernard Holland, "Appraising Ballet Music," *The New York Times,* May 9, 1988.

4. Charles Wuorinen was interviewed by the author by telephone on June 23, 1988.

5. Paul Ingraham was interviewed by telephone on June 6, 1988.

6. Prior to the American Music Festival, Celia Ipiotis led panel discussions before the New York City Ballet Guild. Peter Martins' remarks are drawn from one of these discussions.

7. Paul Dunkel was interviewed by telephone on June 3, 1988.

8. Holland, "Appraising Ballet Music."

9. Anna Kisselgoff, "In A Word, The Festival Was A Workshop," *The New York Times,* May 22, 1988.

10. Two recommended books on Charles Ives are Henry and Sidney Cowell, *Charles Ives and His Music* (New York: Oxford University Press, 1955); and Vivian Perlis, *Charles Ives Remembered: An Oral History* (New York: W. W. Norton, 1974).

11. For an account of the club, see Katherine Teck, "Dear Potential Modern Music Lover," *Music Educators Journal* (December 1969): 31–32, 75–77.

Bibliographic Essay

The literature concerning music for the dance in America is often contained within volumes that have another primary focus. There *is* extensive information in print; however, one must frequently find it a chapter or a page at a time. The works mentioned below were selected as a basic introduction for the general reader.

An excellent survey of recent developments in concert music in the United States is John Rockwell, *All American Music: Composition in the Late Twentieth Century* (New York: Vintage Books, 1984). Its lengthy bibliographic essay is most helpful in locating other sources of information. An unusually lucid volume dealing with complicated technology is Thomas B. Holmes, *Electronic and Experimental Music: History, Instruments, Technique, Performers, Recordings* (New York: Charles Scribner's Sons, 1985).

There is a very readable chapter on American music, giving an overview since colonial times, in Karl Haas, *Inside Music: How to Understand, Listen to, and Enjoy Good Music* (New York: Doubleday & Co., 1984). A more extended exploration is H. Wiley Hitchcock, *Music in the United States: A Historical Introduction* (Englewood Cliffs, N.J.: Prentice-Hall, Inc., 1974). Nevertheless, Mr. Hitchcock warns that: "One of the least-studied areas of early American music is that of the dance" (p. 42).

A slightly different approach is Daniel Kingman, *American Music: A Panorama* (New York: Schirmer Books, 1979), which presents the various ingredients of American musical heritage and includes information about twentieth-century pioneer composers as well. Highly recommended is Eileen Southern, *The Music of Black Americans* (New York: W. W. Norton, 2nd ed. 1983). It includes much unusual and interesting information about music for dancing.

A lovely, illustrated introduction to both contemporary ballet and modern concert dance in the United States is Agnes de Mille, *America Dances* (New York: Macmillan, 1980). Robert Coe has documented the important role of television in *Dance in America* (New York: E. P. Dutton, 1985).

For a general introduction to ballet, two books by Mary Clarke and Clement Crisp are recommended: *Understanding Ballet* (New York: Crown Publishers, 1976); and *The Ballet Goer's Guide* (New York: Alfred A. Knopf, 1981). The essay "How to Enjoy Ballet" appears in George Balanchine and Francis Mason, *Balanchine's Complete Stories of the Great Ballets* (New York: Doubleday & Co., rev. ed., 1977).

For perspective on the earlier history of American theatrical dance, see Lillian Moore, *Echoes of American Ballet* (New York: Dance Horizons, 1976); and Paul Magriel, ed., *Chronicles of the American Dance, From the Shakers to Martha Graham* (New York: Da Capo Press, 1978).

For perspective on modern dance in America, the following volumes are recommended: Walter Terry, *Isadora Duncan: Her Life, Her Art, Her Legacy* (New York: Dodd Mead & Co., 1963); Jean Mirroson Brown, ed., *The Vision of Modern Dance* (Princeton, N.J.: The Princeton Book Co., 1979); Selma Jeanne Cohen, ed., *The Modern Dance: Seven Statements of Belief* (Middletown, Conn.: Wesleyan University Press, 1965); Connie Kreemer, *Further Steps: 15 Choreographers on Modern Dance* (New York: Harper & Row, 1987); Joseph H. Mazo, *Prime Movers: The Makers of Modern Dance in America* (Princeton, N.J.: The Princeton Book Co., 1982, orig. ed. 1977).

For personal impressions of what it is like to dance onstage, also including comments concerning music, see Mikhail Baryshnikov, *Baryshnikov at Work* (New York: Alfred Knopf, 1983); John Gruen, *People Who Dance* (Princeton, N.J.: Dance Horizons/Princeton Book Co., 1988); Christopher d'Amboise, *Leap Year: A Year in the Life of a Dancer* (Garden City, N.Y.: Doubleday & Co., 1982); Toni Bentley, *Winter Season: A Dancer's Journal* (New York: Random House, 1982); and Joan Brady, *The Unmaking of a Dancer: An Unconventional Life* (New York: Washington Square Press, 1983).

Concerning musical collaboration in the earlier part of this century, nothing quite matches Verna Arvey's survey of the American scene in *Choreographic Music: Music for the Dance* (New York: E. P. Dutton, 1941). There are some personal accounts of collaboration in Aaron Copland's memoirs, written with Vivian Perlis, *Copland: 1900 through 1941* (New York: St. Martin's Press, 1984). Also, there is a chapter on work methods of choreographers in Agnes de Mille, *The Book of the Dance* (New York: Golden Press, 1963).

Also of interest on the subject of collaboration are articles by composer Norman Lloyd and choreographer Erick Hawkins in Walter Sorrell, *The Dance Has Many Faces*, 2nd ed. (New York: Columbia University Press, 1966).

Still a good historical introduction to classical styles is Humphrey Searle's *Ballet Music* (New York: Dover, 1973). A historical appreciation of the development of musical collaboration for the dance in Europe is Baird Hastings, *Choreographer & Composer: Theatrical Dance and Music in Western Culture* (Boston: Twayne, 1983). It includes some discussion of Balanchine's collaborations with Stravinsky.

Of further interest concerning collaboration is Elinor Rogosin, *The Dance Makers: Conversations with American Choreographers* (New York: Walter Co., 1980). Jack Anderson has chronicled all the new works premiered in both New London and Durham in *The American Dance Festival* (Durham, N.C.: Duke University Press, 1987).

An extensive treatment of music for studio classes is Elizabeth Sawyer, *Dance with the Music: The World of the Ballet Musician* (Cambridge, Mass.: Cambridge University Press, 1985). There is also an excellent chapter on the place of music in the training of dancers in Karel Shook, *Elements of Classical Ballet Technique as Practiced in the School of the Dance Theatre of Harlem* (New York: Dance Horizons, 1977). Katherine

Teck has two related volumes in preparation: *Musicians in the Dance Studio* and *Music in the Training of Dancers*.

Finally, of timeless interest to both dancers and musicians is the convocation address given by José Limón to the students at the Juilliard School on October 5, 1966: "Dancers Are Musicians Are Dancers," *Juilliard Annual Review* (1966/67): 4–10.

Index

Accent, 12-13, 115
Accompaniment, 145, 154. *See also* Piano accompaniment
Aerodance, 52
Agathe's Tale, 9, 36, 40
Ahab, 17-18
Ailey, Alvin, 36-37, 40, 53, 72-73
Allison, Nancy, 94
American Ballet Caravan, 48-49
American Ballet Theatre, 81, 103-21, 162-63
American Ballet Theatre Orchestra, 103-10, 116-21
American Dance Festival, 53, 78, 181
American Music Festival, New York City Ballet, 126, 199-207
Analysis of music and ballet, 168-69
Apollon, 16
Appalachian Spring, 95
Arranging music for dance, 5-7, 45-49, 74, 109
Audiences, 9-10, 21, 42, 62, 82, 101-3, 106, 110, 120-21, 127, 132, 142, 157, 169, 200-201, 205-7

Balance between sound and movement, 53
Balanchine, George, 6, 15-17, 19-21, 40, 42, 78, 80, 88, 102, 125-27, 139-40, 157, 162-63, 168
Ballet: dancers, 152-58, 160-70; music, 3-5, 15-17, 34-36, 40-44, 48, 67-68, 78-82, 85, 87-95, 103-21; orchestras, 40, 85-121, 157-58, 202-5
Ballet de Santiago, 91-93
Barker, Alan, 111-20, 166-67
Baryshnikov, Mikhail, 110, 177-80
Bayadère, La, 113-20
Bayou, 42
Bennett, Robert Russell, 5, 45
Bennington College, 13, 23, 30
Bernstein, Leonard, 19, 28, 72-73, 105
Birdwell, Edward, 87-89
Black Lake, 151
Boards of directors, 187
Boas, Franziska, 14, 23
Boelzner, Gordon, 205
Bolender, Todd, 53
Bond, Victoria, 195-96
Bonnefoux, Jean-Pierre, 200
Brahms *Quintet,* 156
Brandenburg Concerto No. 2, 94-95
Breath preparation, 138, 154, 173-74
Brigadoon, 45, 49, 152
Broadway shows, 5-7, 11-12, 15, 45-49, 72, 109, 152-54

Brown, Elizabeth, 93-94
Butler, John, 36-37

Cage, John, 32-33, 57-58, 61
Calcium White Light, 206
Cameron-Wolfe, Richard, 51-52
Carlisle Project, 162, 165
Carroll, Edward, 94-95
Changing Woman, 58
Charlip, Remy, 62
Children in dance, 11-12, 75-78, 188-90
Choreographers, 3-26, 55-59
Choreography: for ballet, 3-7; for modern concert dance, 8-15, 17-26, 55-59, 62-64
Christensen, Lew, 40-41
Cisneros, Evelyn, 176
Clark, Larry, 158-60, 170-71, 191
Classical music, 8, 15-17; for ballet, 125-27, 169
Cleveland, Dennis, 103, 108, 118
Cleveland–San Jose Ballet, 67-68, 134, 157-58
Cloven Kingdom, 8-9
Clytemnestra, 135
Collaboration, creative, 3-82, 199-202; for performance, 202-5
Colman, John, 12
Commissioning projects, 8, 17, 24, 71, 193-95
Composers for ballet and modern dance, 3-82
Concerto Barocco, 163
Conducting for dance, 9, 36, 48, 104-5, 111-20, 123-45; skills required, 111-12, 137-40, 161, 204
Conductors, 36, 40-41, 67-82, 104-5, 111-12, 117, 123-45, 161, 163-64
Connelly, Paul, 112, 119-20
Conservatory musicians, 190-91
Contemporary music, 17-22, 28, 33-34, 126, 142-43, 193-207
Copland, Aaron, 3-4, 19, 28, 95
Coppélia, 85, 191
Copyists, 45, 108
Corps de ballet, 114-15
Cortese, Glen, 140-43
Counting time in music and dance, 9, 10, 14-15, 25-26, 29, 153, 164, 174
Cowell, Henry, 8-9, 17, 21, 23, 28, 33-34, 58, 61
Creature on a Journey, 56
Credits in programs, 47
Critics and critical reviews, 21, 40-41, 44, 68-69, 97, 181-82
Cues, 134-35, 138, 140
Cunningham, Merce, 53, 158-59
Cunningham, Ron, 196-98

Dalby, Norma Reynolds, 52-55
Dalcroze Method, 11-13
d'Amboise, Jacques, 75-78
Danbury Mix, 206
Dancers: onstage, 44, 58, 98, 155-57, 162-65; in relationship to musicians, 36, 51, 70-71, 78, 87-88, 90, 98, 110, 130, 133, 141, 143-45, 153-54, 165; viewpoints on music, 149-83
Dance Theatre of Harlem, 72, 74
Dance USA, 187
Danilova, Alexandra, 182
Dankworth, John, 189
Dean, Laura, 62-66, 182
de Coteau, Denis, 127-32, 176
Deep Rhythm, 36-37
de Forest, June, 106-7
Delibes, 16, 85, 91, 100, 191
de Mille, Agnes, 3-7, 28, 40, 45-49, 80, 152-53, 175-76, 187-88
de Ribère, Lisa, 162-66
Diaghilev, Serge, 15, 44
Diamond, David, 17
Diggity, 9, 70-71
Dirge, 31
Dissonance, 14
Distortion of music, 107-8, 112, 124, 133, 141-42
Dlugoszewski, Lucia, 17, 19-21, 151-52
Dougla, 74
Duffy, John, 193
Duncan, Isadora, 7, 20
Dunham, Katherine, 72, 74-75
Dunkel, Paul, 203-4
Dunning, Jennifer, 93-94, 178
Dynamic, 172-74

Electronic music, 22-26, 28-30, 32-33, 62-63, 65-66
Ellington, Duke, 75
Embattled Garden, 36, 39
Emotions in performance, 12, 42-43, 135
Erdman, Jean, 55-59, 60-62, 171
Esplanade, 95
Evanitsky, Stephanie, 52
Evitts, David, 205

Fall River Legend, 4-5
Farber, Viola, 158-59, 170
Farrell, Suzanne, 166
Feast of Ashes, 36-37, 130
Feld, Eliot, 80, 107, 206
Feldman, Morton, 58
Filling Station, 41, 130
Financing music for dance, 8, 22-24, 33, 61, 69, 71, 128, 140, 143, 188, 193-95, 202
Finney, Ross Lee, 17-18, 21
Fiorato, Hugo, 99-102, 124, 163
Flade, Tina, 60
Folk music, 49
Fonseca, Peter, 178
Ford Foundation, 193
Forest of Three, 24
Form in music and dance, 4, 10, 13, 169
Fragments: Tragedy and Comedy, 28
Free-lance instrumentalists, 85-121
Frontier, 28

Gamelan, 59
Gamelan music, 59
Gathering Wood, 93-94
Glass Pieces, 101, 125-26
Glyph II, 55
Gould, Morton, 4-5, 76-77, 78-82, 202
Graham, Martha, 17-19, 27, 30-32, 34-36, 38-39, 41-42, 52; Company, 55-56, 67, 134-37
Gregory, Cynthia, 107, 176

Harkarvey, Benjamin, 133
Harris, Roy, 13-14
Harrison, Lou, 17, 56-62, 171-72
Hawkins, Erick, 17-22, 40, 62, 150-51, 172; Company, 140-43, 149-52
Henry Street Playhouse, 23
Here and Now with Watchers, 151
Heritage Dance Theater, 152-53
Hierarchy of music and dance, 107, 143-45, 165-66
Highwater, Jamake, 20
Hindemith, Paul, 28
Hogan, Kelly, 55
Holder, Geoffrey, 74
Holland, Bernard, 200, 203
Holm, Hanya, 11-14, 46-47, 172-74
Horst, Louis, 27-32, 36, 56-57
Horvath, Ian, 155-58, 193-95
Houston Ballet, 188-90
Hovhaness, Alan, 17, 57
Hubbard, George R., 160
Humphrey, Doris, 7, 27-30, 36
Hurrah, 20
Husa, Karel, 162

Imago, 25
I'm Old Fashioned, 79, 81
Improvisation, 5, 12, 22-23, 46-47, 54-55, 61, 75, 171
Incident at Black Briar, 196-98
Independence of music and dance, 25, 71, 153, 158, 171
The Informer, 152
Ingraham, Jean, 95-96
Ingraham, Paul, 101, 202-5
Instrumental variety, 9-10, 12-13, 21, 23, 29, 31, 60, 197-98
Instrumentation. *See* Orchestration
Interplay, 80-81
Interpretation, 156-57
Io and Prometheus, 57, 60
Irving, Robert, 88, 100-101, 124-27, 163, 167
Ives, Charles, 15, 205-6
Ives, Songs, 205-6
Ivesiana, 15

Jaffe, Susan, 119-20
Jazz, 65, 75, 106, 119-20, 135
Jersey, Cynthia, 91-93
Joffrey, Robert, 59
Joffrey Ballet, 59, 62, 123-24, 139
Johnson, Kate, 206

Johnson, Martha, 113-15
Jones, Alun, 160, 162
Jooss, Kurt, 48
Jowitt, Deborah, 63-64
Judith, 35-36
Juilliard School, The, 190

Kalisch, Joan, 103-5
Kaplow, Maurice, 90-91, 132-34
Kapp, Richard, 94
Kaschmann, Truda, 23-24
Kay, Hershy, 5, 17
The King and I, 45, 47, 49
Kisselgoff, Anna, 20, 205
Kiss Me Kate, 11
Koeneman, Martha, 91
Koppell, Olivia, 110
Krenek, Ernst, 24

Laderman, Ezra, 57-58, 94
Lady in Waiting, 189
Lanchbery, John, 92, 114-17, 163
La Plante, Skip, 159-60
Last Look, 71-72
Lee, Elizabeth, 181-82
Leon, Tania, 72-75
Lerner and Loewe, 11
Librarian's duties, 108-9
Lifestyles of instrumentalists, 86-88, 92-93, 101, 104-7
Light 17: A Dreamcatcher's Diary, 53-54
Limón, José, Company, 52-53
Live music for performance, compared to tape, 55, 62, 64, 93, 97-98, 100, 123-24, 140-41, 153, 155, 191
Lloyd, Ruth and Norman, 30
Loudspeakers in theaters, 131
Louis, Murray, 94
Louisville Ballet, 160
Lowry, W. McNeil, 187
Lubovitch, Lar, 65
Luening, Otto, 28-33

Magnetic, 62-63
Mahler, Donald, 143-45
Makarova, Natalia, 113-15, 120, 179, 183
Martins, Peter, 101-2, 199, 202, 205-6
Mathews, Fred, 52
McBride, Robert, 31
McDowell, John Herbert, 8-9, 68-69
McPhee, Jonathan, 137-40
Meet the Composer's Composer/Choreographer Project, 193-95
Melody in music, 21, 114
Metric Mix, 55
Metropolitan Opera Ballet Company, 143-45
Mills College, 60-61
Minimalist music, 62-66
Minkus, Ludwig, 113-20
Mitchell, Arthur, 73-74
Modern concert dance, 8-15, 17-30, 55-59, 62-66
Modern dance, music for, 7-15, 17-40, 51-66, 149-52
Modern Listeners' Record Club, 206
Monotony, 15
Moog, Robert, 25
Morganstern, Daniel, 106-7
Morganstern, Lucy, 109
Muller, Jennifer, 182
Multigravitational Aerodance Experiment Group, 52
Multimedia, 31-33
Musgrave, Thea, 93-94
Music: appropriate for dance, 6-8, 15-17, 20-21, 80, 153; in relation to dance, 174-75
Musicality in dancers, 70-71, 115, 166, 167-83
Musicians and dancers. *See* Dancers
Musicians onstage, 74-75, 93-94
Musique concrète, 24-25
My Fair Lady, 11, 46-47

Nagy, Ivan, 92
Nahat, Dennis, 67-68, 156
Narration in dance, 3-5, 17-18, 43, 68, 77, 134-35
National Dance Institute, 75-78
National Endowment for the Arts, 87, 187-88
New York City Ballet, 15-16, 78, 87-89, 199-207
New York City Ballet Orchestra, 99-102, 124-27, 202-5
New York City Center, 96

New York International Ballet Competition, 169-70
Night, 62
Night Journey, 34-36
Nikolais, Alwin, 22-26, 187
Norris, Lee, 75-78
Nunlist, Juli, 165
Nureyev, Rudolf, 94, 136

Opera ballets, 143-45
Orchestras, 44, 139, 157, 191. *See also names of specific dance companies*
Orchestration, 9-10, 39-40, 109, 113-14, 116
Orchestrators, 5-6, 45, 114
Organization of dance companies, 187-88
Other Selves, 195-96
Owl and the Pussy Cat, The, 36-37, 135-36

Paradise Gained, 160
Pasquale, Victoria, 123-24
Patron support of live music, 128-29
Penitente, El, 28, 31
Pennsylvania Ballet, 89-91
Pennsylvania-Milwaukee Ballet, 91, 132-34
Percussion for dance, 12-15, 23, 54, 60-61, 65, 74-75, 91, 117, 173
Performing rights, 37
Perilous Chapel, 56
Pettibone, Laura, 151-52
Pew Charitable Trusts, 193
Phrasing in music and dance, 4, 7, 9, 70-71, 169, 175
Piano accompaniment, 5-6, 9-10, 12, 23, 31, 47-48, 113-15. *See also* Accompaniment
Pillar of Fire, 151
Pits. *See* Theater pits
Plains Daybreak, 20
Polaris, 70
Pollins, Harvey, 12
Polyrhythm, 65
Pre-classic forms, 27, 158
Primitive Mysteries, 28
Prince, Robert, 189
Public Domain, 69
Pulse, 56, 135, 172-75; absence of, 26
Purchase, SUNY, College at, 190-91

Radio City Music Hall, 79, 86-87
Recordings of ballet music, 127
Reedy, James, 149-51
Reeve, Holly, 152-54
Rehearsals, 95-98, 99-102, 113-20, 126, 134, 201
Reich, Steve, 63-66
Reiser, Joseph, 160
Rhythm in music and dance, 56, 63
Riegger, Wallingford, 11, 13, 28, 31
Rittmann, Trude, 5-7, 12, 45-49
Robbins, Jerome, 28, 45-47, 79-81, 205-6
Rock music, 21, 66
Rodeo, 3-4, 28
Rodgers, Richard, 5
Rondo Dance Company, 94-95
Rorem, Ned, 19
Rosalinda, 91-93
Ross, Janice, 132
Rubato in music, 133
Rudiakov, Michael, 85

Le Sacre du Printemps, 9-10, 43, 48, 70
St. Denis, Ruth, 27
San Francisco Ballet, 41
San Francisco Ballet Orchestra, 127-32, 176
Sarah Lawrence College, 54
Saturday Morning, 196
Schermerhorn, Kenneth, 104-5, 109
Schuman, William, 28, 31, 34-36, 190
Seawright, James, 25
Shiva, King of the Dance, 172
Signatures, 133
Silence, 17, 58
Silent films, 22
Sinatra Suite, 155
Skylight, 62-63
Sleater, William, 196-97
Sleeping Beauty, 161
Smuin, Michael, 129
Snow White, 69-71
Solaris, 52
Solstice, 57, 59
Sorrell, Walter, 14-15, 28
South Pacific, 45-46
Spoon River Anthology, 160
Squires, Gregory, 86-87

Stage fright, 97
Stanford, Lynn, 177-80
Starr, Helen, 160-62
Steele, Robert, 195-96
Stevenson, Ben, 188-90
Stodelle, Ernestine, 27-28
Stravinsky, Igor, 6, 9-10, 15-16, 85
Stravinsky Festival of the New York City Ballet, 16, 125
Structure in music and dance, 64
Stubbs, James, 106, 116
Student composers, 24
Studio music for class, 12, 67, 111-12, 136-37, 154-55, 177-80, 189
Substitutes, problem of, 111, 128-29
Surinach, Carlos, 9, 36-40
Sussman, Stanley, 67-68, 134-37, 158
Swan Lake, 161-62
Synthesizers, 62-63
Syzygy, 71

Takei, Kei, 53-54
Tanner, Virginia, 55
Taped music, 8-9, 11, 18, 22, 24-26, 28-30, 32-33, 55, 64-66, 75, 96, 98, 123-24, 155. *See also* Live music for performance
Taylor, Paul, 8-11, 36, 40, 68-72, 96, 174-75, 206; Company musicians, 95-98
Tchaikovsky, P. I., 16-17, 21, 51, 85, 113-14
Television, 126-27
Tempo, 95, 98-99, 105-6, 113, 120, 123-25, 130-31, 135, 141, 144-45, 163, 179, 205
Theater pits, 39, 85-86, 95-98, 103, 105, 117-21, 127-28, 204
Theatre Piece No. 2, 28-30
Themmen, Harold, 108-9
Themmen, Ivanna, 109
Thomson, Virgil, 3, 17, 40-44, 76-77
Total theater, 56, 158-60
Touring, 48-49, 89-91, 104-7, 129-30, 134, 139, 141
Trend, 11
Trickster Coyote, 21
Trojan Women, 162
Tudor, Antony, 35-36, 51, 157
Tympani, 62-63

Unanswered Question, The, 206
Undertow, 35

Van Appledorn, Mary Jeanne, 167
Van Tuyl, Marion, 60
Varese, Edgard, 11, 14
Verdy, Violette, 167-70
Video, 60, 115, 180
Visualizing dance, 150
Volkov, Solomon, 16-17

Waring, James, 68-69
Webern, Anton, 7
Weidman, Charles, 27
Weill, Kurt, 5, 49
Weisberger, Barbara, 90
Wen-chung, Chou, 76-77
West Side Story, 28
Wigman, Mary, 13-15, 23, 28, 61
Willenger, Edward, 127
Winter Dreams, 134
Women choreographers. *See* Allison, Nancy; Dean, Laura; de Mille, Agnes; de Ribère, Lisa; Duncan, Isadora; Dunham, Katherine; Erdman, Jean; Farber, Viola; Graham, Martha; Holm, Hanya; Humphrey, Doris; Muller, Jennifer; Pettibone, Laura; St. Denis, Ruth; Takei, Kei; Verdy, Violette; Wigman, Mary
Women composers, 5-7, 12, 17, 19-21, 28, 45-49, 52-55, 62-66, 72-75, 93, 109, 151-52, 165, 167, 182, 195-96, 200
Women conductors, 72-75. *See also* Rittmann, Trude
Women in the theater, 48
Wuorinen, Charles, 200-201
Wu T'ai Shih, 67

York, Donald, 9, 69-72, 95-99

Zwilich, Ellen Taaffe, 200

About the Author

KATHERINE TECK has worked as a pianist for dance at the State University of New York, College at Purchase; at Sarah Lawrence College; the YM-YWHA of Mid-Westchester; and other studios. She has performed as a horn player with orchestras, bands, and chamber ensembles, as well as for ballet and modern dance.

A graduate of Vassar College, she earned a master's degree in composition of music at Columbia University. Subsequently she worked in the concert music department of Broadcast Music, Inc. and then started her own business, The Modern Listeners' Record Club. She has also worked as a newspaper reporter and as an editor of nonfiction books on the arts.

For this volume, she did extensive first-hand interviewing of leading artists in the field over a period of several years. Two companion volumes are in preparation: *Musicians in the Dance Studio* and *Music in the Training of Dancers*.